AMERICA
THE VULNERABLE

Our Military Problems
And How To Fix Them

EDITED BY
JOHN F. LEHMAN
AND HARVEY SICHERMAN

FOREIGN POLICY RESEARCH INSTITUTE
PHILADELPHIA

John F. Lehman and Harvey Sicherman.
ISBN 0-910191-24-7
UA23.A437 2002
Printed in the U.S

Dedication

On a sad note, Colonel Harry G. Summers Jr., U.S. Army (ret.), who penned the article dealing with operations, procurement, and the defense industrial base and sat as a panelist for our second conference, passed away on November 14, 1999. Colonel Summers, a veteran of the Korean and Vietnam Wars, was the recipient of two Legions of Merit, the Silver Star, three Bronze Stars, two Purple Hearts, two Air Medals, and two awards of the Combat Infantryman's Badge, and also authored numerous books, articles, and columns. He was, in short, the quintessential soldier-scholar. We dedicate this volume to his memory.

TABLE OF CONTENTS

PREFACE

In 1996, the Foreign Policy Research Institute convened a Defense Task Force composed of distinguished scholars and practitioners to examine the increasingly important debates over U.S. military capabilities in the post–Cold War era. Issues included the roles and missions of our forces, the defense industrial base, and civil-military relations. We undertook a second conference in 1998 to explore the culture(s) and ethos of our armed services, and in the fall of 1999 we held a final conference on weapons of mass destruction (i.e., nuclear, biological, and chemical weapons) and information warfare. This volume brings together in one place nine essays commissioned for the three major conferences, plus five related essays from the pages of Orbis, FPRI's quarterly journal of world affairs, and an introductory essay that lays out plainly five threats to America's national security and what can be done about them. The views offered here do not reflect a consensus of the task force, for unanimity was not our goal. Rather, we sought—and received—the expert and carefully considered assessments of a diverse group of individuals.

The result is a comprehensive and, we hope, invaluable tool for policymakers, analysts, and the interested public. We argue strongly that our military problems should be seen in the round, rather than approached piecemeal, with each problem considered to the exclusion of the others. The good news is that the United States does not yet face a military crisis. The bad news is that the deficiencies outlined in this report are rapidly eroding our capabilities. We should not wait until a crisis arises before we fix the problems. We have the skill and the resources—financial, industrial, and human—to deal with them now. There can be no excuse for not doing so.

The work of this task force has been made possible by the generous support of the Sarah Scaife Foundation, whose secretary, R. Daniel McMichael, continues his admirable preoccupation with American national security; our trustees Bobbie and Tatnall L. Hillman; and the Merion Fund of the Foreign Policy Research Institute. Walter A. McDougall, Roger Donway, Shaynee Snider, and Stephen Winterstein lent their invaluable editing skills to the various contributions in this volume. Last, but not least, Harvey Sicherman and John Lehman did a masterful job running this project, ably assisted by the project coordinator Michael P. Noonan.

John H. Ball
Chairman, Board of Trustees
Foreign Policy Research Institute
Philadelphia

AMERICA THE VULNERABLE

by John F. Lehman and Harvey Sicherman

A decade has passed since the end of the Cold War. The demise of the Soviet Union concluded the most vulnerable period in American history, a time when the possibility of nuclear attack threatened the very existence of the United States. No wonder then that Americans heaved a mighty sigh of relief, having survived to watch the fall of their country's most powerful enemy.

Our new sense of security led to a predictable course of action. We disarmed. Starting with the first Bush administration and accelerating through both Clinton terms, the United States reduced its military forces by 40 percent. National defense expenditures in real terms (adjusted for inflation) dropped from $302.3 billion in 1992 to $274.8 billion in 2000.[1] The portion of the U.S. gross national product devoted to defense shrank from 6.5 percent in 1985 to just over 3.0 percent, a level not seen since the 1930s. Arguably this defense "dividend" made a major contribution toward ending federal deficits.

Our military, however, was not allowed to rest on its laurels. U.S. forces were engaged abroad with increasing frequency in countries such as Somalia, Haiti, and Bosnia-Herzegovina, culminating in the U.S.-led war with Yugoslavia over Kosovo in 1999. These operations strained falling budgets and smaller forces. Simultaneously, our defense planning was challenged by the so-called revolution in military affairs, which requires keeping U.S. defenses in the forefront of new technologies.

Slowly—very slowly—America's complacency about security has begun to wear off, replaced by growing unease at what the chairman of the Joint Chiefs of Staff, General Henry Shelton, called "the fraying of the force." Among the greatest concerns:

- Problems posed by an all-volunteer force to the American tradition of a citizens' army under civilian control.
- The loss of qualified pilots, sailors, and soldiers in vital jobs throughout the services, and the unreadiness of various units.

---

[1]National defense expenditures are an amalgamation of defense-related spending programs ranging from the Defense Department's budget to nuclear weapons programs in the Energy Department. International Institute for Strategic Studies, *The Military Balance 1999/2000* (London: Oxford University Press, 1999), p. 17.

- The debatable wisdom of humanitarian interventions and their legacy of open-ended commitments.
- An overly consolidated contractor base with hugely inflationary potential.
- New missile threats and the controversy over missile defenses.
- The dangers of biological and chemical weapons.
- The challenge of ensuring computer security in an era of ubiquitous electronic communication and international hackers.

Each of these issues has its own community of partisans who will propose various actions to address it, and pressures on Capitol Hill, the Pentagon, and the White House may produce some progress. In our view, however, this piecemeal approach will obscure a larger issue. While none of these problems is yet at a crisis stage, together they are steadily eroding the U.S. capability to deter war across the spectrum or, should deterrence fail, to win any conflict.

Clearly, U.S. forces that are uncertain of their command and control, subject to operational disruption from computer hackers, and trained more for peacekeeping than warfighting are going to lack the capabilities America needs and expects. A noncompetitive industrial base will be unable to produce weapons in either the numbers or quality needed, but its wares will be outrageously expensive. And if the United States remains vulnerable to biological or chemical threats, or to ballistic missiles, then our government's freedom of action abroad and our safety at home will be equally illusory.

But it is not too late to head off such a fate. We have the opportunity to correct the course, to steer clear of the "Pearl Harbor" cycle whereby only a disaster brings effective action. Doing so will require more resources, but the remarkably improved state of federal finances should ease the way for increased defense spending. We do not ask for a blank check. As the late economist Herbert Stein used to say, we may not have enough to do everything, but we do have enough to do what is necessary.

We also have the advantage of a relatively stable strategic consensus. The United States remains an Asian and European power and, if anything, the end of the Cold War has reinforced America's role as the linchpin of security in those regions. The American people give no sign of wishing to relinquish these responsibilities, which in turn set certain requirements for our force levels.

The notion of intelligent action by government in advance of a crisis may be regarded by some as an oxymoron, but there is no substitute for acting now to forestall a crisis in our military capabilities. Unlike earlier times, we are not burdened by either a lack of resources or strategic confusion. Only a fatal complacency will explain the absence of prudent measures.

To overcome such complacency, our leaders must be willing to educate the public in order to mobilize support. Defense, after all, is the first and most essential of public goods. We are convinced that a defense plan that concentrates on the main threats is the only effective way to proceed. We are also convinced that the American people will support it.

We turn now to the five most serious military problems and what can be done about them.

The Demilitarization of the Military

At the heart of our strategy is the axiom that to keep the peace we must be able to fight and win a war. Our military has as its principal mission the defense of the United States and our interests abroad. Throughout the Cold War, this required the training and deployment of large U.S. forces to other countries. They were held in readiness to fight a war, and from Korea to Vietnam to the Persian Gulf, they occasionally did so.

Surprisingly, despite the demise of our major adversary, U.S. military forces have been deployed overseas at a frenetic pace higher than any in history: thirty-seven separate deployments between 1991 and 1999, or an average of one deployment every eleven weeks. Of these, only eleven (29.7 percent) used military force to deter war or to conduct "traditional" war-fighting missions.[2] The big missions of the past decade have pitched U.S. forces into the murky realms of so-called humanitarian intervention, peacekeeping, and the still murkier territory of "peace enforcement."

This shift in focus could lead to what may be called a "demilitarization" of the military: the emphasis is no longer primarily on war but on contingencies fundamentally different from war. While U.S. forces have always been used to rescue civilians from natural

[2]The previous historical high-water mark for overseas military deployments during peacetime was the period between the Spanish-American War and the First World War. During that time, U.S. forces were also deployed overseas thirty-seven times, but over a seventeen year period. That averaged out to one deployment about every six months. These figures are taken from Michael P. Noonan, "Warfighting vs. Peacekeeping: The Historical Record of U.S. Interventions Abroad, 1798–1999," a paper delivered at the Inter-University Seminar on Armed Forces and Society's Biennial International Conference, Baltimore, Md., Oct. 24, 1999.

disasters (and the Marine Corps in particular has a tradition of so-called small wars of intervention), these have always been a secondary, or lesser, mission. The wide use of American forces to rescue foreign populations from the ravages of bad government or civil war is new and troubling. Among the consequences:

• *Loss of focus.* Concentrating on lower-order problems may come at the cost of innovation in war-fighting tactics, equipment, and organization. Given the great technological changes inherent in the revolution in military affairs, that cost appears prohibitive indeed.

• *Misdirection of talent.* The best officers are always attracted to the "action," and if the action is peacekeeping, we could find ourselves with an officer corps experienced primarily with constabulary and politico-military assignments rather than with warfare.

• *Disruption of training.* Combat arms units involved in peacekeeping may need up to six months of retraining in order to recover their war-fighting skills.

• *Distortion of force strength.* The army in particular justifies some of its end-strength based on the demands of peacekeeping. These are the ways to "remilitarize" the military:

• *Sharpen intervention criteria.* While we do not support a blanket rejection of humanitarian intervention, American forces must be committed in a sensible and prudent manner. Units with logistical, transportation, and command, control, communications, computer, and intelligence (C^{4}I) capabilities should be the first tapped for peacekeeping operations that require U.S. forces. Troops on the ground should be an absolute last resort.

• *Maintain the war-fighting edge.* Training to fight wars must be the focus for most units, while a smaller portion of the force will require training for peacekeeping operations.

• *Integrate intelligence activities.* The United States must better integrate its political and military intelligence activities for the forces engaged in peacekeeping operations.

• *Emphasize proportionality.* Commanders, both civilian and military, must develop a better sense of proportion for the engagement of units supporting such operations. Disproportionality leads to the overuse of certain units and occupational specialties.

The Procurement Dilemma

There are two problems with procurement. One concerns the "sizing" issue, that is, the forces we need to achieve our objectives in the face of whatever threats may arise. The second concerns the industrial base, or how we procure the weapons those forces need.

As stated earlier, American forces have been functioning at a high operational tempo since the end of the Gulf War. During the same period, the number of personnel has shrunk by over 40 percent. Operations and maintenance have been sustained by underfunding training readiness and especially modernization, that is, the replacement and upgrading of matériel. As defense industries have consolidated in response to the drastically smaller market, the competitive spur of multiple procurement sources has disappeared for most systems. The smaller industrial capability of single suppliers cannot provide equipment at a cost that fits a reasonable defense budget.

For example, plans for procurement of the F-22 and Joint Strike Fighters by the air force, navy, and Marine Corps promise to be the largest defense industry contracts in American history—a total of more than $200 billion dollars. Such an enormous outlay of resources for two weapons systems basically guarantees that funding other forms of defense modernization will be difficult in the absence of a huge increase in the defense budget.

In response to these issues, we recommend five steps:

• *Redefine the sizing issue.* The standard for U.S. forces to be able to fight two nearly simultaneous regional conflicts (e.g., in the Persian Gulf and Korea) should be updated. Current forces are "sized" according to the Desert Storm model, a scenario that is highly unlikely to recur. Instead, U.S. military planners should focus on force capabilities that can be used in any theater against multiple threats across the spectrum of conflict.

• *Eliminate nondefense missions.* The Department of Defense should not be tasked with nondefense matters such as environmental clean-up. These activities, costing $5–8 billion annually, should be shifted to other federal agencies.

• *Promote competition in the defense industry.* Costs of defense contracts must be controlled through competition. As procurement levels increase, additional firms will be able to compete. As for defense spending levels, the United States can afford to spend more, but without reform, any increased spending will only represent increased waste.

• *Streamline procurement.* The Pentagon's procurement process, which currently takes more than twenty years from the start of a new system to deployment (the F-22 being a good example), must be radically streamlined. Computing technology in the private sector (according to what is known as Moore's Law) now grows obsolete in less than fourteen months.

• *Avoid the "silver bullet" trap.* Do not assume that some technological revolution can resolve the structure-procurement-readiness dilemma. Advanced technology can bring greater efficiency, but not to the extent expected. For example, precision-guided munitions offer a distinct advantage over "dumb" bombs, but are not so accurate that they can substitute on a larger scale for other munitions. However, evidence does suggest that in the future, smaller, high-tech forces with greater speed and firepower will be most efficient.

The Military-Civilian Cultural Gap

The military and American society interact at two levels: (1) civil-military relations between the civilian political leadership and the uniformed military leadership; and (2) what is typically understood as a culture clash between the military and society at large.

Civil-military relations carry the heavy legacy of Vietnam, where, in the military's view, civilians micromanaged the conflict and failed to support the forces in an unpopular war. This gave birth to numerous attempts to codify when and how U.S. forces should be used abroad, a movement that dovetailed with incessant efforts to centralize the command structure, effectively presenting a unified military position to the civilian leaders. An essential part of this shift was the Department of Defense Reorganization Act of 1986 (Goldwater-Nichols). This legislation centralized military authority among the regional commanders in chief (CINCs) and made the chairman of the Joint Chiefs of Staff the sole principal military adviser to both the president and the secretary of defense. In practice, this limited not only the scope of military advice available to the political leadership, but also the policy- and priority-setting roles of the service chiefs and civilian service secretaries. The legislation also altered personnel policies so that staff experience, particularly on joint staffs, is now mandatory for promotion to the "flag" rank of admiral or general. Consequently, junior officers may infer that staff assignments matter more than command experience.

The problem of the gap between military culture and American society has become more noticeable in the era of the all-volunteer force, now a quarter-century old. Military culture is a crucial if often misunderstood aspect of defense. There will always be a divergence between the discipline required of a fighting force and the free-wheeling individualism of the society it is charged to defend. In fact, an effective military has its own distinctive culture, one that emphasizes honor, courage, and self-sacrifice under a command structure. Attempts to erase this divide by "civilizing" the military, or by making the services the focus of social experiments, risk serious harm to efficiency and morale. Disruptive social innovations, such as allowing women in combat or tolerating openly homosexual personnel, must be evaluated primarily by their effect on readiness, morale, and training.

The cultural issue has been further aggravated by the fact that fewer and fewer American leaders today have any military experience. The all-volunteer force and the absence of military recruiting on many college campuses reinforce the gap in understanding between those who serve and those they defend. In a democracy, it is vital that defense should not become the narrow preserve of a few who remain separate from the rest of society.

Several steps will help address these problems:

• *Change the law.* Title X of the U.S. Code should be amended to increase and diversify the sources of advice available to the president, strengthen civilian control, and emphasize command and leadership rather than bureaucratic skills.

• *Promote short-term service.* The military should target a broader socioeconomic spectrum when recruiting both officers and enlisted personnel. To that end, it should offer shorter commitments to active-duty service and increase opportunities for service members to continue their commitments in the federal reserves or National Guard.

• *Expand military education and familiarization programs.* Establishing military familiarization programs would enable the civilian leadership to understand the military experience and the conduct of warfare. Additionally, more courses on civil-military relations should be introduced to universities, and ROTC programs promoted wherever feasible.

• *Manage the gap.* We must understand that there will always be a gap between the culture(s) of the military and that of civilian society, and recognize that the preferences of would-be social reformers may have negative effects on the professionalism of the military institution. At the same time, it is essential to institute personnel policies that promote those who are best qualified regardless of their race, color, gender, or creed, and that prohibit double standards for the physical, mental, and skills requirements for men and women.

The Threats Posed by Weapons of Mass Destruction

The fourth threat to American national security is the vulnerability of U.S. forces and the civilian populace to nuclear, chemical, and biological weapons. Paradoxically, the dominating performance of the American military in Operation Desert Storm has convinced many potential adversaries that the only way to offset America's conventional military dominance is to acquire weapons that can target the American home front. Despite international efforts to curtail them, many nations have acquired or sought such weapons, particularly nuclear, since the end of the Cold War. Both India and Pakistan publicly joined the nuclear club by testing weapons in 1998. North Korea, Iran, and Iraq are known to be seeking nuclear weapons and long-range missiles to deliver them. The United States must also consider the growing military might of China, including a major expansion of its missile forces. Russian military doctrine also continues to stress the importance of nuclear weapons.

The United States, however, still has no means to defend itself against such dangers except by threatening aggressors with nuclear retaliation, a step fraught with its own moral dilemma, especially when dealing with dictators who have effectively made hostages of their own populations. A broad consensus has developed in the United States that a limited ballistic nuclear defense is a prudent step. Some have argued that the development of such a system may lead the Russians and others to increase their missile arsenals in the interest of sustaining a nuclear balance, that is, to deny the United States the ability to strike them while shielding itself from a counterstrike. But no one has seriously argued for a system of total protection for the mainland United States that will be capable of dealing with all types of missile attack; some missiles will always get through. Rather, a limited system (the only sort that is technically feasible) could offer an additional measure of protection against some threats without upsetting the security of Russia, China, or other major powers—unless, of course, their intentions are hostile.

Biological and chemicals weapons are seen as the "poor man's nuclear weapons," and many states and would-be terrorists are trying to develop them. Despite sensational media coverage, these weapons have proven very difficult to control and have never been decisive on the battlefield. They remain, however, a potentially devastating way to terrorize a society, a danger well illustrated by the Aum Shinrikyo cult's attack on the Tokyo subways in 1995. Fortunately, the United States already has in place the elements for an effective civil defense against such weapons.

To reduce U.S. vulnerability to weapons of mass destruction (WMD), an effective program would do the following:

• *Develop limited national missile defense.* The technical parameters of a limited land-based missile defense should be established and our allies persuaded that it would also help to protect them. To that end, a constructive discussion must be held with Russia regarding the revision of the Antiballistic Missile Treaty, although this should not be allowed to determine our decision about deployment. Also, we should experiment with a theater missile defense based on the navy's Aegis system that may be well suited to regional defenses.

• *Improve existing systems to defend against biological and chemical threats.* These threats, while serious, do not justify vast new expenditures. Most cities and towns have emergency procedures already available (e.g., for controlling chemical and toxic spills) that can be developed to another level. Existing defense systems in cities such as New York need to be studied and duplicated if possible. National Guard capabilities on this front should also be improved and expanded. Local emergency personnel will be the most available and able to respond should such an attack take place.

• *Improve intelligence capabilities in regard to WMD.* In light of the fact that the Indian and Pakistani nuclear weapons tests came as a surprise (as did the last North Korean rocket test), the United States must improve its intelligence capabilities concerning WMD. Specifically, we need people on the ground to supplement other methods of obtaining information.

The Cyberthreat

The United States has moved from an industrial to an information economy. Computers, faxes, and electronic mail are indispensable throughout all segments of our society and constitute the "central nervous system" of the U.S. military. Weapons systems are increasingly sophisticated and rely on the same technologies that made the civilian sector boom throughout the latter half of the 1990s. Unfortunately, such systems can be attacked and disabled with potentially catastrophic consequences.

The National Security Agency has admitted that several crucial spy satellites were disabled due to year 2000 computer glitches, and the Pentagon computer system has been attacked numerous times by hackers, some of whom may have been working for foreign governments. During the air war over Kosovo, for instance, a senior military officer warned that we had withstood our first information warfare attack when someone, presumably a Serb, bombarded e-mail systems within the European Command.

Much like chemical or biological weapons, information warfare is particularly useful to weaker states as they seek to attain tactical advantages over the United States. Information warfare has been called a "weapon of mass disruption" because of its ability to disable systems of both civilian and military importance. Until now, the technological revolution spurred on by the development of the computer has mostly aided the offense, but if military history has anything to teach, a defensive reaction will be forthcoming. America cannot afford to lag behind in either case.

We propose three actions for dealing with this threat:

• *Improve dialogue between the public and private sector.* The government and its agencies can learn much about information warfare and its capabilities from the private sector. Such a dialogue could prove advantageous to both sides for defending the nation's information infrastructure.

• *Explore diplomatic options.* International agreements on the unrestricted global flow of information should be developed and strengthened, and should include safeguards against abuse.

• *Develop information-warfare capabilities in the reserves.* The National Guard and federal reserves offer the best way for the federal government to tap into civilian expertise in information warfare. Guardsmen and reservists have access to information technologies not found in most parts of the U.S. government. The formation of reserve units specializing in information warfare would be cost effective, play to reservists' core competencies, and improve our defenses against such attacks.

A Note on Money

This report would be remiss without a comment on the costs of the program outlined above. The defense budget is a rather esoteric subspecialty of political economy, and the only thing that can be said definitively about it is that the numbers never stay still. According to the latest estimates from the Congressional Budget Office, a "sustaining budget" of $340 billion (about 15 percent higher than in 1999) will be necessary to support current and projected forces. This reflects the bulge in procurement to replace aging weapons systems that were neglected because of operations and readiness spending over the past decade. Others have suggested smaller increases of anywhere from 2 to 10 percent.[3]

Our view is that when we evaluate the next defense budget, we should be sure to ask the right questions. Does it reduce the vulnerabilities we have described? Does it reverse, or at least halt, the erosion in our military capabilities? Is it coupled with sufficient reforms in the Pentagon so that the money is wisely spent, or is it merely throwing more money at the wrong problems in the same old way? Our security and the security of our children depend on the right answers.

[3]See, for example, the Council on Foreign Relations, *Future Visions of U.S. Defense Policy*, John Hillen, project director (New York: Council on Foreign Relations, 1998); and Steven M. Kosiak, *Analysis of the FY 2001 Defense Budget Request* (Washington, D.C.: Center for Strategic and Budgetary Assessments, Feb. 2000).

ROLES AND MISSIONS

by Donald Kagan

Since the fall of the Berlin Wall, American military forces have been used to remove the ruler of Panama, to drive the Iraqi army out of Kuwait and later to deter its return, to alleviate a famine in Somalia, to remove a military junta from Haiti and restore the elected president to power, to compel warring ethnic factions in Bosnia to stop fighting and then to enforce the resulting truce until elections could be held, and to deter a threat from China against Taiwan, among other interventions.[1] At the same time, American forces have been stationed in Korea to deter an attack from the north and in the Persian Gulf to deter aggressive actions by either Iran or Iraq.

Two Constrained Visions

The end of the Cold War has removed the danger of a war between the two superpowers, but plainly it has not removed the need for strong and competent American military forces to deal with problems around the world that engage the attention of the United States. The relative clarity that underlay America's Cold War policy and strategy is gone, replaced by confusion, debate, and a denial of reality. At the extreme is a call to bring America home, to focus attention on domestic problems, and to cut the budget for international affairs and military forces to the bone in order to pay for domestic programs and tax cuts. This call is often connected to the assertion that there is no credible threat to American security, that American military power and expenditure are colossal compared with those of any other state, and that no danger to the general peace and security is anywhere in view. Such problems as arise, it is said, can be dealt with by regional powers or the United Nations. The United States should stand aloof and avoid unilateral intervention; it should not even involve itself as the senior partner of an alliance.

More common than this view are less-extreme demands for

---

[1]This essay originally appeared in *Orbis*, Spring 1997, and arose from the Foreign Policy Research Institute conference "The Demilitarization of the Military?" Philadelphia, Pa., July 17–18, 1996.

limiting American involvement. These assert that America cannot afford the cost of widespread engagement, and that involvements abroad for the purpose of humanitarian intervention or for establishing and keeping the peace run a high risk of "mission creep," military escalation, and descent into a deadly quagmire similar to Vietnam. To avoid such mistakes, advocates of this position insist, a set of rigid requirements should be met before any engagement of American forces. But these requirements are so rigid that they would, in practice, prevent any use of American military power in instances short of a direct attack on the United States or its allies.

Advocates of both these arguments agree that American military forces should be used only in defense of the country's vital interests, which are generally defined in a limited fashion to include only the defense of the United States, its allies, and its critical economic interests. That is the place to begin considering the missions for the various elements of American military forces: What are the country's interests? Which are most important? Need interests be "vital," a matter of life and death for the country, before military force can be used? What strategy should the United States adopt to protect its interests, and where does the use of military power fit? A discussion of the proper missions for military forces must respond to these questions, and a responsible policy must follow from the answers.

America in Today's World

American grand strategy must begin with the recognition that the United States is a satisfied power. It has no desire to extend its territory and no unsatisfied territorial claims. It has the world's largest and most powerful economy and has achieved that status under the current rules of the game. Even after making severe cuts in expenditures, it is by far the world's greatest military power. Historically, such predominance causes fear and jealousy among other states, who usually band together to balance and oppose such hegemony, but that has not been the response to American preeminence. The United States is allied with most of the world's wealthiest nations, many of whom possess impressive military forces of their own. The United States is the world's leading democratic state and the exemplar of free enterprise and trade at a time when these values are admired and widely shared. Though annoyed from time to time by America's policies and its ability to have its way, U.S. allies do not fear American aggression, but rather fear the United States will withdraw from active involvement and leadership.

Few, if any, nations in the history of the world have ever enjoyed such a favorable situation. It stands to reason that the keystone of American strategy should be an effort to preserve and sustain the situation as well and as long as possible. America's most vital interest, therefore, is maintaining the general peace, for war has been the swiftest, most expensive, and most devastating means of changing the balance of international power. But peace does not keep itself, although one of the most common errors in modern thinking about international relations is the assumption that peace is natural and can be preserved merely by having peace-seeking nations avoid provocative actions. The last three-quarters of the twentieth century strongly suggest the opposite conclusion: major war is more likely to come when satisfied states neglect their defenses and fail to take an active part in the preservation of peace.

It is vital to understand that the current relatively peaceful and secure situation is neither inevitable nor immutable. It reflects two conditions built up with tremendous effort and expense during the last half-century: the great power of the United States and the general expectation that Americans will be willing to use that power when necessary. The diminution of U.S. power and credibility, which would follow on a policy of reduced responsibility, would thus not be a neutral act that would leave the situation as it stands. Instead, it would be a critical step in undermining the stability of the international situation. Calculations based on the absence of visible potential enemies would immediately be made invalid by America's withdrawal from its current position as the major bulwark supporting the world order. The cost of the resulting upheaval in wealth, instability, and the likelihood of war would be infinitely greater than the cost of continuing to uphold the existing international structure.

The Main Task

The chief mission of American military forces, therefore, must be to maintain their superiority, that is, their ability (in cooperation with their allies) to fight and win wars at such a level as to deter possible disturbers of the peace from seeking to change the international situation by violence or the threat of violence. That is no easy task, especially for modern democratic countries at this moment in history. The achievements of deterrence are always hard to see and to appreciate. If there is no war and no immediate threat in sight, opponents of the policy will denounce it as an unnecessary expense diverting resources from more desirable causes. They will regard the peaceful international situation as natural and unconnected to what has helped produce it: the effort and money expended on military power. The only time in its history that the United States has steadily maintained powerful military forces in order to deter war was from 1950 through the end of the Cold War, a period that concluded with the peaceful collapse of its major rival. Throughout that time, the policy was under domestic attack on the grounds that it was either unnecessary or provocative, or both. In the absence of an obvious, already-powerful opponent, it is even harder to convince many people that the current advantageous situation rests on a base to which preponderant American military power is essential.

Yet it is remarkable how swiftly an apparently secure peace can be shattered by a sudden challenge to the complacency of the satisfied states from an unexpected source. In 1919 Germany was defeated, isolated, disarmed, and strategically contained. The situation was fundamentally unchanged when Adolf Hitler's Nazi regime came to power in 1933. Yet by 1941 Germany had launched a world war, conquered France and all of Western Europe, and was on the point of bringing the entire continent under its control.

As late as the 1920s, the notion that Japan might be a threat to peace seemed absurd even to the former first lord of the Admiralty, Winston Churchill. As chancellor of the Exchequer (1924–29), he repeatedly reduced naval appropriations to help pay for social programs, dismissing future dangers in the Far East: "Why should there be a war with Japan? I do not believe there is the slightest chance of it in our lifetime." The Admiralty, he said, should make plans "on the basis that no naval war against a first class Navy is likely to take place in the next twenty years."[2] In 1931 Japan invaded Manchuria. Several years later it launched an invasion of China, and in 1941 it attacked British, French, and Dutch colonies and American forces at Pearl Harbor and elsewhere, bringing World War II to the Pacific.

In 1990, few would have believed that a third-rate power such as Iraq would offer a military challenge to the sole remaining

---

[2]Quoted in Telford Taylor, *Munich: The Price of Peace* (New York: Doubleday, 1979), p. 203.

superpower, but in that year Saddam Hussein's army invaded Kuwait, compelling the United States to send a vast military force to drive the Iraqis out, at enormous expense.

Lesser Tasks

Deterrence of war at the level of at least theater campaigns—through strength and the evident willingness to use it—must be the most important mission of America's armed forces. It cannot, however, be the only one, as the uses of American forces abroad in the last decade show. Neither the Bush nor the Clinton administration can fairly be described as looking for trouble. Both made deep cuts in expenditures for defense, and both faced serious domestic opposition to interventions abroad. Thus, whatever the wisdom of any particular involvement, each one resulted from a decision by a government not eager to take it. There is little reason to doubt that similar problems and challenges will continue to arise in the future. Challenges to peace and security arise naturally from the conflict for power between and within states. Some conflicts, like the fighting in Bosnia and the Chinese menace to Taiwan, involve principally the interests and security of America's friends and allies. But a consistent American refusal to take action to meet threats to peace and security that fall short of invasions or similarly obvious dangers will raise questions about the U.S. willingness and ability to do so, undermining the confidence and support of friends and allies. The current, unusually stable condition of the world rests heavily on the belief in America's military power and commitment. If these are seen to decline, the stability and security of the world will decline apace. The United States need not involve itself in every challenge that arises; it need not take action whenever it takes part. However, it must face the fact that whenever it chooses to stand aloof from challenges that may concern it, there is a price to pay in damage to the credibility of its policy of deterrence.

Still, decisions to intervene or not must be made. And the nice calculations needed to make the decision in each case are far from the various rigid checklists that some analysts wish to have filled out before any use of military force is undertaken. Serious and continued study and discussion of basic principles and historical experience will always be needed to alert decision makers to the risks of both intervention and abstention, but there is no magic formula that can make decisions in advance. That is what statesmen are for.

What seems clear, however, is that interventions on a scale smaller than war should and will take place from time to time. Opinions differ on how frequent these will be, but experience suggests that they will be most frequent and most difficult when the powers that wish to preserve peace are, or seem to be, unable or unwilling to resist its breach. The Korean War, for instance, broke out when the United States appeared both unable and unwilling to defend its South Korean ally. Swift and enormously deep reductions in the size and quality of the U.S. Army right after World War II brought it down in just a few years from some 10 million to about 552,000, half of them on occupation duty overseas serving as clerks and policemen, the other half in the United States performing various administrative tasks. General Omar Bradley, who inherited this army in 1948, described it as one that "could not fight its way out of a paper bag."[3] Early in 1950, the American secretary of state gave a speech that mentioned a number of states in the Far East that the United States would fight to defend. South Korea was not among them. The combination of America's evident military weakness and its apparent lack of will encouraged North Korea to launch an attack and its Soviet sponsor to permit and support it. The ensuing war almost ended in swift defeat and disaster for South Korean and American forces. In any case, it lasted for years, cost a great fortune, and took thousands of American lives before ending in a stalemate that has required the emplacement of American forces in Korea for more than four decades.

Iraq's invasion of Kuwait in 1990 took place at a time when American military power was far stronger—the foremost in the world, the power of the Soviet Union having declined. Saddam Hussein could nevertheless challenge U.S. might because he had good reason to doubt American willingness to use its military power to prevent or reverse an invasion of Kuwait, a doubt strengthened by the absence of significant American ground forces in the vicinity.

There is good reason to believe that the violence and loss of life involved when Yugoslavia disintegrated, and the threat that these have posed to the stability of Europe, could have been avoided by timely intervention on the part of the United States and its allies. Given the power of American military forces, then recently demonstrated in the war in the Persian Gulf, there would probably

[3]Omar N. Bradley and Clay Blair, *A General's Life* (New York: Simon and Schuster, 1983), p. 474.

have been no need to use those forces had the United States and NATO made clear that violence would not be tolerated. Instead, both attempted to avoid the responsibility of intervention, thus permitting and encouraging the horrors and disruptions that followed, only to decide in due course that these were not tolerable. When at last NATO resorted to intervention, it required the serious use of arms and the deployment of a considerable force for at least a year. But all of that happened after the Bosnian horrors had taken place. And the end of the difficulties and of American involvement are far from evident.

These examples show that the denial of American interest and attempts to avoid involvement, such as the threat or use of military force, can have a result opposite to what is desired. Instead of preventing the expenditure of resources and the risk of American lives, such avoidance may encourage conditions that cause greater expenditure and risk. There is no realistic alternative to the requirement that America's armed forces be able both to fight and to win real wars, as well as to engage in smaller actions to deter war, to establish peace, and to keep the peace for some period after it has been established.

The Checklist Illusion

Unimpressed by such proposals, yet fearful that peacekeeping and similar assignments would seriously degrade the army's warfighting ability, some people propose an approach that would keep these involvements to a minimum and, indeed, make them rare events. To this end, they insist that an established canon of criteria be met before American armed forces are introduced abroad. One set of suggestions, not meant to be unduly restrictive, requires a determination prior to any intervention (1) that the action has some reasonable chance of success; (2) that the United States has resources adequate for its execution; (3) that its purpose is to protect American interests; (4) that the U.S. government is able to define and explain the mission; and (5) that the mission solves a greater problem than it creates. These are all sensible considerations, and no government should commit armed forces abroad without thinking about them, among others. But they do not help much. The third item will almost always be debatable, and the fourth amounts to little more than an exercise in rhetorical skill. And determinations about the others cannot be made in advance. Statesmen responsible for deciding will have to act on their best judgment, as they have in the past. There can be no guarantee that they will make the right decision, but there is no escape from deciding.

The one criterion not yet discussed, common to most lists of requirements, presents the greatest difficulty. It would require evidence of a national, or at least political, consensus before a decision is made to use armed force. This suggestion arises from the understandable desire to avoid involvements that have been seen as disasters in the past and that have arisen from the commitment of American armed forces in situations short of declared war. The instance most frequently cited is Vietnam; another is the peace-keeping intervention in Lebanon during the Reagan years, which led to the death of 241 marines. The humanitarian mission to Somalia is a third example.

The purpose of this requirement is to make such interventions impossible, or at least highly unlikely. In retrospect, it may seem improbable that the American people or their representatives would have given advance approval to missions of this kind, but the proviso offers no guarantee against unsatisfactory involvements. The interventions in Vietnam and Korea earned both political and popular support as long as the government was seen to be aiming at victory. Presidents Ronald Reagan and George Bush would surely have won support had they sought public approval for the missions to Lebanon and Somalia, and there is no reason to be certain that the dismay caused by the mishaps in those places would not have been overcome and forgotten had the government in each case found a good reason to persist in the mission. The main effect of such a requirement would be similar to the effect of Bush's decision to gain congressional support before launching a military effort against Iraq—to give America's opponent further reason to doubt U.S. resolve and to refuse a peaceful conclusion to the crisis, and to give him time to improve his military or diplomatic situation.

The unspoken assumption underlying this and other restrictions meant to hamper interventions is that inaction is safer than action. But the history of this century does not support that opinion. In 1936 Adolf Hitler violated both the Versailles and Locarno treaties by sending a military force to occupy the demilitarized Rhineland. Had the leaders of France and Great Britain, or even France alone, acted to drive out his pitiful contingent they might well have destroyed his regime on the spot and avoided a war that ultimately caused some 40 million deaths. At the very least they would have made impossible the swift German defeat of France in 1940. Given the climate of opinion at the time, leaders of Great Britain and France might have found it hard to convince their publics to support military action. But that will never be known, because the leaders were paralyzed by the bitter memories of World War I and believed that restraint and the avoidance of the use of military force were the only way to preserve peace. They found excuses for inaction, and the Nazis were able to take the first major step on the road to war and conquest.

Iraq's invasion of Kuwait is also instructive. The U.S. military leadership, badly scarred by public criticism and unsatisfactory outcomes during the Vietnam War, as well as by the affair in Lebanon, advised inaction. The chairman of the Joint Chiefs of Staff recommended that a line be drawn to defend Saudi Arabia, leaving Kuwait in Saddam's hands. Many members of the political opposition vigorously and publicly opposed military intervention. Had President Bush been guided by the need to test public support before deciding to take action he would not have acted. Instead, he decided at once that Saddam's *coup de main* "would not stand." With great effort, and the passage of valuable time, he was able to win, by only a few votes in the Senate, congressional support for the use of force to drive the Iraqis from Kuwait. But that was accomplished after he had already decided on action; mustering support would have been impossible had he not already made his decision. To win the congressional vote the president undertook a last attempt at diplomacy, and that had consequences. For one thing, it took time. For another, any chance that visible resoluteness and serious military preparations might convince Saddam to retreat without a fight was undercut by the efforts at last-minute negotiation, forced by the need to sway domestic opinion.

Moreover, if these diplomatic efforts had succeeded, if Saddam had withdrawn before the fighting began, the result would have been almost as bad as leaving him in place. He could have retreated with his large military force intact, a force that included chemical weapons and possibly nuclear and biological ones as well. He also could have retreated with the prestige of his forces undiminished. Doubt about American resolve and willingness to fight would have lingered and grown, undermining the confidence of friendly and moderate elements in the Middle East. The threat to peace and American interests would not have been defeated but only delayed. What was needed was a swift military response as soon as possible after Iraq's violation of Kuwait's frontier. Public support would have been available, as it was once the president made his decision clear. Delay caused by the desire to win such support in advance could have been very costly had not Saddam proved to be such a convenient opponent.

These examples, and they could readily be multiplied, show that there may be dangers not only from military involvement but also from a refusal to undertake such involvement. Indeed, in countries like the Western democracies, there may be more danger from the latter than from the former. The avoidance of interventions short of full-scale war, therefore, is not a safe refuge but an illusion. In any case, there is no way to know in advance whether it is safer to stay out or go in, no escape from the judgment of statesmen, and no security in tying their hands. It is necessary, therefore, to seek the best ways to meet the challenge of varied and unforeseeable missions in a manner compatible with maintaining a military force capable of fighting and winning major conflicts.

Trends Eroding U.S. Strength

Still, the question remains: can the armed forces carry out these smaller assignments without damaging their ability to carry out their primary mission—to win major wars? In particular, can the army do so? For it is to the army that these secondary assignments present the most serious difficulties; the other services find little in them that runs the risk of degrading their war-fighting capacities. But commitments of tens of thousands of soldiers to peace-making and peacekeeping missions for periods of months or years place a serious strain on the army, whose numbers are already below those of the inadequate force available at the outbreak of the Korean War.

Budget cutting. Yet the desire to cut military expenditures has created pressure to reduce the army's numbers even further. That is justified by the assertion that wars of the future will rely heavily on new "smart" and "stealthy" weapons, many of them unmanned and many others released from ships and airplanes at a great distance, thus making large numbers of soldiers unnecessary.

But one must be cautious about claims that new technology will make traditional ground forces marginal or irrelevant. Previous advances in military technology, even when they have had important effects on the character of warfare, have produced exaggerated claims and expectations. After the Franco-Prussian War, the officers of the German general staff ignored the complexities of traditional grand strategy and put their hopes and faith in mastery of the new technology. "Theirs was a narrow world of technical marvels: cartography, railroads, communications, weapons systems. They mastered statistical tables, devised intricate mobilization schedules, formulated complicated plans," all of which, however, was not enough to overcome the traditional disadvantages of numbers and geography.[4]

Similarly, British advocates of air power in the interwar years thought they could deter war or win it without the use of ground forces by developing the new technology of "strategic" aerial bombardment. "To the British Government rearmament came to seem almost a question of air power alone. Cabinet discussions tacitly assumed that the next war, if it came, would take the form of a direct, almost a private duel between the British and German Air Forces."[5] The ensuing war nevertheless lasted more than five years, involved bitter warfare between enormous armies, and ended only when ground forces marched into the German capital.

The war to drive Iraqi forces from Kuwait brought swift victory to the side with an overwhelming advantage in modern technology, including the first significant use of "smart" and "stealthy" weapons. Yet that victory required the employment of hundreds of thousands of ground troops even after a month-long pounding of Iraqi forces from the air. An air force colonel who flew in the Persian Gulf War rightly observed: "Airpower can only do so much; the Army must go in on the ground to defeat the enemy's ground forces to finally win the battle."[6] It is also true that the placement of ground forces in significant numbers is one of the most effective means of deterring breaches of the peace. But with inadequate numbers the army will be unable to perform its vital part in these jobs.

Unfortunately, the army is an attractive target for budget cutters because manpower, especially in the form of professional volunteers, is very expensive, and the army has by far the largest number of men and women. However, the United States must resist the temptation to save money by assuming that ground

[4]Holger H. Herwig, "Strategic Uncertainties of a Nation-State: Prussia-Germany, 1871–1918," in *The Making of Strategy: Rulers, States, and War*, ed. Williamson Murray, MacGregor Knox, and Alvin Bernstein (Cambridge, U.K.: Cambridge University Press, 1994), p. 251.

[5]Correlli Barnett, *The Collapse of British Power* (New York: Morrow, 1972), p. 4.

[6]Quoted in John Pimlott and Stephen Brady, *The Gulf War Assessed* (London: Sterling Publishers, 1992), pp. 122–23.

forces in future wars will play a less important role, at least until it is clear that some better substitute will be available. Until that time, it would be reckless to assume that a modernized ground force of considerable size will not be needed to fight (and deter) the wars of the future.

The problem of numbers is intensified by financial considerations. Already there is broad agreement that currently projected forces will be inadequate to carry out the strategy of the Clinton administration's Bottom-Up Review. Some analysts suggest that forces for the current strategic plan are underfunded for the period 1997–2002 by some $130 billion. If they are right, then even without involvement in missions short of war U.S. forces' capacity to do their job in both the short run and long run will be undermined.

The problem is also exacerbated by the need to keep pace with the advance of military technology. Whether or not America finds itself in the midst of a true revolution in military affairs, there is no doubt that the continued effectiveness of U.S. armed forces will require expensive investments to replace worn and obsolete equipment with the weapons and defenses of the future. There is already considerable tension within the armed forces over the need to maintain the forces at an adequate state of readiness to cope with current challenges and those of the near future, and the need for research, development, and procurement of the weapons of the next generation.

Numerous non-war assignments. The erosion caused by budget cutting is multiplied by involvement in secondary missions. The practice has been to carry out these missions without providing adequate additional funds, so that the decision to engage in them comes at the expense of general readiness and modernization. America's peacekeeping force in Bosnia, for example, will cost at least $3.5 billion for its first year of deployment.[7] The temptation, therefore, is to resist involvement in such missions in order to avoid degrading the war-fighting capacity of the armed forces.

Opponents of secondary missions also fear another source of degradation. They point to the danger that a focus on these lesser activities could undermine the army's war-fighting capacity in more subtle, yet fundamental, ways. The skills and qualities needed for peacekeeping are not the same as those required for war fighting. The toughness, aggressiveness, and ferocity that are essential for the latter are the opposite of the tact, patience, and caution often needed for the former. The fear is that the training

---

[7]"Bosnia Force Costs U.S. $3.5 Billion a Year," New York Times, Aug. 8, 1996.

needed to produce effective peace-keepers would degrade the trainees' capacity for war fighting. Some believe that the kind of soldier who excels in one assignment, regardless of training, is less well suited to the other. There is thus concern that as peace-keeping becomes more frequent, the peacekeeping type of soldier will be more readily favored and advanced, at the expense of the army's war-fighting capacity. This tendency, it is feared, will be increased if the army looks to the new, smaller missions as a means for building or protecting the size of the army against current and future reductions.

Various proposals have been suggested to meet these threats. One is to divide the army into two kinds of soldiers, each with its distinct kind of training. This plan would reduce at once the number of available fighting men, and in time it would create a sense that one group consisted of "real" soldiers while the other did not, with devastating consequences for morale. Most people believe that this would produce the worst possible degradation of the army's effectiveness, and they argue for a single kind of soldier with uniform training in both assignments. They place their hopes in a new kind of training that would allow soldiers to move comfortably and effectively from one kind of assignment to the other after a period of transitional preparation.

Another approach is to make greater use of reserves and guardsmen for peacekeeping purposes. That could increase the numbers available, since political support for these troops is strong. To make this approach work, however, training of reserves and guardsmen would need to improve to something like that employed by the marines with their reserves. Nevertheless, questions arise. If these auxiliaries are to be used in both types of assignments, will their training and duality be adequate for war fighting? If not, would not a two-tiered army emerge with the problems discussed above?

In sum, there is no real choice but to produce a doctrine and training program that will allow the army to carry out the range of missions that America's situation requires. Peace and American security depend on it.

This assignment is not easy and calls for both resolve and clear, hard thinking. The military and civilian leaders planning America's defense policy must be prepared to make the kinds of organizational changes, even radical ones, that may be needed in the new era, and to institute training to meet the new conditions. They also need to find better ways to reduce and control the cost of acquiring and maintaining needed weapons, for financial restrictions will always be serious.

However, they must face the fact that more money than is now budgeted or anticipated will be needed to meet the challenge. Their natural tendency to withdraw from as much responsibility as possible as soon as possible, and to shape defense expenditures to meet domestic political rather than strategic needs, has twice in this century put the Western democracies at risk. The major responsibilities facing America's leaders today are to resist that tendency and to educate the American people and their representatives as to what is needed for peace and security and what it will cost.

A New Strategy Is Needed

None of that can happen without the formulation of a clear national grand strategy to suit the international situation. In 1950, Paul Nitze (then head of the State Department's Policy Planning Staff) was charged with producing a comprehensive statement of national security policy. The document, known as NSC-68, became the general foundation of the containment strategy that shaped American policy in the next half century. The policy of containment laid out in those years was a rare example of a state making a rational evaluation of the problems it faced, the nature of its opponent, and the character of the threat that opponent posed to stability and peace, and then deciding on a reasoned course of action, including the sacrifices and commitments needed for success. It was a realistic approach that rested on an understanding of the need for military power and the manifest willingness to use it when necessary. Yet it was a subtle approach that gave full weight to the importance of ideas, economics, institutions, culture, and the need to adapt to change.

The adoption of the fully shaped policy of containment required a sharp break with America's past. Contrary to its traditions, the United States joined in a continuing alliance with nations in Europe and, later, in other parts of the world. It consciously undertook the chief burden of preserving the peace, under conditions tolerable to itself and its allies, gearing its economy for the purpose and adopting military conscription in peacetime. American leaders took these taxing and extraordinary measures to meet what they believed to be a serious and imminent threat. But the policy of containment was also shaped by their understanding of the origins of World War II. That war, they had concluded, originated in the failure of the Western democracies to meet their responsibilities after World War I, their withdrawal into isolation, and their unwillingness to bear the costs of keeping the peace, which required the capacity and will to resist detrimental changes in the balance of power caused by dissatisfied states that use subversion, threats, and military force to achieve their purpose.

To define the missions for America's armed forces in the decades to come requires a new NSC-68. There needs to be a full national debate, followed by the adoption of a grand strategy of continued engagement in the new constellation of international relations. The United States must take the lead in preserving the peace by deterring the resort to armed violence and intervening to prevent or stop it when necessary. With that goal established and understood, American military and civilian leaders can better turn to the difficult task of anticipating potential missions and preparing the means to make them successful.

SUPERPOWERS DON'T DO WINDOWS

by John Hillen

Since the collapse of the Soviet Union, American foreign policy thinkers have been striving to define a role for the United States in the post–Cold War world.[1] Their proposals have ranged from "strategic independence" on the isolationist pole to "assertive multilateralism" and "benevolent hegemony" on the interventionist pole. The sheer volume of labels and taxonomies, far from suggesting a wealth of ideas, is clear evidence of what Jonathan Clarke dubbed America's "conceptual poverty."[2]

Nonetheless, the majority of proposed post–Cold War strategies appear to seek a sensible course that lays out an active international role for the United States as a global superpower while avoiding the dreaded specter of the "global cop"—wasting American lives and resources, tilting at windmills, and minding everyone's business but its own. Robert Tucker has called this quest for the middle road "the great issue of American foreign policy today. It is the contradiction between the persisting desire to remain the premier global power and an ever deepening aversion to bear the costs of this position."[3] Another way to understand it is to consider Americans' desire for a reasonable policy of global engagement: one that preserves American involvement in global activities that benefit the United States but does not squander U.S. resources on global gendarmerie.[4] As former secretary of defense James Schlesinger noted, "The reality of the post–Cold

---

[1]This essay first appeared in *Orbis*, Spring 1997. While some of the numbers herein are dated, and some of the circumstances have changed, the author is confident that the basic argument and theoretical thrust of this piece remain relevant.

[2]Jonathan Clarke, "The Conceptual Poverty of U.S. Foreign Policy," *Atlantic Monthly*, Sept. 1993, pp. 54–66.

[3]Robert W. Tucker, "The Future of a Contradiction," *National Interest*, Spring 1996, p. 20.

[4]See the results of polling in John E. Reilly, ed., *American Public Opinion and U.S. Foreign Policy 1995* (Chicago: Chicago Council on Foreign Relations, 1995), p. 6; and Center for International and Security Studies, *An Emerging Consensus: A Study of American Public Attitudes on America's Role in the World* (College Park, Md.: Center for International and Security Studies at the University of Maryland, July 1996), p. 5. See also Steven Kull, "What the Public Knows That Washington Doesn't," *Foreign Policy*, Winter 1995, p. 104.

War world is that the U.S. has limited capital for foreign ventures. . . . The clear inference is that we should husband that political capital for those matters that are of vital interest to the United States."[5] To that end, Washington must promote a new security compact for America's alliances, for without substantial reworking to accommodate recent geopolitical and military trends, America's alliance system threatens to be a burden rather than a boon. Specifically, the system should demarcate a division of labor that takes advantage of allies' differing interests and military capabilities, with the fundamental dictum for the United States being "superpowers don't do windows."[6]

Currently, America's military alliances take many different forms. In its strictest sense, an alliance is a commitment for mutual military support against some external actor(s) in a specified set of circumstances.[7] Conversely, collective security organizations like the United Nations, the Association of Southeast Asian Nations (ASEAN) and the Organization for Security and Cooperation in Europe (OSCE) are not military alliances. Formal alliances are usually based on treaties and can range from highly institutionalized multilateral arrangements like NATO to dormant multilateral arrangements such as the Rio Treaty, to active bilateral defense alliances such as those with Korea and Japan, to latent bilateral agreements such as that with the Philippines, to de facto bilateral alliances like that of Australia and the United States, to moribund multilateral alliances like the Southeast Asia Treaty Organization.

The United States also maintains informal military alliances based upon other types of security cooperation, including the supply of military training and equipment, basing rights for U.S. troops or pre-positioned equipment, military training exchanges, and combined military exercises. These informal alliances can, in times of need, become frameworks for establishing coalitions, as demonstrated by the informal alliance between the United States and its partners in the Persian Gulf. Lastly, the United States participates in some de facto military alliances in cases where the

[5]Harry Summers, "Achilles Heel of Keeping the Peace," *Washington Times*, Oct. 17, 1996.

[6]This organizing imperative was summed up by the former chief of the Central Intelligence Agency's Afghan Task Force. When asked why the CIA had no intention of sorting out the squabbles of Afghan tribal leaders after the organization had been so active in helping to evict the Soviets from Afghanistan, the agent replied that "superpowers don't do windows." Jonathan Clarke, "Don't Keep U.S. Troops in Bosnia," *Los Angeles Times*, July 8, 1996.

[7]See Stephen Walt, *The Origin of Alliances* (Ithaca, N.Y.: Cornell University Press, 1987).

U.S. national interest is so obvious that a commitment to the defense of an ally is implicit, even absent a formal defense agreement. That is the case with countries such as Israel and Taiwan.

The United States needs this flexible array of alliances to protect its interests around the globe. But however extensive and varied they may be, U.S. vital interests are finite. So, too, are U.S. resources. Hence, the critical questions that any new strategy must address are where, when, why, and how the United States ought to be willing and able to intervene militarily—and where, when, why, and how it ought *not* to be willing to deploy its forces. In the post–Cold War world, perhaps the best metaphor for the proper U.S. role in alliances is the role the Mayo Clinic plays in health affairs, or the FBI plays in law enforcement. That is, the United States should take the lead in the hierarchy of global security, but within a cooperative system in which allies play supporting roles. The Mayo Clinic and the FBI undertake only those essential duties that are in keeping with their unique talents and resources, leaving routine health care and law enforcement to local hospitals and police. For otherwise, those elite agencies would not only drown in minutiae and waste their resources, they would soon lose their capacity to perform the challenging tasks for which they were formed.

If the United States is to avoid both damaging isolationism and wasteful activism in foreign affairs, it must recognize that it cannot and should not attempt to do everything. That means America should focus on security problems in its "jurisdiction," leaving its allies and like-minded states to play the roles of local doctor and cop. The United States also must recognize that it, and it alone, can perform the unique, expensive, and demanding task of deterring or defeating major-power aggression in any region of the globe. To maintain the skills necessary to execute this function requires strategy, doctrine, training, and force structure focused on deterrence and war fighting, not on peacekeeping missions. Lastly, the United States must realize that a failure to be prepared to combat serious security threats will sooner or later have consequences so catastrophic as to dwarf the problems of muddling through a Bosnia-, Haiti-, or Somalia-type mission.

The U.S. Defense Posture and Strategic Strain

Unilateral disarmament is a recurring pattern of American history, and the post–Cold War years are no exception. Since 1991, the U.S. military has suffered at least a 35 percent decrease in both force structure and defense funding. As a result, the force is the smallest fielded by the nation since 1940.[8] Unfortunately, these slashing cuts have occurred only on the supply side. On the demand side—commitments overseas—the military has actually been saddled with new responsibilities. In short, the U.S. armed forces, like so many downsized institutions, are being asked to do more with less, leading to two severe consequences. The first is a disparity between stated U.S. security commitments and the forces fielded by the nation, which has been the focus of recent intense debates.[9] The second is the resulting strain (on both personnel and matériel) the armed forces suffer as they attempt to compensate with an accelerated operational tempo. Their effort to do so has deprived the armed services of a prudent balance among current operations, training, readiness, and funding for future operations and equipment, owing primarily to overseas deployment require-ments for the myriad missions they are being asked to perform. For instance, on any given day in 1996 the army has some 105,000 soldiers permanently stationed overseas and another 40,000 on temporary duty in some sixty countries.[10] This demand, coupled with reductions in force size, means that many soldiers are deploying at a rate 300–400 percent higher than during the Cold War. In a time of relative peace, nearly 15 percent of active-duty army soldiers are deployed on twelve-month hardship tours of duty. A General Accounting Office (GAO) investigation in fact found that some army units were deployed more than 210 days per year.[11]

The other services face similar dilemmas. Expressing his con-cern about the high operational tempo, the U.S. Air Force chief of

[8]The 1997 end-strength goal for the active-duty military is 1.418 million. *FY 1997 Budget Briefing* (Washington, D.C.: Department of Defense [hereafter DOD], Mar. 4, 1996), slide 14. The next-lowest active-duty military strength number since 1940 was 1.444 million in 1948. Office of the Secretary of Defense, Comptroller, *National Defense Budget Estimates for FY 1997* (Washington, D.C.: DOD, Apr. 1996), p. 160.

[9]See Baker Spring, *Will Clinton Pay the Price for America to Remain a Global Power?* Backgrounder, no. 1083 (Washington, D.C.: Heritage Foundation, May 16, 1996); Andrew Krepinevich, *Bottom-Up Review: An Assessment* (Washington, D.C.: Defense Budget Project, 1994); Don Snider, Richard Betts, Andrew Krepinevich, et. al., "The Coming Defense Train Wreck and What to Do About It," *Washington Quarterly*, Winter 1996, pp. 89–131. There are also several critical reports by the General Accounting Office [hereafter, GAO], including *Bottom-Up Review: Analysis of Key DoD Assumptions*, Jan. 31, 1995; and *Future Years Defense Program: Optimistic Estimates Lead to Billions in Overprogramming*, July 29, 1994.

[10]DOD, *Defense Almanac* (Washington, D.C.: DOD, 1996), p. 18; G. E. Willis, "On the Road Again," *Army Times*, July 1, 1996.

[11]GAO, *Military Readiness: A Clear Policy Is Needed to Guide Management of Frequently Deployed Units* (Washington, D.C.: GAO, Apr. 1996).

staff set a target of a maximum of 120 days of temporary duty per unit. That target was drastically exceeded by many units, including airborne warning and control system units (average of 136 days), RC-135 units (168 days), combat air controllers (160 days), EC-130E units (175 days), and some electronic-warfare units that spent more than 300 days annually on deployments.[12] The navy has also exceeded its budgeted operations tempo for the past several years and predicts that it will do so again in fiscal year 1997.[13] With the decline in the number of its warships, the navy has been forced to "gap" the assignment of aircraft carriers and other warships, meaning that other forces must forgo routine training, maintenance, and rest in order to cover the gap left by the absence of a carrier. That happened in the spring of 1996, when the USS *Nimitz* was rushed from the Persian Gulf to cover the Taiwan-China crisis, requiring the United States to deploy a squadron of air force F-15s to Jordan to continue coverage of the no-fly zone over Iraq. Even more recently, the USS *Enterprise* left the Adriatic in September 1996 to reinforce the U.S. presence in the Persian Gulf during the latest confrontation with Saddam Hussein. The sudden absence of the *Enterprise* forced the land-based aircraft supporting the implementation force in Bosnia to make up for the hundreds of weekly sorties flown by the carrier-based aircraft.

These requirements are literally wearing out men and matériel, and former Pentagon planner Robert Gaskin has noted that the military is "approaching burnout."[14] The high rate of current operations has strained budgets, equipment, and units to the point where all services have cancelled required wartime training exercises. In one such instance, peacekeeping support duties in 1995 forced three air force fighter wings to cancel critical combat training exercises.[15] As a result of these trade-offs, 28 percent of the services' frequently deployed units are not "combat ready."[16]

Moreover, the Department of Defense (DOD) is unable to invest in the recapitalization of the armed forces. Procurement accounts have dropped some 70 percent in the past ten years, precipitating a 1996 rebellion by the Joint Chiefs of Staff, who

[12]Ibid. Additional information from author's interview with the U.S. Air Force Chief of Staff Operations Group, Washington, D.C., Aug. 1996.

[13]Chief of Naval Operations, *Department of the Navy 1997 Budget* (Washington, D.C.: Department of the Navy, 1996), p. 2-2.

[14]Art Pine, "U.S. Military Highly Rated, But Strains Begin to Show," *Los Angeles Times*, Mar. 19, 1996. See also Steven Komarrow, "Smaller Forces, More Missions Add Up to GI Stress," *USA Today*, Oct. 8, 1996.

[15]Author's interview with U.S. Air Force Chief of Staff Operations Group.

[16]GAO, *Military Readiness*, p. 12.

begged Congress to restore $20 billion in funding for new weapons systems. In the meantime, the current stocks of equipment are wearing down with heavy use. The C-130 aircraft supplying the Bosnia mission are at least twenty-six years old and are flying at twice their normal use rate. European-based C-130s had to be supplemented by a squadron from North Carolina because, in the words of one aircraft commander, the European-based squadron "ran their aircraft into the ground." New C-130s are not expected until 2005 at the earliest.[17] Overall, projected DOD budgets continue to live off the capital investments of the Reagan-era military buildup. As a result, by 2005 all of the tanks and most of the U.S. military aircraft will be older than the soldiers and pilots using them.

Lastly, the strain on the armed forces is lowering morale and the quality of military life. The GAO investigation noted that "officials in major commands revealed pronounced concerns about personnel problems such as divorces . . . and lowered retention."[18] The drop in retention rates is especially worrying given the time and money spent training service members. In 1995, the navy failed to reach its target on first-, second-, and third-term reenlistments.[19] This problem was somewhat ameliorated by the shrinking force structure, but threatens to become acute when the navy finishes its post–Cold War drawdown.

History suggests that military powers should use the breathing space between major conflicts to replenish their military stocks, train (and rest) their personnel, and aggressively experiment with new doctrines and equipment. Instead, the U.S. military is being driven into the ground by an already high operating tempo compounded by a series of peripheral peace operations. Speaker of the House Newt Gingrich (R-Ga.) has recognized that this effort is "stretching our military [to] the verge of the breaking point." He noted that

> at some point somebody needs to stand up and say there is a minimum size to being the world's only superpower, and we have gotten smaller than that in terms of our regular units, and we have an obliga-

[17]Bryan Bender, "Bosnia Mission Highlights Need for Improved C-130, Pilots Say," *Defense Daily*, Oct. 9, 1996.

[18]GAO, *Military Readiness*, pp. 3, 13. See also Leonard Wong, Paul Bliesse, and Ronal Halverson, "Multiple Deployments: Do They Make a Difference?" paper presented at the Inter-University Seminar on Armed Forces and Society Biennial Conference, Baltimore, Md., Oct. 21, 1995.

[19]Tom Philpott, "Is the Navy Now Too Small to Meet the Challenges of an Unstable World?" in *Seapower Almanac*, ed. Jim Hessman (Washington, D.C.: U.S. Navy League, Jan. 1996), p. 6.

tion to insist on a military in which people can serve without being burned out by the sheer constancy of their being used.[20]

Diverging Military Competencies

Since the end of the Cold War, U.S. allies, especially in Europe, have increasingly debated the need to develop capabilities for military operations that do not rely so heavily on the United States. In general, Washington has welcomed this movement toward greater self-reliance, although the Bush administration initially sent conflicting signals about European-only defense initiatives such as the Franco-German Corps and the Western European Union (WEU). The growing enthusiasm for U.S. allies' assuming a greater share of regional security burdens was clearly expressed in 1991 when then-president of the European Union Jacques Delors triumphantly proclaimed that solving the Bosnian crisis would prove to be the "hour of Europe."

Unfortunately, the rhetoric has not matched reality. As Professor Eliot Cohen has noted,

> Two seemingly contradictory trends seem to be at work: a formal effort to develop more independent forces that can operate outside traditional frameworks and operational environments, on the one hand, and on the other increased dependence on the United States in key areas of military power.[21]

The International Institute for Strategic Studies (IISS) recently concluded that "without the US, European NATO member-states do not have the capability to mount a combined arms operation of more than 30,000 troops, with air and naval support, capable of engaging in a full-scale military conflict outside NATO borders."[22] Moreover, the core competencies of the American military and those of America's allies are diverging. While the United States focuses on deterrence and war fighting, many of its allies are refocusing their shrinking militaries on peacekeeping and operations other than war.

As with the United States, monetary concerns are a driving force behind the changing military capabilities of many U.S. allies. While Korea and Japan have increased their defense spending since the end of the Cold War (Japan markedly so), America's

---

[20]Speaker of the House Newt Gingrich, Address at the Center for Security Policy's annual award dinner, Washington, D.C., Sept. 18, 1996.

[21]Eliot Cohen, "The U.S. and Alliance Strategies," paper presented at the 38th annual conference of the International Institute for Strategic Studies, Dresden, Germany, Sept. 1–4, 1996.

[22]International Institute for Strategic Studies, *The Military Balance 1996/97* (Oxford: Oxford University Press, 1996), p. 32.

European allies have cut defense spending as a percentage of gross domestic product (GDP) by an average of one-third.[23] Most of these cuts have been precipitated by the stringent fiscal requirements of EU monetary integration. (As of September 1996, only Luxembourg and Ireland met the Maastricht treaty conditions of having a budget deficit that is less than 3 percent of GDP and a national debt that is less than 60 percent of GDP.[24]) Given these spending cuts, many European militaries have recently changed from the conscript system to all-volunteer forces, a move that typically halves the size of a force. And in the absence of a clear and present danger from a major power, many allies have shifted their focus away from territorial defense. Canada's new defense minister recently stated, "I am a peacekeeper, not a warrior"[25]; and at an August 1996 ceremony to celebrate the end of conscription in the Netherlands, the Dutch defense minister noted that "the draft no longer fitted with the army's role in a world where peacekeeping has taken over from combat."[26]

Moreover, with few exceptions, European allies are not investing in strategic airlift and sealift; strategic logistics systems, space-based command, control, communications, and intelligence (C^3I) networks; and modern weapons systems based on revolutionary advances in information technology—capabilities that allow for power projection and sustained war-fighting campaigns.[27] The percentage of European defense spending devoted to research and development is half that of the United States, and expenditure on procurement is equally low. Many European defense analysts have noted that the decision not to invest in expensive systems has relegated their nations to reliance on the United States in campaigns outside of Europe and war-fighting contingencies even within Europe.[28] Yet only a few Europeans, mostly defense industrialists, have criticized the lack of investment.[29]

[23]Statistics taken from 1991–96 annual editions of International Institute for Strategic Studies, *The Military Balance* (Oxford: Oxford University Press).

[24]Fred Barbash, "Europe's Quest of Common Currency by 1999 Proving Divisive but Fervent," *Washington Post*, Sept. 23, 1996.

[25]Howard Schneider, "Canada's Military under Attack," *Washington Post*, Oct. 5, 1996.

[26]"Dutch End Military Draft," *International Herald Tribune*, Sept. 1, 1996.

[27]See R. L. Kugler, *U.S.–West European Cooperation in Out-of-Area Military Operations: Problems and Prospects* (Santa Monica, Calif.: RAND, 1994); Ronald Asmus, Richard Kugler, and Stephen Larrabee, "What Will NATO Enlargement Cost?" *Survival*, Autumn 1996, pp. 5–26.

[28]See Philip H. Gordon, "Recasting the Atlantic Alliance," *Survival*, Spring 1996, pp. 50–51; Rick Atkinson and Bradley Graham, "As Europe Seeks Wider NATO Role, Its Armies Shrink," *Washington Post*, July 29, 1996.

[29]See, for example, Robert Bussiére, "A Europe of Security and Defence," *NATO Review*, Sept. 1995, pp. 31–35.

Hence, the divergence between U.S. and allied military capabilities grows ever more acute. The United States holds both a qualitative and an enormous quantitative advantage over its allies. For example, the United States is the only member in its many security alliances that possesses large aircraft carriers, long-range strike aircraft, stealth aircraft, a network of space-based C^3I satellites and sensors, advanced aerial surveillance and reconnaissance systems, global lift capabilities, strategic logistics systems, and advanced weaponry based on information technology and the nascent "revolution in military affairs." However, Philip Gordon of IISS has noted that "this dependence isn't unpleasant enough to inspire the Europeans to do what they have to do to get around it."[30]

Consequently, many U.S. allies, particularly the European ones, though they remain valuable as political partners, are of rapidly diminishing use as military partners in war-fighting coalition operations such as the war in the Persian Gulf. The United States dominated the military force structure of that thirty-one-state coalition, providing not only the high-tech weaponry and logistics support but also more than 70 percent of the ground troops. The only other members with ground forces of comparable quality, Great Britain and France, had to scramble to mobilize a division and large brigade, respectively.[31] The United States also provided 76 percent of the in-theater combat aircraft and two out of every three warships, including all six coalition aircraft carriers. The command and support functions for launching air strikes also came predominantly from U.S. forces—on January 20, 1991, the third day of the air campaign against Iraq, every electronic warfare aircraft in theater was American. In addition, only American warships and a few British frigates had the technology necessary to operate together in the dangerous waters of the northern Persian Gulf.[32] The political value of the broad coalition aside, the basic management philosophy behind the distribution of coalition forces was to take advantage of the special capabilities that each state brought to the table. For Germany, Japan, and Kuwait that meant money; for Saudi Arabia and other Gulf states it meant money, basing, and national infrastructure; and for Islamic coun-

[30]Atkinson and Graham, "As Europe Seeks Wider NATO Role." See also Brooks Tigner, "Europeans Resist AGS Fast Track," *Army Times*, Oct. 14, 1996.

[31]See Jeff McClausland, *The Gulf Conflict: A Military Analysis*, Adelphi Paper 282 (London: International Institute for Strategic Studies, 1993).

[32]DOD, *The Conduct of the Persian Gulf War* (Washington, D.C.: Government Printing Office, 1992), pp. 70–81. See also Department of the Navy, *The U.S. Navy in Desert Shield and Desert Storm* (Washington, D.C.: Government Printing Office, 1991).

tries such as Egypt, Syria, and Morocco it meant political support and limited military contributions.

With decreasing support available from allies, the United States must continue to fund, provide, and train large forces for the war-fighting capabilities needed to protect the vital interests of America and its allies. That is why America's regional allies must take the lead in future Somalias, Haitis, and Bosnias—missions of regional peacekeeping, crisis management, and humanitarian relief—so as to leave the United States free to focus its energies on global power projection and large-scale combat operations.

Diverging Interests

American partnership with regional powers expected to play the role of "the cop on the beat" is not a novel idea. The Nixon Doctrine rested in part on such devolution of responsibility to certain states, such as Iran under the shah, on the assumption that these locally powerful allies could spare the United States the need to intervene directly. But in those days of the Cold War, a commonly perceived threat made for a confluence of interests between the United States and its allies. Today the situation is very different, and as the Iraq crisis of September 1996 highlighted, even a Saddam Hussein is not enough to ensure common cause in a key region. If anything, the latest round of confrontations with Iraq underscored an historical truism: alliances and coalitions tend to weaken as soon as the perception of threat diminishes. Thus, in comparison with his aggression against Kuwait and threat to the entire Arabian peninsula, Saddam's limited assault on an Iraqi Kurdish faction in August and September of 1996 elicited vastly different responses—the unilateral U.S. cruise-missile strike was unsupported or openly criticized by close allies such as France, Turkey, and Saudi Arabia. Similarly, during the Cold War, the overwhelming threat posed by the Warsaw Pact was the centripetal force holding NATO together. Today, absent that unifying threat, the stakes in local crises such as that in Bosnia are different for the United States and Europe. Bosnia may be the primary European security problem and it may touch the vital national interests of European powers, but it is not a primary concern of the United States, and the large U.S. engagement there serves only to erode the sole superpower's ability to discharge its primary functions.

What are those functions? They are to prevent, deter, or confront security challenges of the first order—from the world's great military powers such as Russia and China—and of the second order—from aggressive and well-armed rogue regimes such as those in Iran, Iraq, and North Korea. Bosnia, while a compelling issue, is a third-order security challenge on the periphery of U.S. interests, and the U.S. commitment to do the heavy lifting for a peacekeeping force there only misconstrues the true American role in European and global security. The United States should be involved militarily, but in a supporting rather than a lead role.

So far, most post–Cold War security challenges have been well below the threshold of a major-power threat necessitating significant U.S. involvement and leadership. It follows that regional devolution should be implemented in handling local threats. That is, allies closest to the problem and whose interests are most affected should be prime movers in mitigating the threat and should not be overly dependent on an ally that may have little interest in addressing the crisis. An "all for one and one for all" approach to every security dilemma, no matter what size, does not make sense for U.S. alliances. Instead, Washington must promote structures, like NATO's new combined joint task force (CJTF), that empower regional allies to tackle local crises. As Owen Harries writes,

> In deciding when to deploy [military force], Washington should practice the sound federal principle of subsidiarity—that is, allowing problems to be handled at the level closest to the problem. This way, a sense of responsibility can be developed throughout the international system and the United States can reserve its own intentions for the great issues involving its vital interests, acting as a balancer of last resort rather than a busybody and bully.[33]

However, America's Cold War military alliances still dominate the international arena, and until other security apparatuses emerge, U.S.-led alliances are often the default mechanism for responding to local problems. In Bosnia, NATO was called upon to solve the crisis, and the United States was thereby thrust into the political and military lead. But such quasi-military missions in areas of marginal importance are unpopular with the American public and offer little return for the investment of scarce national security resources. Many Americans question the utility of alliances in which the imperative of leadership forces the United States into operations and actions it might not otherwise undertake. That was the case in Bosnia, where preserving the credibility of NATO and the United States became the motivation for what

---

[33]Owen Harries, "Dole's Calculated Pragmatism," *New York Times Magazine*, Sept. 22, 1996.

Clinton administration officials characterized as a regrettable mission, the U.S.-led intervention.[34] Clearly the alliance and U.S. leadership were not functioning as the means to the ends of U.S. foreign policy, but became the end in themselves.

The confluence of these trends does not augur well for the continued management of international peace and security through an enduring alliance system. Alliances are intended to be a cost-effective means of protecting and promoting American interests. But the United States is no longer able to discriminate among security priorities, and the alliance system is hampering the effectiveness of U.S. national strategy. To reverse this slide, the United States must take charge of reforming the system instead of mistaking defense of the status quo for a manifestation of leadership.

Moreover, U.S. alliance leadership should not become a shibboleth for crisis management worldwide. Much as domestic policy analysts have questioned the utility of federal leadership in areas such as education and welfare, American foreign policy leadership should recognize a similar imperative in the global security hierarchy and not use America's leading role to usurp the responsibility, or discourage the capability, of alliance partners to take decisive action on minor regional affairs. Heeding these caveats, Washington should promote a security compact built on the following two principles.

Focus on Collective Defense

The majority of security challenges in the post–Cold War world are likely to be local crises requiring a protracted yet low-level military commitment. The United States should not squander its power on these tangential missions, though they may be the media rage of the moment. Rather, it must focus on deterring and defeating major-power threats (such as state-to-state aggression) in key regions.

With the exception of the U.S. role in North and Central America, Washington's commitment to regional security in Europe, the Middle East, the Persian Gulf, East Asia, and the Western Hemisphere is one of collective defense, not collective security. An alliance of collective defense (such as NATO) is a collaborative effort to defend against threats to the balance of power in a region through precisely focused missions.

[34]See John Pomfret, "U.S. Builds Arc of Alliances to Contain Serbia's Power," *Washington Post*, Dec. 19, 1995.

An alliance of collective security (such as the United Nations, OSCE, or ASEAN), on the other hand, provides a forum through which members can organize cooperative responses to various problems of peace and security, not just major-power threats. Collective security missions are broadly defined, sometimes anticipate problems, and can encompass nonmilitary efforts as well as limited or quasi-military interventions, including humanitarian intervention, support to nation building, peacekeeping, and peace enforcement. Collective security does not offer the same unambiguous goals as collective defense and often results in disputes among alliance members, as seen in the imbroglio among NATO allies about the U.N. mission to Somalia in 1993.[35] Overall, these alliances tend to be substantially less cohesive and decisive than those of collective defense.

The critical distinction between collective defense and collective security has been lost in recent years, especially in Europe, where local problems have thrust themselves onto NATO's agenda in the "threat vacuum" left by the dissolution of the Soviet Union. Using NATO for peripheral, ambiguous, and inconclusive security missions, such as that in the Balkans, could eventually erode U.S. public support for an American role in Europe. "Bring the boys home" will be the rallying cry if the *raison d'être* for an American military presence in Europe becomes policing local troubles on behalf of prosperous European allies.

Make the U.S. Role Unique and Decisive

With few exceptions, no U.S. allies have global security responsibilities. (Great Britain and France do, albeit in a more limited fashion.) Thus, as the world's only superpower with a full range of such commitments, the United States should play a unique and decisive role in its military alliances, and not needlessly duplicate the capabilities of its allies.

During the Cold War, America and its allies had qualitatively similar operational capabilities for territorial defense. While the United States had more forces and unique strategic capabilities, America's allies were able to field interoperable capabilities on the battlefield (tactical aircraft, artillery, tanks, personnel carriers, and, in the case of Great Britain and France, nuclear weapons). But the evolution of core military competencies has altered this calculus. A new security compact should focus U.S. military capa-

---

[35]See Kenneth Allard, *Somalia Operations: Lessons Learned* (Washington, D.C.: National Defense University Press, 1995), pp. 56–57.

bilities on missions of deterrence and war fighting where the presence of U.S. forces can alone provide the decisive edge.

In some cases the United States can make a decisive contribution with only a limited deployment of small but special capabilities (e.g., logistics or intelligence assets) that multiply the effectiveness of a coalition otherwise dominated by allies. The United States should be enthusiastic about providing a limited but decisive edge to an operation led by allies so long as it does not undermine the U.S. ability to meet more important security commitments elsewhere. In broader missions, such as the war in the Persian Gulf, the United States might be called upon to dominate the force structure, command-and-control arrangements, and operational planning. In management guru Peter Drucker's words,

> Effective leaders delegate a good many things; they have to or they drown in trivia. But they do not delegate the one thing that only they can do with excellence, the one thing that will make a difference, the one thing that will set standards, the one thing they want to be remembered for. They do it.[36]

Leadership in the alliance system naturally devolves on the United States, owing to the major-power security guarantee that only America can deliver and the enormous power it can bring to bear. Along with the unique and decisive military capabilities it can deploy for almost any operation, these constitute the immutable pillars of U.S. leadership in military alliances, a role that cannot be delegated. But a failure to delegate any responsibilities risks turning the alliance system into what political scientist Benjamin Schwarz calls a "wasting proposition" that needlessly siphons off American resources.[37]

The United States therefore must not feel trapped into leading all ambiguous missions. A Herculean effort to provide the preponderance of resources in every alliance would only sacrifice U.S. resources and determination, while giving its allies carte blanche to concentrate on "productivity, market penetration, wealth, and innovation: the kind of power that matters most in today's world."[38]

[36]Peter Drucker, "Not Enough Generals Were Killed," *Forbes ASAP*, Apr. 8, 1996, p. 104.

[37]Benjamin C. Schwarz, "The Arcana of Empire and the Dilemma of American National Security," *Salmagundi*, Winter/Spring 1994, p. 195. Schwarz's case is a variant of the theme of "imperial overstretch" raised in Paul Kennedy, *The Rise and Fall of the Great Powers* (New York: Random House, 1987).

[38]Ronald Steel, *Temptations of a Superpower* (Cambridge, Mass.: Harvard University Press, 1995), p. 5.

Fixing the Alliances

If the United States is to counteract the trends eroding the alliance system and avoid being bankrupted by trying to play clinician, cop, and social worker to the world, it must insist on a fair apportioning of responsibilities and costs with its allies. Washington must devise new approaches to some alliances, reject the proposed restructuring of others, perhaps conclude some new ones, and in every case subject its alliances to scrutiny designed to determine how they can best support American interests.

Europe. In post–Cold War Europe and the Mediterranean, NATO remains the premier fact of life in the security arena. And even with the collapse of the Soviet Union, the collective defense of Europe is an enduring American interest. Moreover, NATO's unprecedented levels of institutionalization and cooperation make it the most credible, functional, and useful military alliance of all time. As the war in the Persian Gulf highlighted, the work that has gone into NATO standards, interoperability, and defense cooperation can be an enormous advantage in operations outside of NATO as well.

Nonetheless, the continued success of the alliance will depend on the will and ability of NATO's European (and Canadian) members to practice increased self-reliance in local missions. This shifting must in turn be bolstered by mechanisms such as the combined joint task force, an organizational framework that will allow European allies to borrow NATO resources for European-led missions. The CJTF was proposed by the United States in 1993 and finally approved by NATO in June 1996. It need only be taken off the drawing board and put into practice.

Once implemented, the CJTF structure will allow NATO and Europe to abandon the Cold War paradigm of "all for one and one for all" by tailoring packages for specific missions. A CJTF operation can be composed of almost any mix of allied units and led by either an American (as in NATO's war-fighting structure) or European commander. An operational force can even be formed outside of NATO and led by other European security organizations, for example, the WEU or the OSCE. In that case, the CJTF could temporarily "lease" NATO units that would be "separable but not separate." A CJTF would also allow non-NATO European states to contribute troops, as many have done for the implementation force in Bosnia.

The U.S. ambassador to NATO, Robert Hunter, called the CJTF "the first significant change in the way the alliance does business since 1966" (when the French left the military structure of the alliance).[39] Not only does the CJTF's flexibility permit allies with the greatest interest in local crises to take the lead and help to equip them for the necessary missions, it can be equally valuable to NATO's traditional task of providing a credible combat capability to deter a major-power threat in Europe. For once CJTF is put in charge of handling lesser security dilemmas, the United States will be free to concentrate on its singular role as NATO's war-fighting leader. That is why the CJTF must not be allowed to atrophy in the committee rooms at NATO headquarters but should manage the follow-on force in Bosnia through 1997 and beyond. The United States might still contribute support capabilities to this European-led CJTF, but the bulk of the troops would come from NATO allies. In 1998, any residual Bosnia force would become entirely European. It would still be a CJTF, but it would be led by a European organization and would no longer be officially connected with NATO.

Of all the U.S. alliances, both formal and informal, NATO is most in need of reform aimed at a clear division of labor. America's NATO allies are prosperous and democratic states. Though they chose to cut defense spending, cut capabilities, and follow ineffective half-measures in Bosnia for four years, they are more than capable of handling European peacekeeping missions with support in key areas from the United States. Mechanisms such as the CJTF will allow European allies to pick up the slack in missions like Bosnia, freeing the United States for more important security tasks.

East Asia. During the Cold War, the U.S. bilateral alliance with Japan was the cornerstone of American strategy in East Asia. The alliance remains critical today, especially because China and North Korea pose two of the most salient threats in a region of increasing importance to U.S national security. Over the years, however, many have criticized the structure of this relationship.[40] Some observers believe that the United States pays too much to maintain some 47,000 troops in Japan when many Japanese (especially the Okinawans) want the troops to leave. Others argue that the Japanese take advantage of America's security blanket to invest would-be defense funds in economic production that eventually harms the United States in unfair trade deals. Still others

---

[39]"NATO Acquires a European Identity," *Economist*, June 8, 1996, p. 51.

[40]See, for example, Ted Galen Carpenter, *Paternalism and Dependence: The U.S.-Japanese Security Relationship*, Policy Analysis, no. 244 (Washington, D.C.: Cato Institute, Nov. 1, 1995).

maintain that in a major-power crisis in East Asia, the Japanese would not support U.S. combat operations unless Japan itself were attacked.

All these points deserve consideration in an ongoing reassessment of the U.S.-Japanese alliance. Nonetheless, the basic structure of the alliance serves America well. The U.S. mission in the alliance focuses on collective defense, while Japan's Self-Defense Force is committed to defending Japan and the sea lanes out to one thousand nautical miles from the home islands. U.S. military forces based in Japan also deter regional threats, as they did in March 1996 when the deployment of two U.S. aircraft carrier battle groups to the area around Taiwan convinced China that the United States was still determined to hold Beijing to its promise not to pursue coercive unification. And with Japan contributing more than $5 billion to the basing of U.S. troops and facilities, the alliance is by far the best cost-sharing arrangement with any ally. (The Clinton administration maintains that it would be more expensive to base those troops back in the United States.)[41]

In April 1996, the United States and Japan concluded additional defense cooperation arrangements that would marginally increase Japan's role in Asian security affairs. These steps were intended to make Japan a better partner in regional contingencies, and not to precipitate a reevaluation of each country's distinct role.

But many observers dismissed these steps as cosmetic and still call for Japan to assume an even greater Asian security role. Yet traditionally a fully militarized Japan with a unilateral defense policy has been destabilizing to the region. Moreover, Japan's remilitarization would not further the alliance goals of the security treaty and could even work against U.S. strategy in the Asia-Pacific region. The United States therefore should not ask Japan to assume the role of deterring major-power conflict in the region. In East Asia, as elsewhere, the job of confronting threats to the balance of power is uniquely America's. But Washington should encourage Tokyo no less than London, Paris, or Bonn to contribute to regional missions. Japanese participation in the U.N. peacekeeping mission in Cambodia in 1993 was a valuable first step. So long as Japan does not assume a grand strategic role, or build weapons or intelligence systems conducive to grand strategy, its Asian neighbors need not fear—and may in time welcome—a Japanese "cop" on the local police force.

[41]DOD, *United States Security Strategy for the East Asia–Pacific Region* (Washington, D.C.: DOD, Feb. 1995), p. 24.

The U.S.–South Korea alliance, by contrast, is more narrowly conceived since it exists to defend against a sole scenario: invasion of South Korea by North Korea. Some critics have questioned the presence of 34,000 American troops in Korea, labeling them redundant given the large size of the South Korean defense forces. However, the United States does not maintain ground troops in Korea because South Korea needs another infantry division to defend itself. Rather, U.S. ground troops are the embodiment of a commitment to peace in what is perhaps the most volatile corner of the great-power international system. It is there, on the borders of Korea, that Russia, China, Japan, and the United States meet. It is there that a rogue regime possesses the capability, and perhaps the intention, to light the fuse of great-power war. Were the United States to withdraw, no other power could provide a reassuring presence. Indeed, any effort by Russia, China, or Japan to do so would risk sparking the very conflict it was meant to repress.

The Middle East. Ad hoc coalitions drawn from de facto alliances are not only useful but preferable to formal de jure alliances like NATO in regions comprised of disparate states divided by religion, ideology, and geopolitics. The United States maintains such a "coalition in waiting" in the Persian Gulf, where security agreements with Kuwait, Saudi Arabia, and other Gulf states are marked by low-key defense cooperation agreements regarding basing privileges, defense training and supply, and combined military exercises. Though there is no treaty requirement—and little in the way of positive inducements to alliance—it is well understood that the negative inducement to unity afforded by the threat of Iraqi (or Iranian) aggression suffices to preserve the balance of power implicit in the strategy of "dual containment." Saudi Arabia and other Gulf states provide invaluable ports, bases, supplies, and key infrastructure. Germany and Japan chipped in billions to help finance the war in the Persian Gulf and would be asked, in need, to do so again. NATO allies and others provide air, sea, and ground assets to complement the U.S. forces. Islamic countries such as Egypt, Syria, Morocco, Afghanistan, Pakistan, and others contribute forces that may have been militarily irrelevant to past coalitions but were politically viable.

Local allies aside, the Gulf is clearly a case where the United States must be directly engaged by reason of its own interest—oil, most obviously, and the desire to shelter Israel and friendly Arab states from regional chaos—and by reason of threat from rogue regimes known to crave missiles and weapons of mass destruction. But in the Middle East no less than in the Balkans, the United States cannot assume responsibility for deterring or punishing the equivalent of "street crime"—for instance, the violence among rival Kurdish factions. For to try to do so and fail would destroy the superpower's credibility, while to deploy the forces needed to succeed would once again erode the strapped U.S. military's ability to perform its indispensable war-fighting mission. That is why the United States must take vigorous and immediate steps to support local allies, Turkey above all, in assuming leadership roles in the Middle East.

Elsewhere. There are, to put the point bluntly, no other regions of the world in which U.S. vital interests are directly threatened at present or will be in the near future. There are therefore no other regions of the world in which U.S. military forces need to be engaged through a military alliance. That is not to say that a future Russian (or Chinese) thrust into Central Asia would not be a scary signal that American power may have to be invoked. But Americans are not prepared to die for Tajikistan, and Washington certainly cannot broker an effective alliance in that region. U.S. diplomatic offices may be of use in South and Southeast Asia, but the American public is not willing, nor is the U.S. military prepared, to ally with or coerce India, Pakistan, or China—or Vietnam—in case of regional strife. Africa is very much on the map of charitable Americans but is completely off the map of the Pentagon. Latin America, of course, remains a U.S. bailiwick, but everyone is happier when needed interventions are performed by Canadians or regional states rather than by "Yankee imperialists."

But if the United States refrains from entering military alliances and takes no more than a supporting role in ethnic and religious conflicts or humanitarian disasters in most of the Third World, who will undertake these tasks? It is simply up to regional powers, with or without cooperation from the United Nations, to walk the beats in their neighborhoods. To the extent those powers need occasional U.S. assistance in logistics, intelligence, or other specialized capabilities, let them seek U.S. help, rather than vice versa. Let them ask Washington for an "alliance" or understanding, instead of the other way around. And the candidates for the roles of local leaders are obvious. In Latin America, the standouts are Argentina, Brazil, Chile, and Venezuela. In South Asia, India and Pakistan have no choice but to mend their fences or prepare to suffer forever. In Africa, the present prospects for regional leaders of any sort are dim. In the ex-Soviet world, the only possible policeman is, yes, Russia, assuming that unhappy country proves willing and able to take its place as a responsible regional power in league with the West. Filling out this roster of local "G.P.s" and "cops on the beat" may take many decades. But if there is to be a new world order, that is how it will come about, not through increased and indiscriminate American intervention, but through precisely the opposite. That is so, first, because an America whose military chases every ambulance will soon be unable to prevent the big calamities and, secondly, because it will soon exhaust Americans' tolerance even for seeing to little contingencies.

That does not mean that the United States will not participate in lesser interventions that have clear goals and a chance for success. It also does not preclude aggressive U.S. diplomatic and economic strategies for those areas where the United States does not have a military alliance. Regional devolution, as an alliance strategy, merely means that all members should box at their own weight level to get the most out of the team.

Conclusion

Most Americans would agree that the United States must be active in the world, but not so active that the effort wastes American resources and energies in interventions that yield little or no payoff and undermine military preparedness. The need for a policy of highly selective engagement is all the more acute owing to the numerous security challenges that the United States must address with a shrinking pool of military resources. There is just no alternative, therefore, to reforming U.S. alliances in ways that forestall further confusion about the U.S. role in minor post–Cold War security challenges. The way to begin is simply to announce to America's allies and partners the criteria that will define when, where, why, and how the United States might choose to use military force and, by implication, the situations in which it will expect its partners to assume leadership. In other words, America proclaims that "superpowers don't do windows," so if you want your local windows washed, you had better gear up to do them yourselves.

Such an "agonizing reappraisal" might shock some, especially in Europe, but it is based on a commonsense recognition that there is a hierarchy in international security composed of local military powers, regional powers, global powers, superpowers, and entities such as alliances and international organizations. The hierarchy conduces to order rather than chaos when each constituent part has roles and responsibilities that match its interests and capabilities. If an organization tries to do too much, it fails. That has been evident for the past few years with the United Nations. Similarly, if the United States attempts to do too much, as it does now, its forces become overstretched and lose sight of their most significant roles.

Consequently, the United States should focus its security policies on major threats such as other great powers or rogue regimes that can upset the local balance of power in key regions. America's allies should take the lead in local crisis management, peacekeeping, and humanitarian relief operations. History shows that another major conflict is never far away and is usually unpredictable. The United States is the only nation capable of forestalling or fighting that conflict. It must remain focused on doing so, for that is the task no one else can do.

THE U.S. PRESUMPTION OF QUICK, COSTLESS WARS

by Andrew P. N. Erdmann

Since the early 1980s, the presumption that the United States must end future military conflicts quickly and at minimum cost has achieved almost the status of orthodox dogma.[1] That military operations must be brief and efficient in terms of the human and economic price paid is not merely desirable, but held to be necessary in order to maintain the support of the American public.

Whether explicit or implicit, this quick, costless war presumption shapes policy pronouncements by leaders of the defense establishment, formal statements of military doctrine, analyses made by civilian strategists, and informal conversations throughout the armed services. In 1993 Secretary of Defense Richard Cheney argued that in "regional conflicts" where the nation's "stake may seem less apparent," the American response must be "decisive, requiring the high-quality personnel and technological edge to win quickly and with minimum casualties." The U.S. Army's central doctrinal statement, Field Manual 100-5, *Operations* (1993), echoes such sentiments in its characterization of the American View of War: "The American people expect decisive victory and abhor unnecessary casualties. They prefer quick resolution of conflicts and reserve the right to reconsider their support should any of these conditions not be met." In a similar vein, the oft-cited civilian strategist Edward Luttwak stresses that "the prospect of high casualties, which can rapidly undermine domestic support for any military operation, is the key political constraint when decisions must be made on which forces to deploy in a crisis, and at what levels." More bluntly, as recently recounted in *Parameters*, the quarterly of the U.S. Army War College, a military conference audience applauded when a young officer remarked that the U.S. military may someday suffer defeat in spite of its superior preparation and equipment because "the American people have lost the warrior's edge."[2]

[1]This essay first appeared, in slightly different form, in *Orbis*, Summer 1999.
[2]See Dick Cheney, *Defense Strategy for the 1990s* (Washington, D.C.: U.S. Government Printing Office, 1993), p. 15; U.S. Army, *Field Manual 100-5: Operations*

This presumption then came to the fore during the Kosovo campaign in 1999. Most fatefully, at the outset of the military campaign President Bill Clinton and his national security team pointedly emphasized that ground options to stop Serb atrocities in Kosovo were not being contemplated. As General Wesley Clark later acknowledged, the civilian leadership "felt that air was easier to get public support for than ground operations." Outside the administration, many observers also shared the quick, costless war mindset, as epitomized by CNN commentator Steve Roberts's assertion that "the American people does not have much of a stomach for these things."[3]

Whence did this presumption come? And, more important, is it valid?

Origins of the Quick, Costless War Presumption

The current belief that Americans lack the requisite fortitude to endure prolonged military operations is ironic, because their history has been defined by success in such conflicts. The United States itself was born of a protracted war, preserved its unity in a savage civil war eighty years later, helped defeat Japanese militarism and European fascism in the greatest conflagration in history, and, finally, sustained for over four decades an unprecedented global engagement to contain the Soviet empire until it collapsed under the weight of its own internal contradictions. The origins of the quick, costless war presumption, however, are not found in these broad contours of American history, but rather in the specific context of the Vietnam War's aftermath.

The search for "the lessons" of Vietnam dominated strategic discussions in the years following the inglorious evacuation of the U.S. embassy in Saigon. For those looking to prevent another such debacle, Vietnam stood as a reminder of the dilemmas war poses

(Washington, D.C.: Headquarters, Department of the Army, June 14, 1993), pp. 1–3; Edward N. Luttwak, "A Post-Heroic Military Policy," *Foreign Affairs*, July/Aug. 1996, p. 36; David Tucker, "Fighting Barbarians," *Parameters*, Summer 1998, p. 74. The drafting of the new doctrinal statement *Field Manual 3-0: Operations* to replace FM 100-5 (1993) has been recently completed. Significantly, the 1986 edition of FM 100-5 did not contain any such assessment of the "American View of War." See U.S. Army, *Field Manual 100-5*: Operations (Washington, D.C.: Headquarters, Department of the Army, May 5, 1986).

[3]Gen. Wesley Clark interview for "Frontline: War in Europe" (http://www.pbs.org/wgbh/pages/frontline/shows/kosovo/interviews/clark.html); "CNN Late Edition with Wolf Blitzer," Apr. 11, 1999, 12:00 a.m. (Eastern Time) broadcast, Lexis-Nexis transcript no. 99041100V47. The Clinton administration's declared intention to avoid using ground troops in Kosovo became "one of the chief errors in the campaign" because it reassured Serbian leaders that a NATO ground operation would not be forthcoming. Tim Judah, *Kosovo: War and Revenge* (New Haven, Conn.: Yale University Press, 2000), p. 269.

for democratic governments. A democratic regime cannot indefinitely sustain an inconclusive, unpopular war. Yet some drew a slightly different lesson from the Vietnam experience, namely, that *any* protracted military engagement must become unpopular with the American people and, therefore, be unsustainable. Such reasoning was embedded in the pronouncements of Secretary of Defense Caspar Weinberger, including his famous "The Uses of Military Power" address of November 1984.[4] Weinberger's criteria for the use of American force hinged upon securing domestic support. And since he questioned whether the American public would support protracted operations, he insisted that "if combat forces are required, they should be introduced rapidly and in the strength necessary to achieve our objective at the least possible cost."[5] In the words of Samuel Huntington, the author of the seminal study of American civil-military relations *The Soldier and the State*, military leaders by the mid-1980s did "not want to act because they fear[ed] the absence of public support."[6] Emphasizing the liberal democratic nature of the American polity, Huntington agreed with Weinberger that "public opinion will not support a prolonged 'slow bleed' of American blood." Huntington concluded that duration would be a critical factor in planning future military operations. "The United States must pursue objectives it can hope to achieve quickly and use means that minimize the time required to achieve those objectives," he wrote. "We must aim for a first round knockout."[7] As embodied in the so-called Weinberger-Powell-Cheney Doctrine of "overwhelming" or "decisive" force, this stress upon the immediate success of military operations continues to shape military policy down to the present day.[8]

---

[4]Caspar W. Weinberger, "The Uses of Military Power," Remarks to the National Press Club, Nov. 28, 1984, News Release No. 609-84, Office of Assistant Secretary of Defense (Public Affairs); Caspar W. Weinberger, "U.S. Defense Strategy," *Foreign Affairs*, Spring 1986, pp. 684–90.

[5]Weinberger, "U.S. Defense Strategy," p. 688.

[6]Samuel P. Huntington, "Playing to Win," *National Interest*, Spring 1986, p. 12.

[7]Ibid., p. 14.

[8]For the development and application of the doctrine of "decisive force," see Kenneth J. Campbell, "Once Burned, Twice Cautious: Explaining the Weinberger-Powell Doctrine," *Armed Forces and Society*, Spring 1998, pp. 357–74; Christopher M. Gacek, *The Logic of Force: The Dilemma of Limited War in American Foreign Policy* (New York: Columbia University Press, 1994), pp. 220–336; Frank G. Hoffman, "'Decisive Force': A New American Way of War?" *Strategic Review*, Winter 1995, pp. 23–34; Colin Powell, "U.S. Forces: Challenges Ahead," *Foreign Affairs*, Winter 1992/93, pp. 32–45; Colin Powell with Joseph E. Persico, *My American Journey*, with new afterword (New York: Ballantine, 1996), pp. 128–29, 139–45, 200, 280–81, 292–93, 420–21, 543–48, 559–62; Caspar W. Weinberger, *Fighting for Peace: Seven Critical Years in the Pentagon* (New York: Warner Books, 1990), pp. 159–60, 401–2. See also the official statements of military strategy issued by the Joint Chiefs of Staff during the 1990s: Colin L. Powell, *National Military Strategy of the United States* (Washington,

Unquestionably, this emphasis on the need for public support of military operations was a healthy corrective to some earlier theories of limited war that tended to downplay the public dimension of the use of force.[9] However, the more extreme form of this "lesson" of Vietnam—that the American public's will was the weak link in the strategic chain and the ultimate cause of failure in Vietnam—should not have endured. As Harry Summers argued in *On Strategy*, and as recent studies that rely upon newly declassified documents reaffirm, the sources of American failure in Vietnam were not found in the public will, but in the failure of the nation's civilian and military leadership to develop a coherent, viable strategy.[10]

Although triumph in the Persian Gulf War expunged many lingering concerns about U.S. military prowess, in recent years doubts about the staying power of the American people have increased to the point that the quick, costless war presumption now permeates discussions about the future national security policy of the United States.[11] The fact that both sides in recent debates over the merits of neo-isolationism,[12] the "revolution in military

D.C.: Joint Chiefs of Staff, 1992); John M. Shalikashvili, *National Military Strategy of the United States of America 1995: A Strategy of Flexible and Selective Engagement* (Washington, D.C.: Joint Chiefs of Staff, 1995); John M. Shalikashvili, *National Military Strategy of the United States of America 1997: Shape, Respond, Prepare Now—A Military Strategy for a New Era* (Washington, D.C.: Joint Chiefs of Staff, 1997).

[9]See the insightful analysis of Stephen Peter Rosen, "Vietnam and the American Theory of Limited War," *International Security*, Fall 1982, pp. 83–113.

[10]Harry G. Summers Jr., *On Strategy: A Critical Analysis of the Vietnam War* (New York: Dell, 1984); Robert Buzzanco, *Masters of War: Military Dissent and Politics in the Vietnam Era* (New York: Cambridge University Press, 1996); H. R. McMaster, *Dereliction of Duty: Lyndon Johnson, Robert McNamara, the Joint Chiefs of Staff and the Lies that Led to Vietnam* (New York: HarperCollins, 1997); Robert S. McNamara, *In Retrospect: The Tragedy and Lessons of Vietnam* (New York: Times Books, 1995); Brian Vandemark, *Into the Quagmire: Lyndon Johnson and the Escalation of the Vietnam War* (New York: Oxford University Press, 1995).

[11]The argument that follows does not focus upon the issue of casualty aversion per se. It does accord closely, however, with the assessment of Richard Betts: "It has become axiomatic that Americans will not tolerate many body bags in the course of an intervention where vital interests are not at stake. There is no clear evidence for this conventional wisdom, however, and ample evidence to the contrary." Richard K. Betts, "What Will It Take to Deter the United States?" *Parameters*, Winter 1995–96, p. 76. For a useful investigation of the relationship between casualties and domestic support for U.S. military operations since the Second World War, see Eric Larson, *Casualties and Consensus: The Historical Role of Casualties in Domestic Support for U. S. Military Operations* (Santa Monica: RAND, 1996).

[12]In arguing *against* the "renewed threat" of isolationism, Arthur Schlesinger Jr., expresses concern over evidence of decreasing public willingness to support military operations abroad which risk American casualties. Arthur Schlesinger Jr., "Back to the Womb? Isolationism's Renewed Threat," *Foreign Affairs*, July/Aug. 1995, pp. 2–8. Harvey Sapolsky also emphasizes this purported aversion to casualties, but he employs this aversion to argue *for* a fundamental retrenchment of American military commitments. This advocacy of neo-isolationism is implied in Harvey M. Sapolsky and Jeremy Shapiro, "Casualties, Technology, and America's Future Wars," *Parameters*, Summer 1996, pp. 123–26. More recently, Sapolsky explicitly advocated a policy of

affairs" (RMA),[13] and the culture of future warfare[14] have taken for granted the American lack of will for protracted military operations only underscores its prominence and widespread acceptance. Some RMA proponents, for instance, allude to the decline in American will in order to reinforce their arguments for a *need* for new high-tech methods of warfighting. Thus, it is not just that technological developments are pushing evolution of a new mode of warfare, but that American political culture necessitates the search for a capacity to wage swift military campaigns with minimal casualties. For example, Alvin H. Bernstein and Martin Libicki exploit this rhetorical tactic when they argue that

> distance [i.e., RMA-style] warfare, because of its relative safety, may offer an antidote to our persistent post-Vietnam aversion to the use of force in international affairs and to growing sensitivity about casualties among our own and even enemy soldiers. Indeed, in an era of rising isolationist sentiment, the tactics of distance warfare are likely to become the most muscular and credible tools available to the architects of American foreign policy.[15]

"restraint," which entails U.S. military disengagement from Europe and Asia as well as a 50 percent reduction in the defense budget. Eugene Gholtz, Daryl G. Press, and Harvey M. Sapolsky, "Come Home, America: The Strategy of Restraint in the Face of Temptation," *International Security*, Spring 1997, pp. 5–48.

[13]In a critical appraisal of over-reliance upon the RMA, Charles J. Dunlap Jr. argues that American adoption of the RMA conception of warfare will create vulnerabilities which a ruthless adversary will then exploit with ingenious asymmetric strategies. Such an enemy might focus upon undermining the weak American public will, for example, by transmitting on global television the mutilation of female prisoners of war. Edward Luttwak agrees that the American public no longer has the stomach to endure significant casualties. However, he advocates increased reliance upon RMA-type weapons systems since these are the only weapons whose use the public might then support. Although they stand on different sides of the RMA debate, therefore, both Dunlap and Luttwak invoke the assumptions that undergird the quick, costless war presumption. Charles J. Dunlap Jr., "How We Lost the High-Tech War of 2007," *Weekly Standard*, Jan. 29, 1996, pp. 22–28; Luttwak, "A Post-Heroic Military Policy," pp. 40–44.

[14]For analyses that suggest that future conflict will be less state-centric, more likely in "complex" terrain favoring the defense, more primitive and barbaric, and, thus, a special challenge for Americans and their values, see Dunlap, "How We Lost the High-Tech War of 2007"; Charles J. Dunlap Jr., "21st-Century Warfare: Four Dangerous Myths," *Parameters*, Autumn 1997, pp. 27–37; Luttwak, "A Post-Heroic Military Policy"; Steven Metz and James Kievit, *The Revolution in Military Affairs and Conflict Short of War* (Carlisle Barracks, Pa.: Strategic Studies Institute, U.S. Army War College, 1994), pp. 12–16; Steven Metz, "Which Army After Next? The Strategic Implications of Alternative Futures," *Parameters*, Autumn 1997, pp. 15–26; Ralph Peters, "The Culture of Future Conflict," *Parameters*, Winter 1995–96, pp. 18–27; Ralph Peters, "The Future of Armored Warfare," *Parameters*, Autumn 1997, pp. 50–59; Ralph Peters, "Our Soldiers, Their Cities," *Parameters*, Spring 1996, pp. 43–50; Martin L. Van Creveld, *The Transformation of War* (New York: Free Press, 1991). For an assessment that suggests American public will should not be underestimated in the face of such challenges, see Tucker, "Fighting Barbarians."

[15]Alvin H. Bernstein and Martin Libicki, "High-Tech: The Future Face of War? A Debate," *Commentary*, Jan. 1998, p. 31. See also Jeffrey Shaffer and Benjamin Ederington, *The Military Technical Revolution: A Structural Framework* (Washington, D.C.: Center for Strategic and International Studies, 1993), pp. 10–12.

And the ramifications of accepting the logic of the quick, cost-less war presumption can be profound, because some defense ana-lysts now argue that the supposed decline in American will man-dates that the primary criterion for the evaluation of weapon sys-tems should be whether these systems offer the prospects for min-imum allied casualties.[16]

How is this purported decline in American will explained? The current diagnosis invokes pathologies beyond the dilemmas that protracted warfare pose for democracies or the specific legacy of Vietnam. Conventional wisdom now identifies a profound cultural shift linked to the prosperity and relative passivity of life in the post-industrial/information age. "Warrior culture" has declined, eroding Americans' willingness to tolerate the sacrifices neces-sary to sustain international leadership. The expectation of rela-tively cheap, antiseptic wars such as that in the Persian Gulf, the rapid reassessment of American policy in Somalia following the death of eighteen Americans in the October 1993 Mogadishu fire-fight, and American hesitation in responding to the Bosnian crisis all conveniently reinforce the notion that deeper trends are at work. According to this argument, Americans have become "soft" relative to their more primitive adversaries. The exact nature of these "trends" remains for the most part elusive. Some have spec-ulated that demographic changes—specifically, declining birth rates, smaller family sizes, and less personal contact with death—are making Western societies less willing to accept casualties.[17] Others point the finger at a new generation of left-leaning, tech-nologically oriented "culture warriors" who do not understand and, therefore, disparage the "warrior spirit."[18] Nevertheless, in its most recent form the logic of quick, costless war presumption suggests that a confluence of economic, social, and cultural forces will gather momentum in the future, thus eroding further the American will to sustain costly military operations abroad.[19]

A proper understanding of the historical development of "war-rior culture" in American history and its relationship to public will, however, reveals that the evidence to sustain the quick, cost-

[16]Luttwak, "A Post-Heroic Military Policy," pp. 40–44.

[17]Edward N. Luttwak, "Where Are the Great Powers? At Home with the Kids," *Foreign Affairs*, July/Aug. 1994, pp. 23–28; Edward N. Luttwak, "Toward Post-Heroic Warfare," *Foreign Affairs*, May/June 1995, pp. 115–116. For a rebuttal, see James Burk, "Public Support for Peacekeeping in Lebanon and Somalia: Assessing the Casualties Hypothesis," *Political Science Quarterly*, Spring 1999, pp. 53–78.

[18]William C. Moore, "The Military Must Revive Its Warrior Spirit," *Wall Street Journal*, Oct. 27, 1998.

[19]See also John A. Gentry, "Military Force in an Age of National Cowardice," *Washington Quarterly*, Autumn 1998, pp. 182–84.

less war presumption is lacking. And since poor diagnosis leads to poor prescription, the presumption is potentially dangerous.

The Eclipse of Traditional "Warrior Culture," 1898–1940

Although the notion of "warrior culture" is familiar, a working definition is necessary to prevent any confusion with the other "cultures" commonly invoked in contemporary public debate. A warrior culture is one that celebrates martial training and skill, patriotism, national service, and above all, demonstrated valor in combat. Such values are sustained and reaffirmed through shared traditions, symbols, and other cultural practices and artifacts, including history, literature, and art. They can also be reinforced through both informal and formal mechanisms, such as privileged social status or the franchise. In the purist forms of warrior culture such values may be preeminent and provide the foundation for a nation's social and political order. The nineteenth-century Zulu or Lakota Sioux, for instance, represented nearly absolute warrior cultures. This concept, however, should not be confused with "military culture," a term frequently employed in contemporary strategic discourse to refer to the "prevailing values, norms, philosophies, customs, and traditions of the armed forces."[20] Warrior culture, by contrast, encompasses shared societal values broadly speaking, not just those within specific military institutions. In other words, peoples possessing a warrior culture are—to employ historian John Keegan's succinct definition—"brought up to fight, think fighting honorable, and think killing in warfare glorious."[21]

Despite their martial heritage, Americans have never come close to embracing a pure warrior culture. Nonetheless, anyone who has walked the battlefield at Gettysburg feels viscerally that the men of the First Minnesota Regiment or Pickett's division were unlike Americans of today. Michael Shaara's *The Killer Angels* succeeds as historical fiction precisely because it recaptures a world so different from our own—one distinguished by dif-

---

[20]Joseph J. Collins, "The Complex Context of American Military Culture: A Practitioner's View," *Washington Quarterly*, Autumn 1998, p. 213. On the various definitions of "military culture" in the current discussions of American military policy, see Don M. Snider, "An Uninformed Debate on Military Culture." On the importance of "military culture" historically and in the current context, see Williamson Murray, "Does Military Culture Matter?"; and John Hillen, "Must U.S. Military Culture Reform?" The latter three, originally from *Orbis*, Winter 1999, are republished in this volume.

[21]John Keegan, "The Warrior's Code of No Surrender," *U.S. News and World Report*, Jan. 23, 1995, p. 47. See also his discussion of cultures centered upon warfare in *A History of Warfare* (New York: Knopf, 1993), pp. 24–46.

ferent conceptions of personal honor, heroic sacrifice for one's friends and cause, and the battlefield as the ultimate test of one's virtue and strength.[22] Looking back from our vantage point at the start of the twenty-first century, we perceive that many of the elements of warrior culture common 140 years ago no longer characterize American society. The place of warrior culture in American life has indisputably changed. Yet this change did not occur during the past few decades, as often implied by those who cite recent developments in news media, demographic trends, or the impact of post-industrial society. Rather, it was the First World War that eclipsed America's traditional warrior culture.

At the dawn of the twentieth century many Americans still considered the battlefield the ultimate testing ground of a nation's and individual's virtue. To be sure, the American people never possessed a monolithic culture with regard to military affairs. A vibrant tradition of dissent that stressed anti-expansionism, exhibited a profound suspicion of military institutions and operations abroad, and sometimes came close to pacifism dated back to the founding of the republic.[23] Yet as late as 1898, the war with Spain could still be described without irony as a "Splendid Little War," and many Americans, including prominent cultural leaders such as Theodore Roosevelt, imagined war a romantic activity. Although often portrayed as a master of realpolitik in histories of American foreign relations, Roosevelt remained a Victorian romantic who wholeheartedly embraced warrior culture, stressed the virtues of personal valor, and considered war the preeminent test of manhood. He famously resigned his position as assistant secretary of the navy to join the Rough Riders in Cuba, but more dramatically, he wished for his own sons to be tested in battle in the Great War, and confided to a friend his hope that they might even be wounded or lose a limb as a mark of valor.[24] Such ideas must seem utterly alien to most Americans today, but they reflected the nation's previous embrace of warrior culture.

The First World War, however, extinguished the flame of this

[22]For an assessment of the latest scholarship of motivation during the Civil War, see Mark Grimsley, "In Not So Dubious Battle: The Motivations of American Civil War Soldiers," *Journal of Military History*, Jan. 1998, pp. 175–88.

[23]Robert David Johnson, *The Peace Progressives and American Foreign Relations* (Cambridge, Mass.: Harvard University Press, 1995), pp. 10–33.

[24]Kathleen M. Dalton, "Theodore Roosevelt's Great War, 1917–1918," Charles Warren Center Colloquium, Harvard University, Apr. 2, 1997. See also Edward J. Renehan Jr., *The Lion's Pride: Theodore Roosevelt and His Family in Peace and War* (New York: Oxford University Press, 1998); and Gerald F. Linderman, *Embattled Courage: The Experience of Combat in the American Civil War* (New York: Free Press, 1987), pp. 275–97.

romanticized warrior culture for the reason that it represented a qualitatively different kind of conflict from any that came before. President Woodrow Wilson's dream of making the world anew in an image of amity and cooperation helped sustain Americans' crusading zeal temporarily, but the failure to ratify the Treaty of Versailles and join the League of Nations, followed by the collapse of stability in Europe and the Pacific by the early 1930s, led Americans to doubt whether their battlefield sacrifices had served any good purpose whatsoever. In the public mind the singular heroic battlefield act lost its significance and was replaced instead by the image of mechanized slaughter in which the individual— whether on the home front or the battlefront—was merely a minor cog in a machine that dealt mass and pointless death.

In their disillusionment over the origins and results of Wilson's crusade, most Americans by the 1930s came to consider traditional warrior culture primitive and dangerous. This was the era of the Neutrality Acts, Senator Gerald Nye's Munitions Committee investigation, and the height of isolationism, when the congressional leadership of both parties and the leading voices in the press agreed that never again should the United States be duped into costly military adventures abroad, whether by "merchants of death" or idealists. Films and novels such as *All Quiet on the Western Front*, as well as popular revisionist histories of the American entry into the First World War, captured these themes and gave them a wide audience.[25] Unlike today, the central foreign policy debates of the 1930s hinged upon prohibiting U.S. military involvement abroad altogether. And unlike today, few believed that U.S. interests extended beyond the Western Hemisphere. Americans' ostrich-like reaction to German, Italian, and Japanese expansion only seemed to confirm their sense of isolation from the storms whipping the rest of the world.

Indeed, by 1940 it seemed on the surface that Americans no longer possessed the stomach for war. Their geographic isolation allowed them to become insular and self-absorbed, while urbanization and mass entertainment reduced their frontier heritage to a trivial Hollywood genre. Despite its industrial potential, therefore, the United States appeared weak and decadent when compared to

[25]John Whiteclay Chambers II, "'All Quiet on the Western Front' (1930): The Antiwar Film and the Image of the First World War," *Historical Journal of Film, Radio and Television*, 1994, pp. 377–411; Warren I. Cohen, *The American Revisionists: The Lessons of Intervention in World War I* (Chicago: University of Chicago Press, 1967); Manfred Jonas, *Isolationism in America, 1935–1941*, reprint ed. (Chicago: Imprint Publications, 1990).

nations still predicated upon the warrior ethos—Germany, Italy, and Japan. How could a democratic political system dependent upon the will of such a people ever hope to assume leadership in the international arena? Lacking the requisite will for a long, bitter struggle, the fascists assumed, Americans would undoubtedly negotiate a peace rather than challenge true warrior cultures on the battlefield. Thus, Hitler dismissed Americans as venal, weak-willed non-factors in his strategic calculus, while the Japanese leadership hoped that the American public would accept the fait accompli at Pearl Harbor and accommodate themselves to Japanese hegemony in the Greater East Asian Co-Prosperity Sphere.[26] As events soon proved, however, a traditional warrior culture such as those stoked by Hitler and Tojo was not sufficient, or even necessary, for military success, and the remarkable American triumph over the Axis speaks to us today, highlighting the true foundations for successful international leadership.

The Great Transformation, 1940–1950

Between 1940 and 1950 a Great Transformation occurred. A large majority of Americans renounced isolationism and concluded that their nation had no choice but to accept international leadership. By 1950 Americans supported unprecedented military commitments abroad as well as the subsidization of Europe and Japan's economic rebirth. All this occurred despite the eclipse of traditional warrior culture following the First World War. This remarkable transformation, which defied all linear predictions based upon the trends of the 1930s, underscores the role that leading statesmen played in redefining Americans' conceptions of national security and reigniting their will to preserve it.

The most impressive collection of American statesmen since the Founding Fathers led the Great Transformation. By the late 1930s Franklin Roosevelt concluded that for the United States to assume leadership internationally the American people's vision of their place in the world needed to be transformed. So FDR assiduously educated the public to an appreciation of the need for a more active national security policy in the face of Axis aggression, rallying support for such departures as Lend-Lease and the

[26]Nobutaka Ike, ed., *Japan's Decision for War: Records of the 1941 Policy Conferences* (Stanford, Calif.: Stanford University Press, 1967), pp. 133–63, 190, 199–239, 247–49, 281–83; Akira Iriye, *The Origins of the Second World War in Asia and the Pacific* (London: Longman, 1987), pp. 140–86; Gerhard L. Weinberg, *Germany, Hitler, and World War II: Essays in Modern German and World History* (New York: Cambridge University Press, 1995), pp. 30–53, 160, 182–89, 194–204.

first peacetime draft in U.S. history.[27] During the Second World War, Democratic and Republican leaders waged campaigns on the home front to convince the party faithful that the United States must remain engaged in international affairs following victory in order to insure the peace.[28] Concurrently, the nation's military leadership distinguished itself by devising and managing a strategy that exploited American economic superiority to crush the Axis powers. The deliberate, efficient "genius" of George C. Marshall epitomized the American approach to the war much more than did the anachronistic histrionics of "warriors" such as George Patton.[29] Following the war a formidable coalition composed of government officials, leaders from both political parties, and military officers then formulated the American response to the Soviet challenge and completed the redefinition of Americans' conception of national security. Harry Truman, Arthur Vandenberg, George Marshall, Dean Acheson, George Kennan, Paul Nitze, Dwight Eisenhower, Douglas MacArthur, Lucius Clay, James Forrestal, Robert Lovett, and John McCloy, and other such "Wise Men" sometimes disagreed about tactics, but together they convinced the American people that their basic values and way of life depended upon their willingness to preserve political and economic stability in Europe and Asia.[30]

This outcome was not inevitable. The fascist and then communist challenges alone did not foreordain a transformation in U.S. strategic culture. Many powerful voices, especially within the Republican Party, advocated withdrawal behind the Monroe Doctrine and creation of a Fortress America. Such an alternative would have accorded well with the American tradition of "entangling alliances with none."[31] Yet a unique constellation of personalities coalesced to articulate and promote the new global conception of national security. Who doubts, for example, that events

[27]Robert Dallek, *Franklin D. Roosevelt and American Foreign Policy, 1932–1945* (New York: Oxford University Press, 1979); Waldo Heinrichs, *Threshold of War: Franklin D. Roosevelt and American Entry into World War II* (New York: Oxford University Press, 1988).

[28]Robert A. Divine, *Second Chance: The Triumph of Internationalism in America during World War II* (New York: Atheneum, 1967).

[29]Eliot Cohen, "The Strategy of Innocence? The United States, 1920–1945," in *The Making of Strategy: Rulers, States, and War,* ed. Williamson Murray, MacGregor Knox, and Alvin Bernstein (New York: Cambridge University Press, 1994), pp. 464–65.

[30]R. May, "Cold War and Defense," in *The Cold War and Defense,* ed. Keith Neilson and Ronald G. Haycock (New York: Praeger, 1990), pp. 7–73.

[31]It should be recalled that a primary motive behind Dwight D. Eisenhower's decision to seek the Republican presidential nomination in 1952 was his fear that Robert Taft might lead the nation toward isolationism if elected. Stephen E. Ambrose, *Eisenhower,* vol. 1, *Soldier, General of the Army, President-Elect, 1890–1952* (New York: Simon and Schuster, 1983), pp. 510–41.

may have turned out much differently if during the critical days of 1940 and 1941 the United States had not been led by FDR, a man possessing a unique combination of strategic vision, cunning political skills, and a keen understanding of the American public? Likewise, imagine how different the world might be if FDR had not replaced Henry Wallace with Truman as his vice president on the 1944 election ticket.

The Great Transformation between 1940 and 1950 in how Americans conceived of their national security ultimately reveals three basic conclusions relevant to current discussions regarding American will in the post–Cold War era.

First, what Americans consider a "national interest" for which they will expend blood and treasure can change over time. This may appear self-evident, but many analysts still assume that national interests are defined exclusively by timeless features of international relations (such as preserving territorial integrity) or the result of simple cost-benefit calculations of material interest. National interests encompass, but go well beyond, such tangible concerns. They also include moral values and ideals, the preservation of the American "way of life," and assessments about how the world works politically, economically, diplomatically, militarily, socially, and culturally. In sum, national interests are ultimately ideas, ideas that can change as values and beliefs about the world change.

Secondly, Americans' acceptance of a broader conception of national security—one that carried an unprecedented risk of future military operations abroad—was not constrained by the decline of traditional warrior culture. In other words, even though traditional values of the pre-1917 warrior culture were not rekindled, Americans resolutely faced international realities including the necessity of making significant sacrifices to preserve their expanded notion of national security.

Thirdly, human beings shape their own destiny. The American experience between 1940 and 1950 underscores the dangers of assuming that certain trends cannot be checked, redirected, reversed, or overcome by forceful leadership. In 1940 a person focusing upon the trends of the previous decade could have easily concluded—as did the Axis leadership—that the American people would never support another major war effort. Likewise, when the war finally ended in 1945, many anticipated that the United States would again disengage from the world. But history is not defined simply by the linear projection of trends into the future. Instead, as demonstrated by American statesmen during the 1940s, sustained and deliberate leadership can transform the public's conception of national security *in spite of* historical traditions and previous social, economic, and cultural trends.

American Will in the Cold War Era, 1950–1989

The expanded notion of national security that was developed in the 1940s provided the foundation for American foreign and defense policy through the decades of the Cold War. A review of the long era of containment is well beyond the scope of this essay, but suffice to say that the American people did not reembrace warrior culture during the Cold War.[32] The idea of the Second World War as "the Good War"—an idea reinforced by such images as John Wayne's portrayal of Sargent Stryker in *The Sands of Iwo Jima*—did become a powerful presence in American culture. Nonetheless, James Jones's ironic dedication to *The Thin Red Line* succinctly and more accurately captures how the Second World War generation of Americans viewed the experience of war in a fundamentally different way than did Teddy Roosevelt five decades before.[33] Instead of raising their children "to fight, think fighting honorable, and think killing in warfare glorious," Americans in the 1950s and '60s reveled in their material prosperity and enjoyed a standard of living unprecedented in human history. These might have been considered debilitating handicaps to those who stress the significance of warrior culture. The American public, however, supported for four decades unprecedented commitments abroad with corresponding defense expenditures to sustain them—all without becoming a "garrison state."[34]

[32]See John Lewis Gaddis, *Strategies of Containment: A Critical Appraisal of Postwar American National Security Policy* (New York: Oxford University Press, 1982).

[33]"This book is dedicated to those greatest and most heroic of all human endeavors, WAR and WARFARE; may they never cease to give us the pleasure, excitement and adrenal stimulation that we need, or provide us with the heroes, the presidents and leaders, the monuments and museums which we erect to them in the name of PEACE." James Jones, *The Thin Red Line* (New York: Delta Paperback, 1962). For a recent essay surveying the evolution of the World War II film genre, see Roger J. Spiller, "In the Dark," *American Heritage*, Feb./Mar. 1999, pp. 41–51.

[34]See Tom Englehardt, *The End of Victory Culture: Cold War America and the Disillusionment of a Generation* (New York: Basic Books, 1995); Aaron L. Friedberg, "Why Didn't the United States Become a Garrison State," *International Security*, Spring 1992, pp. 109–42; Aaron L. Friedberg, *In the Shadow of the Garrison State: American Anti-Statism and Its Cold War Grand Strategy* (Princeton, N.J.: Princeton University Press, 2000); Michael J. Hogan, *A Cross of Iron: Harry S. Truman and the Origins of the National Security State, 1945–1954* (New York: Cambridge University Press, 1998); Michael S. Sherry, *In the Shadow of War: The United States since the 1930s* (New Haven, Conn.: Yale University Press, 1995); Stephen J. Whitfield, *The Culture of the Cold War* (Baltimore, Md.: Johns Hopkins University Press, 1991).

American public support during the "limited wars" in Korea and Vietnam deserves special attention. With images of the Second World War still fresh, Americans approached these conflicts with grim realism, not the romance of the first decades of the twentieth century. Nevertheless, based upon their significant sacrifices in these secondary theaters of the Cold War—including nearly one hundred thousand combat deaths—it is hard to argue that Americans displayed a debilitating sensitivity to casualties. Public support as measured in opinion polls started high in both conflicts and only waned to the degree that both conflicts dragged on inconclusively and casualties mounted. This parallel decline in support for the Korean and Vietnam Wars suggests, as political scientist John Mueller noted over twenty-five years ago, that public disenchantment was not a function of uncensored television broadcasts from Vietnam. Rather, support declined when reasonable questions emerged as to whether the costs were proportional to the objectives.[35] Is it surprising that the American public became restless over the prolongation of the Korean War when the principles and processes surrounding the repatriation of prisoners of war emerged as the crucial stumbling block in the armistice negotiations? Similarly, as the objective of preserving an independent South Vietnam continued to be frustrated years after the commitment of American ground forces, was not a reassessment in order? As Richard Betts emphasizes, the examples of Korea and Vietnam reveal that casualties alone do not undermine public support; rather, "casualties in an *inconclusive* war, casualties that the public sees as being suffered indefinitely, for no clear, good, or achievable purpose" lead to an erosion of support.[36]

In retrospect, what is most striking about public support during the Korean and Vietnam Wars is not that it declined, but rather that it did not decline further and much more rapidly. In the case of Korea the public did not demand the withdrawal of American forces from the Korean peninsula after the signing of the armistice in 1953 and has not done so during the subsequent forty-eight years. Indeed, public support for an American presence along the DMZ continues despite the fact that a serious military confronta-

---

[35]More precisely, public opinion as measured by polls correlates better with the logarithm of the number of casualties suffered than with either the number of casualties or the duration of the conflict. John E. Mueller, *War, Presidents and Public Opinion* (New York: Wiley, 1973), pp. 42–65, 167; John Mueller, "The Common Sense," *National Interest*, Spring 1997, pp. 82–83. See also the refinement of Mueller's study offered in Scott Sigmund Gartner and Gary M. Segura, "War, Casualties, and Public Opinion," *Journal of Conflict Resolution*, June 1998, pp. 278–300.

[36]Betts, "What Will It Take to Deter the United States?" p. 76.

tion, potentially involving nuclear weapons, remains a real possibility.[37] Similarly, the images of the vocal and sometimes violent Vietnam anti-war movement often overshadow the fact that many Americans, while desiring disengagement from the Vietnamese conflict, still did not favor unconditional, unilateral withdrawal, even as late as the 1970s. The notion of "Peace with Honor" still resonated after seven years of war.[38] Accepting for the sake of discussion the hypothetical scenario of a viable South Vietnamese government's emerging and securing its borders around 1970, it is conceivable that U.S. forces might be standing watch today over the Seventeenth Parallel just as they do along the Thirty-eighth.

The foregoing observations should not minimize the detrimental impact the Vietnam conflict had upon the American polity and military. American leadership during the Vietnam era squandered public support, sowing the seeds of discord and skepticism in civil-military relations and public life more generally. And, of course, this failure of judgment and leadership further discredited the last exponents of warrior culture. Nonetheless, the rebound in American self-confidence and assertiveness during the 1980s demonstrated that American will, when combined with compelling public leadership, remained sound and resilient. Considered against the broader historical backdrop of the entire Cold War, therefore, the American public consistently demonstrated its will to defend its interests.

Misplaced Pessimism in the Post–Cold War Era

Perhaps the end of the Cold War changed all of this. Perhaps the American will to sacrifice disappeared along with the Soviet Union. After all, Americans had sacrificed blood and treasure in secondary theaters such as Korea and Vietnam not as ends in themselves, but as part of the global strategy of containing the Soviet challenge. Without the clear and present danger posed by an obvious ideological and military "peer competitor" to hold them in check, other forces might come to the fore and erode the

[37]For example, the 1996 Foreign Policy Leadership Survey revealed that 63 percent of the respondents favored the use of U.S. troops to resist a North Korean invasion of South Korea. Table 3 in Ole R. Holsti, "Continuity and Change in the Domestic and Foreign Policy Beliefs of American Opinion Leaders," paper at 1997 annual meeting of the American Political Science Association, Aug. 28–31, 1997.

[38]In May 1971, for instance, 55 percent of Americans opposed the withdrawal of all U.S. troops from Vietnam by the end of 1971 if it meant a communist takeover of South Vietnam, while 75 percent opposed such a withdrawal if it threatened the lives or safety of the U.S. prisoners of war held by the North Vietnamese. Mueller, *War, Presidents and Public Opinion*, pp. 97–98.

public's will. Recent analyses finger the usual suspects that might weaken American will, namely, the intertwined factors of Americans' lack of warrior culture, materialism bred of prosperity, relative isolation from the savage realities of international life, and new information-age lifestyles. Consequently, they suggest, the will to tolerate anything beyond minimal casualties will decline in the future, thus limiting future U.S. military policy to quick, relatively low cost operations. On the surface, such fears sound compelling. However, evidence from the four most significant post–Cold War military crises—the Gulf War, Somalia, the Bosnian conflict, and the Kosovo intervention—confirms that reports of the demise of the American will have been greatly exaggerated.

The widespread public support for the Persian Gulf War undercuts the simplistic notion that Americans will only support military operations that promise minimal casualties. While it is true that Americans sustained relatively light casualties in Desert Storm, what matters is the public expectation of casualties *before* Desert Storm. In the months leading up to the allied offensive, no public consensus emerged regarding the potential costs of liberating Kuwait. Although few opinion leaders expected defeat, many offered pessimistic assessments of the potential costs of a ground offensive against Iraq. Military experts estimated casualty figures ranging from the thousands to tens of thousands, depending upon the particular scenario.[39] Testifying before Congress in November 1990, for example, Edward Luttwak cautioned that his analysis, based upon "the most optimistic assumptions of the most optimistic briefer," predicted "thousands of killed in action, wounded, and the inevitable quotient of missing-in-action."[40]

[39]Testimony in December 1990 before the House Armed Services Committee displayed a representative range of casualty estimates by well-informed military observers. Col. Trevor N. Depuy reported that his computer simulation of different ground offensive scenarios predicted total American casualties ranging from 6,000 to 18,000, with 1,000–3,000 fatalities. He estimated that an air campaign would result in 1,800 American casualties, 300 of them killed in action. U.S. Air Force Gens. Charles L. Donnelly Jr., and Russell E. Dougherty considered Depuy's estimates reasonable. James A. Blackwell Jr., of the Center for Strategic and International Studies, stated that allied casualties could reach 30,000, and Col. Harry S. Summers supported this more pessimistic estimate. However, Les Aspin, summarizing his personal assessment of the testimony, concluded "the prospects for a rapid victory with light to moderate American casualties, perhaps three to five thousand including five hundred to a thousand or so fatalities, are high." *Crisis in the Persian Gulf: Sanctions, Diplomacy and War, Hearings Before the Committee on Armed Services, House of Representatives, 101st Congress, Second Session* (Washington, D.C.: U.S. Government Printing Office, 1991), pp. 336, 419, 462–63, 488, 916–17. See also Powell, *My American Journey*, p. 485.

[40]Edward N. Luttwak testimony, *The Persian Gulf Crisis: Joint Hearings before the Subcommittee on Arms Control, International Security and Science, Europe and the*

Public expectations reflected these concerns. From the beginning of the Kuwaiti crisis in August 1990, the majority of Americans believed that if war with Iraq should occur, it would be over within one year, but would not be an easy operation. Polls taken in early January 1991 revealed that over 60 percent of Americans expected the war would result in "a high number of American deaths," while only 10–13 percent anticipated fewer than a thousand combat deaths. As late as February 10, 1991, 47 percent believed that Americans would suffer casualties in the range of "several thousand" or "tens of thousands."[41] Despite such concerns, a clear majority supported the use of force to compel Iraqi withdrawal from Kuwait.[42]

The minimal casualties suffered during the Gulf War pleasantly surprised the American people. Their surprise, however, highlights their willingness to endure a much higher cost to secure the national interest. Moreover, the subsequent terrorist attacks against the Khobar Towers in Saudi Arabia and the U.S. embassies in Kenya and Tanzania have generated no calls for withdrawal from the Persian Gulf region.[43] If anything, the protracted dispute with Iraq has increased the demand for more forceful policies aimed at toppling Saddam Hussein.[44] The American people, therefore, continue to demonstrate a will to tolerate the costs of defending their conception of the national interest.

By contrast, the rapid reevaluation of U.S. policy toward Somalia following the Mogadishu firefight that left eighteen Americans dead is commonly cited as proof that public will to sustain U.S. policy is absent. This reasoning, however, overlooks the fundamental cause of the reversal in Somalia, namely, the lack of a coherent policy. Indeed, the Somali case is analogous to the Lebanese disaster ten years before. In both cases, U.S. forces were initially deployed on a peacekeeping or humanitarian mission. As the political context changed, decision makers in Washington

Middle East, and on International Operations of the Committee on Foreign Affairs and the Joint Economic Committee, 101st Cong., 2nd Sess., Nov. 28, 1990 (Washington, D.C.: U.S. Government Printing Office, 1991), p. 328.

[41] Tables 223, 224, 226, and 228 in John E. Mueller, *Policy and Opinion in the Gulf War* (Chicago: University of Chicago Press, 1994), pp. 305–7.

[42] The Jan. 13, 1991, ABC/*Washington Post* poll, for instance, found 76 percent of Americans approved the congressional resolution authorizing President Bush to go to war. The same poll also revealed that 55 percent of Americans expected the war would result in a "high number of American deaths." Tables 65 and 227 in Mueller, *Policy and Opinion in the Gulf War*, pp. 222, 307.

[43] The author would like to thank Stephen Peter Rosen for suggesting this point.

[44] For the skeptical evaluation of such proposals, see Daniel Byman, Kenneth Pollack, and Gideon Rose, "The Rollback Fantasy," *Foreign Affairs*, Jan./Feb. 1999, pp. 24–41.

altered policy, but without systematic reevaluation of military deployments on the ground. In both cases, the shock of unexpected casualties—in Lebanon the bombing of the Marine Corps barracks that left 241 Americans dead, in Somalia the costly mission to capture warlord Mohammed Farrah Aideed—forced thorough reviews of U.S. policy. These reviews concluded that the risks of further casualties were not proportionate to the interests at stake. Consequently, in both cases, after waiting long enough to avoid signaling panic, the respective administrations withdrew American forces.[45]

The public outcry in the case of Somalia was not the result of weakness of will or a "CNN effect."[46] Whether the visual images of the carnage in the streets of Mogadishu were carried live or broadcast hours or days later was less relevant than the Clinton administration's failure to explain why a policy entailing the risks of such casualties had merit. If a convincing case had been forthcoming, the American people conceivably could have "rallied around the flag" and supported a military escalation that promised worthwhile results and restored the nation's honor. Indeed, some poll data indicate that a majority of Americans supported more forceful action in Somalia in the immediate aftermath of the October firefight.[47] But, just as in Lebanon, the president concluded that no compelling justification existed and decided that a swift exit was the lesser of evils. American policy failed the American people in Somalia, not vice versa.

Likewise, in the Bosnian crisis that unraveled after 1992, prevailing wisdom portrayed public support for involvement in the conflict as meager at best. However, this notion that the American people were hostile to more forceful action in Bosnia does not hold up in the face of systematic examination. In the most thorough and sophisticated analysis to date of poll data and media

[45]On the development of American policy leading to the Lebanon tragedy, see George P. Shultz, *Turmoil and Triumph: My Years As Secretary of State* (New York: Charles Scribner's Sons, 1993), pp. 196–234; Weinberger, *Fighting for Peace*, pp. 115–17, 135–74.

[46]As Assistant Secretary of Defense for Public Affairs Kenneth Bacon has argued, "It wasn't because the press was there that we've had disastrous stories; it was because we got into a disastrous situation, which was covered by the press." "Covering the War," *NewsHour with Jim Lehrer*, Apr. 20, 2000 (http://www.pbs.org/newshour/bb/media/jan-june00/vietnam-_4-20.html). For a debunking of the myth of the "CNN effect" in the Somalian case, see Larson, *Casualties and Consensus*, pp. 45–46, 71. See also Mueller, "The Common Sense," pp. 83–85.

[47]Steven Kull and I. M. Destler, *Misreading the Public: The Myth of a New Isolationism* (Washington, D.C.: Brookings Institution Press, 1999), pp. 104–8; Tucker, "Fighting Barbarians," p. 76; Burk, "Public Support for Peacekeeping in Lebanon and Somalia," pp. 53–78.

coverage, Richard Sobel debunks the myth of a fundamentally weak American public will regarding the Bosnian conflict. It is true that before the Dayton accords Americans consistently opposed *unilateral* military action in Bosnia, and public support for any involvement in the crisis was volatile. Such volatility, however, was more a function of the lack of leadership, especially from the president, than anything else. Nonetheless, before Dayton a reservoir of public support existed for U.S. participation in *multilateral* military operations under the auspices of the United Nations or NATO, such as facilitating the delivery of humanitarian assistance or using force to protect U.N. peacekeepers from Serbian attacks. This support reflected a combination of realism and humanitarianism, that is, a desire to prevent the conflict from expanding beyond Bosnia while relieving the suffering of those directly affected by the war. Sobel's analysis reveals that systematic bias in the major news media promoted the inaccurate "conventional wisdom" that no public support existed for American action in Bosnia. American media consistently underreported or inaccurately reported the true complexities of public opinion and emphasized instead the most vehement and vocal opposition to involvement in Bosnia. The American public possessed a more mature and skeptical, yet activist, mindset regarding Bosnia than has been credited. Thus, whatever the conventional wisdom may say, U.S. policy toward Bosnia has not been fundamentally constrained by either a paralytic fear of casualties on the part of the American public or demands for rapid disengagement.[48]

Lastly, the American public's response to the 1999 NATO intervention in Kosovo discredits further the quick, costless war presumption. When Operation Allied Force began in March 1999, most Americans could not even identify which side the United

[48]Richard Sobel, "U.S. and European Attitudes toward Intervention in the Former Yugoslavia: *Mourir pour la Bosnie?*" in *The World and Yugoslavia's Wars*, ed. Richard H. Ullman (New York: Council on Foreign Relations, 1996), pp. 145–81; Richard Sobel, "Portraying American Public Opinion toward the Bosnia Crisis," *Harvard Journal of Press/Politics*, Spring 1998, pp. 16–33; Richard Sobel, "United States Intervention in Bosnia," *Public Opinion Quarterly*, Summer 1998, pp. 250–78; Kull and Destler, *Misreading the Public*, pp. 108–9. Contrary to the opinion of many, European public opinion throughout the Bosnia crisis in fact supported more vigorous military action than their respective political leaders offered. See Sobel, "U.S. and European Attitudes toward Intervention in the Former Yugoslavia." On the generation of congressional and public support for the deployment of American forces to Bosnia, see Richard Holbrooke, *To End a War* (New York: Random House, 1998), pp. 316–18. Three years after their initial deployment, 63 percent of Americans still approved of the presence of U.S. troops in Bosnia, even though a majority mistakenly believed that American soldiers had been killed by hostile fire in Bosnia during the previous year. Program on International Policy Attitudes, "Americans on Kosovo: A Study of US Public Attitudes," May 19, 1999 (http://www.pipa.org/OnlineReports/Kosovo.kosovo.html).

States was supporting and which it opposed. However, as attention to and understanding of the conflict increased, public support for U.S. participation in the NATO military campaign rose to 60 percent by mid-April 1999. A majority never considered Kosovo a "vital interest," but perceived a moral obligation to protect Kosovar civilians from the Serbian campaign of ethnic cleansing.[49] Accordingly, a majority of Americans, after weighing the costs of the engagement against their determination to succeed, approved of an operation that they thought would be neither quick nor costless. After initial hopes for a quick capitulation by Milosevic faded, the public supported continuing the operation "as long as necessary" while remaining skeptical that air strikes alone would bring peace. It is especially noteworthy that more than half of Americans not only expected that U.S. ground troops would be necessary, but supported that option despite the perceived high risk of U.S. casualties. Americans opposed a bloody, protracted war, but accepted the risk of casualties as the cost of returning the Kosovar refugees to their homes.[50]

The public's support of the operation's objectives owes very

[49]*Los Angeles Times* Poll Alert, Study #425, Mar. 26, 1999 (http://www.latimes.com/news/timespoll/national/lat_tpoll990326.htm); Pew Research Center for the People and the Press, March 1999 News Interest Index, Mar. 24–28, 1999, "Few See Strategic Interests, Humanitarian Concerns Cited; Support for NATO Air Strikes with Plenty of Buts," Mar. 29, 1999 (http://www.people-press.org/marchrel1.htm); Pew Research Center, Kosovo News Interest Index, Apr. 15–18, 1999, "Clinton Ratings Dip; Continued Public Support for Kosovo, But Worries Grow," Apr. 21, 1999 (http://www.people-press.org/kosovorpt.htm); Pew Research Center, May 1999 News Interest Index, May 12–16, "Collateral Damage Taking Its Toll; Americans Disengaging from Kosovo," May 18, 1999 (http://www.people-press.org/may99rpt1.htm); Gallup Organization, "Kosovo in Crisis: U.S. Role and Clinton Approval" (http://www.gallup.com/poll/indicators/Indkosovo.asp); *Washington Post*–ABC News polls, Apr. 8 and May 18, 1999 (http://washingtonpost.com/wp-srv/politics/polls/vault/stories/data040899.htm and /data051899.htm); Gary Langer and Ben Fitzpatrick, "Tempered by Risk," Apr. 8, 1999 (http://abcnews.go.com/sections/world/dailynews/kosovo_pol990409.htm); *New York Times*/CBS News poll, Apr. 5–6, 1999 (http://www.nytimes.com/library/national/040899poll-results.html); CNN, "Poll: Americans Split on NATO Airstrikes," Mar. 25, 1999 (http://www.cnn.com.US/9903/35/kosovo.poll/index.html); Program on International Policy Attitudes, "Americans on Kosovo." An insightful preliminary analysis of American public opinion during the Kosovo intervention is Robert D. Killebrew and Javid Ali, "Air Power and Public Opinion in Operation Allied Force," study prepared for the Association of the United States Army, 1999. The author wishes to thank Col. Killebrew for providing a copy of this unpublished report.

[50]Mark Gillespie, "Support Grows for Kosovo Mission, But Public Still Divided," Gallup Poll Release, Mar. 26, 1999 (http://www.gallup.com/poll/releases/pr990326.asp); *Los Angeles Times* Poll Alert, Study #425; *New York Times*/CBS News Poll, Apr. 5–6, 1999; Dan Balz, "Consensus Grows to Send Ground Troops," *Washington Post*, Apr. 6, 1999; *Washington Post*-ABC News Polls, Apr. 8 and 28, 1999 (http://www.washingtonpost.com/wp-srv/politics/polls/vault/stories/data040899.htm and /data042899.htm); Pew Research Center, Kosovo News Interest Index, Apr. 15–18, 1999, "Clinton Ratings Dip; Continued Public Support for Kosovo, But Worries Grow," Apr. 21, 1999; Gallup Organization, "Kosovo in Crisis"; Program on International Policy Attitudes, "Americans on Kosovo."

little, however, to presidential or congressional leadership, which remained lackluster throughout the eleven-week campaign. Indeed, President Clinton never convinced most Americans that he possessed a coherent strategy in Kosovo.[51] They supported the intervention because their moral outrage and resolve overcame their skepticism. The public shifted its support to a bombing pause and opening negotiations only when the air campaign continued into May 1999 without any sign of success or a change in military strategy. This shift, however, reflected concern not about potential American costs, but about the air campaign's failure to halt the depradations inflicted upon Kosovar civilians. Even then, the American public preferred continuing the military campaign to accepting a settlement that abandoned the Kosovars to their fate at Serb hands.[52]

After the air campaign ended on June 10, 1999, Americans supported continued U.S. involvement in Kosovo, despite their considerable misgivings as to the region's long-term prospects for peace. Only two Americans in five considered Operation Allied Force a "victory," and roughly half concluded that it had not been "worth it." Nevertheless, a clear majority favored U.S. participation in the peacekeeping operation even though most felt it would likely become a long-term commitment with a risk of future casualties.[53] Thus, Americans proved again that they would not recoil from the costs of upholding their international obligations. While conflicted over their government's strategy, a majority remained determined to reverse the ethnic cleansing of the Kosovars. Although a rapid deterioration of the situation might lead to a reevaluation of the risks and stakes in the Balkans, the Kosovo experience demonstrates that the presumption of quick, costless war exists more in the minds of some policymakers and pundits than in the minds of the American people.

[51]*New York Times*/CBS News Poll, Apr. 5–6, 1999; Gallup Organization, "Kosovo in Crisis."

[52]Frank Newport, "Support for U.S. Kosovo Involvement Drops," Gallup Poll Release, May 26, 1999 (http://www.gallup.com/poll/releases/pr990526.asp); Pew Research Center, "Collateral Damage Taking Its Toll"; *Washington Post*–ABC News Poll, May 18, 1999.

[53]Gallup Organization, "Kosovo in Crisis"; Gary Langer, "Doubting Americans," June 11, 1999 (http://more.abcnews.go.com/sections/world/dailynews/kosovo_langer990611.html); Frank Newport, "New Poll on Kosovo Finds Underwhelmed Public," Gallup Poll Release, June 11, 1999 (http://www.gallup.com/poll/releases/pr990611c.asp); Pew Research Center, "Muted and Mixed Public Response to Peace in Kosovo," June 15, 1999 (http://www.people-press.org/nato99rpt.htm).

The Dangers of Misjudging American Will

A nation's will provides the foundation upon which military policy is built. The American experience in the twentieth century belies the simplistic notion that the lack of a pervasive warrior culture translates into weakness of will in the international arena. It would be ironic, therefore, if now, at the time of our greatest strength, we underestimate our own will because we overemphasize the significance of certain cultural, economic, or demographic trends. Moreover, this would be doubly ironic because our past enemies grossly misjudged American will for the same reason— and paid dearly for their errors. If we fall into this trap, the potential dangers for the United States could be no less serious.

The dangers will arise both at home and abroad. Domestically, continued acceptance of the quick, costless war presumption risks becoming a debilitating, self-fulfilling prophecy. After all, how can we expect the American public and military to cope with future exigencies requiring protracted operations or entailing significant casualties if such contingencies are defined away as beyond American will? Even if a crisis posing such dilemmas should never occur (an unlikely eventuality), the quick, costless war presumption threatens civil-military relations. The passing of the torch of leadership from the generation that came of age during the Great Transformation to one defined by Vietnam has already strained these relations.[54] However, the corrosive effects upon civil-military relations will be even more profound if future military leaders mature within an organizational culture that believes the American people represent the weak link in the chain of military policy.

Abroad, our allies will be discouraged and our enemies

[54]For the current debate surrounding the state of civil-military relations, see A. J. Bacevich, "Tradition Abandoned: America's Military in a New Era," *National Interest*, Summer 1997, pp. 16–25; Andrew J. Bacevich and Richard H. Kohn, "Grand Army of the Republicans," *New Republic*, Dec. 8, 1997, pp. 22–24; Eliot A. Cohen, "Civil-Military Relations," *Orbis*, Spring 1997, pp. 177–86 (reprinted in this volume); Ole R. Holsti, "A Widening Gap between the U.S. Military and Civilian Society? Some Evidence, 1976–96," *International Security*, Winter 1998/99, pp. 5–42; Douglas Johnson and Steven Metz, "Civil-Military Relations in the United States: The State of the Debate," *Washington Quarterly*, Winter 1995, pp. 197–213; Richard Kohn, "Out of Control: The Crisis in Civil-Military Affairs," *National Interest*, Spring 1994, pp. 3–17; "An Exchange on Civil-Military Relations," *National Interest*, Summer 1994, pp. 23–31; Edward N. Luttwak, "Washington's Biggest Scandal," *Commentary*, May 1994, pp. 29–33; Edward N. Luttwak, "From Vietnam to *Desert Fox*: Civil-Military Relations in Modern Democracies," *Survival*, Spring 1999, pp. 99–112; Pew Research Center for the People and the Press, "The Civilian-Military Gap Flap," poll analysis, Dec. 10, 1999 (http://www.people-press.org/99watch3.htm); Thomas Ricks, "The Widening Gap Between the Military and Society," *Atlantic Monthly*, July 1997, pp. 67–78; "A Symposium on Civil-Military Relations," *Armed Forces and Society*, Spring 1998, pp. 375–462.

encouraged. In the future the United States will more often than not participate in multilateral military operations for reasons of legitimacy, both international and domestic, and efficacy. Yet predicating American capabilities and policy upon the quick, costless war presumption will inevitably call into question the credibility of the American commitment to its allies, thus making the formation of multilateral military initiatives considerably more difficult. Why should our allies commit themselves to operations that we are not willing to undertake alongside them?[55] If we choose to rely upon others to do the heavy lifting, the lifting might never get done. And, naturally, our prospective adversaries hope for exactly this outcome. As numerous analysts have suggested and recent wargames conducted by the U.S. military confirm, a cunning opponent will develop so-called asymmetric strategies and tactics to force Americans to choose between undertaking costly, protracted operations or capitulation.[56] Over the long term, therefore, continued adherence to the quick, costless war presumption could well become the United States' Achilles' heel.

The most insidious danger, however, is the belief that a decline in American will is foreordained and that therefore no opportunity exists to recast the public's conception of its national interests and stoke its will to preserve them. Economic, cultural, and demographic trends may then be used as an excuse not to exercise leadership when leadership is most urgently needed.

Only sustained, articulate, and farsighted leadership, prefer-

[55]Even so unorthodox a thinker as Ralph Peters succumbs to the quick, costless war presumption when contemplating burden sharing between the U.S. and its allies. For instance, he offers as one of his ten "tenets" for future U.S. military operations in urban areas: "Do the job fast. If the job can't be done fast, get somebody else to do it." Peters, "The Future of Armored Warfare," p. 59.

[56]During the 1998 spring wargame of the U.S. Army Training and Doctrine Command's Army After Next Project, the adversary planned his campaign (set in the year 2021) with precisely this intent. Before American forces could deploy in theater, enemy forces seized strategic urban areas, dug in, and then called for a cease-fire and negotiations. The American leadership was thus presented with the unpalatable choice of either dislodging the enemy from "hedgehog" positions, which would strain both domestic and alliance support, or negotiating a settlement with an opponent who held many trump cards. The adversary further complicated American planning by positioning prisoners of war, foreign nationals, and civilians in, around, and on top of strategic facilities. The U.S. leadership decided to eject the enemy from its fortified positions at the cost of thousands of American casualties. Such a campaign could easily prove difficult for the military to accomplish and shocking to the public if both expect a quick, costless war in the years ahead. Author's observations at the Army After Next Project 1998 Spring Wargame, Apr. 20–29, 1998. In light of such findings, the Army After Next's 1998 annual report to the Chief of Staff of the Army notes that "short wars and short campaigns are not guaranteed in the future." *Knowledge and Speed: Battle Force and the U.S. Army of 2025* (Ft. Monroe, Va.: TRADOC, 1998), p. 3. On the Army After Next Project, see the special feature in *Military Review*, Mar.–Apr. 1998, pp. 2–57; Richard J. Newman, "Bombs Get Smarter; What About Generals?" *U.S. News and World Report*, May 18, 1998, pp. 42–43.

ably by the president, can counter these dangers of misjudging American will. The time for such leadership is now, as the military policy for the next century takes shape. For just as the will of the American people ought not be underestimated, neither can it be taken for granted. The public will to sustain difficult, costly military operations cannot be manufactured after a crisis emerges by spin control, sound bites, and televised rallies, which at worst become embarrassing spectacles, as exemplified by the Ohio State University "town meeting" during the flare-up of tensions with Iraq in February 1998.

How can the will to sustain necessary but expensive long-term commitments be cultivated? The answer does not lie in nostalgia for a past warrior culture. How many Americans, including members of the armed forces and veterans, would want to resurrect the culture that led Teddy Roosevelt to hope that his own children would be maimed in war? Instead, our national leaders—elected officials, career and appointed government administrators, and military officers alike—must foster a realistic public understanding of the challenges, opportunities, and potential *costs* of leadership in international affairs. As weapons of mass destruction proliferate, these potential costs include the real risk of prolonged operations with casualties well beyond the few hundred the United States has suffered since Vietnam. The popular enthusiasm for quick technological solutions should always be tempered by a realistic appraisal of the fundamental nature of warfare. Especially while debating the merits of the RMA, the temptation to use the quick, costless war presumption as a rhetorical trump card must be resisted. What is needed instead is a program of "strategic candor." This is not the easy path, but it is the only one in our democratic system that will lead to long-term success.[57]

Admittedly, recent developments do not inspire optimism. Domestic affairs have consumed the attention of the nation's executive and legislative leadership. Whether one approves or disapproves of the enlargement of NATO or the extension of the American peacekeeping presence in Bosnia, the fact that neither policy stimulated vigorous public debate is discouraging. Even

---

[57]The phrase "strategic candor" is adapted from Bacevich, "Tradition Abandoned," pp. 20–21. In this case, the idea of "candor" hearkens back to the abortive Project Candor during the first year of Eisenhower's presidency. The initial intent behind this initiative, which was eventually reduced to Eisenhower's "Atoms for Peace" proposal before the U.N. General Assembly in December 1953, was to explain to the American public the realities of international relations in the thermonuclear age in order to prevent alarm, panic, or malaise, and, correspondingly, to generate continued support for American international leadership.

more disappointing is the lack of sustained consideration of the long-term implications of NATO's commitments in Kosovo. Indeed, the prediction in May 2000 by the top American commander there that NATO peacekeepers might be needed in the Balkans "for at least a generation" scarcely caused a ripple.[58] A shallow understanding of such expansions of our foreign obligations will weaken public support should a serious crisis erupt in the future. Yet it is not too late. Americans consistently place more confidence in the military than in any other major institution in society.[59] They are also not as introverted or isolationist as some fear and others hope, however reticent they may be to search abroad for dragons to slay.[60]

In the years ahead, Americans' will to endure the costs necessary to secure themselves and their interests can be sustained, but only through dedicated, farsighted statesmanship. Is the current "baby boom" generation of leaders up to the task? Our allies and enemies wait to find out.

---

[58] John Donnelly, "US General Sees Long Role in Balkans," *Boston Globe*, May 2, 2000. See also Lenard J. Cohen, "Kosovo: 'Nobody's Country,'" *Current History*, Mar. 2000, pp. 117–23; David Rohde, "Kosovo Seething," *Foreign Affairs*, May/June 2000, pp. 65–79.

[59] Leslie McAneny, "Military on Top, HMOs Last in Public Confidence," Gallup Poll Release, July 14, 1999. For polling data reflecting public confidence in the military during the past decade, see George Gallup Jr., *The Gallup Poll: Public Opinion 1997* (Wilmington, Del.: Scholarly Resources, 1998), pp. 128–33.

[60] Aaron L. Friedberg, "Are Americans Becoming Isolationist?" *Commentary*, Nov. 1998, pp. 45–48; Ole R. Holsti, "Continuity and Change in the Domestic and Foreign Policy Beliefs of American Opinion Leaders"; Bruce W. Jentleson and Rebecca L. Britton, "Still Pretty Prudent: Post–Cold War American Public Opinion on the Use of Military Force," *Journal of Conflict Resolution*, Aug. 1998, pp. 395–417; Andrew Kohut and Robert C. Toth, "Arms and the People," *Foreign Affairs*, Nov./Dec. 1994, pp. 47–61; Kull and Destler, *Misreading the Public*; Mueller, "The Common Sense," pp. 81–88; John E. Reilly, ed., *American Public Opinion and U.S. Foreign Policy 1999* (Chicago: Chicago Council on Foreign Relations, 1999); U.S. Commission on National Security/21st Century, *New World Coming: American Security in the 21st Century— Supporting Research and Analysis* (Washington, D.C.: U.S. Commission on National Security/21st Century, Sept. 15, 1999), pp. 116–30.

OPERATIONS, PROCUREMENT, AND INDUSTRIAL BASE

by Harry G. Summers Jr.

One need not look far afield to see the devastating effect that the post–Cold War drawdown in the U.S. military could have on America's ability to fight and win on the battlefield.[1] The former Soviet military, once the most feared in the world and for almost a half century the very criterion by which the U.S. military judged itself, has virtually collapsed. Like the U.S. military, Russia's armed forces have suffered draconian cuts. In 1988, during the Cold War, the Soviet military (which then included not only the Russian military but also the military forces of the other Soviet republics) had more than 5 million soldiers, sailors, and airmen under arms. By 1995, Russia, the successor to the Soviet Union, had only 1.5 million military personnel on active duty. This decline in the physical aspects of Russian combat power is only part of the story. The precipitous decline in soldier morale is even more telling. As one former officer said, "The armed forces had become a disaster area" with the soldiers "separated in spirit by the total lack of a common purpose or unified goals."[2] The results were apparent in the debacle in Chechnya, where lightly armed Muslim guerrillas held the Russian military at bay for almost two years.

The Hollow Army

Could a similar scenario of military decline unfold in the United States? As then army chief of staff General Gordon Sullivan, who presided over the U.S. Army's post–Cold War drawdown, emphasized in 1991, it almost did in July 1950 in the opening days of the Korean War. At that time, America's lead element,

---

[1]This essay originally appeared in *Orbis*, Spring 1997, and arose from the Foreign Policy Research Institute conference "The Demilitarization of the Military?" Philadelphia, Pa., July 17–18, 1996.

[2]Vadim Makarenko, "'I Realized Something Had Broken Down,'" *U.S. News and World Report*, Aug. 26, 1996, p. 35.

Task Force Smith (the First Battalion, Twenty-First Infantry Regiment commanded by Lieutenant Colonel Charles B. Smith), was decimated by the advancing North Korean army, which had the American troops outgunned and outmanned. In the early days of the war, the United States was behind on the weapons-technology curve. American 2.36-inch antitank rocket launchers, for instance, could not stop the North Korean army's Soviet-supplied T-34 medium tanks, and neither could the light tanks of the divisions coming from Japan.

I witnessed this tragedy first-hand as a young corporal in a tank company in the Twenty-Fourth Infantry Division, Task Force Smith's parent unit. We lost all of our 75mm-gun M24 Chaffee tanks within the first week of the war. My platoon sergeant, who had fought the Nazi panzers as a tanker in World War II, shot twelve rounds into an advancing T-34, only to see them bounce harmlessly away. The enemy tank then blew out his entire engine compartment with one round from its high-velocity 85mm gun.

As if that were not demoralizing enough, two close friends and my company commander died for want of a seventy-five-cent starter solenoid on the company tank retriever when it stalled after the driver was shot in a North Korean roadblock. Unable to restart the retriever, the three were all gunned down as they tried to escape.

Like the untrained Russian conscripts in Chechnya, we had not been prepared for the terrible realities of war. As historian T. R. Fehrenbach put it, "In the first six months [of the Korean War] America suffered a near debacle because her Regular Army fighting men were the stuff of legions, but they had not been made into legionaries."[3] But it was not the first time that had happened.

From its beginning, the United States has followed a pattern of being caught unprepared, hastily mobilizing at great cost, then rapidly cutting back its forces after the crisis has passed. A few months after the end of World War I, Major George C. Marshall said in words that ring true today, "The public ran away from the tragedies of the War . . . and became obsessed with the magnitude of the public debt and the problems of its reduction. Forgetting almost immediately the bitter lessons of unpreparedness, they demanded and secured the reduction of the Army."[4]

[3] T. R. Fehrenbach, *This Kind of War: A Study in Unpreparedness* (New York: Macmillan, 1963), p. 438.

[4] Maj. George C. Marshall, "The Effect of School Histories on National Defense," in *Report of the Tenth Annual Conference of the Association of Military Colleges and Schools of the United States*, Washington, D.C., Mar. 7–8, 1923, p. 32.

Citing examples from the Revolutionary War, the War of 1812, the Mexican War, and the Philippine Insurrection, as well as World War I, Marshall ruefully pointed out that there are numerous instances of the same general nature. But the astonishing fact is that America continues to follow a regular cycle in the doing and undoing of measures for the national defense. Americans start in making adequate provisions and then turn abruptly in the opposite direction and abolish what has just been done.[5]

Marshall must have recalled those words in September 1939 when he was appointed army chief of staff and took charge of a force completely unprepared for World War II. As his soldiers of the First Infantry Division in France had in 1917, these soldiers paid the price in blood at Bataan and Corregidor in the Philippines, and at the Kasserine Pass and the Fa'id Pass in North Africa as they bought time for the U.S. mobilization capability to catch up. And when he took over as secretary of defense in the Korean War, Marshall must have thought of those words again as American soldiers once more paid the price for a hollow army. Eventually the prototype weaponry that for budgetary reasons had not been procured earlier, including 3.5-inch antitank rocket launchers and 90mm-gun M46 Patton medium tanks, made its way to the battlefield. But for thousands of soldiers it was too late.

"No More Task Force Smiths"

When he took over as army chief of staff in 1991, Sullivan adopted the motto "No more Task Force Smiths." It was a motto more provident than he realized. By the time General Sullivan left office in 1995, the army had declined from 770,000 soldiers and sixteen active combat divisions at the end of the Cold War to 495,000 soldiers and ten active divisions, almost 100,000 fewer than the 590,000 soldiers of the hollow army at the beginning of the Korean War.

But Sullivan had been true to his word. Though smaller than its Korean War predecessor, the post–Cold War army had no "Task Force Smiths." The army of 1950 had been gutted internally. None of its ten divisions had a wartime complement of weapons: the infantry regiments had only two of their three rifle battalions, the field artillery battalions had only two of their three firing batteries, and the divisions had only light-tank companies rather than the authorized medium-tank battalions. While also ten divisions

[5]Ibid.

strong, the active army of 1995 had not been skeletonized. Budget cuts had somewhat degraded unit readiness, but the force was not a hollow one. Instead, the entire army was armed, manned, and trained for combat.

Back to Basics

While much has been made of the current revolution in military affairs, with its emphasis on Information Age technology and computer warfare, the real revolution took place almost a quarter-century ago in response to the debacle in Vietnam. In 1972, under Admiral Stansfield Turner at the Naval War College, a "back to basics" movement began that swept the military. The false doctrines of the civilian nuclear war strategists, who preached that nuclear weapons had transformed the nature of war, were thrown out. So were the teachings of the social scientists, who argued that guerrilla insurgencies were the wave of the future and that nation building should be the principal military task.

These civilian-bred fallacies had almost destroyed the military's ability to wage conventional war. Admiral Turner insisted that the military again become the master of its own profession, and there emerged a renewed emphasis on conventional war-fighting doctrines and training fundamentals. To that end, the army formed its Training and Doctrine Command; the air force began Project Warrior and formed its Center for Aerospace Doctrine, Research, and Education; and the navy initiated its Naval Doctrine Command. Training was revitalized, combat-maneuver training centers were established, and training simulators and computer war games were introduced to hone combat skills.

All the services also reworked their basic battle doctrines, concentrating on conventional war-fighting operations and tactics. Driven by then navy secretary John Lehman's emphasis on offensive rather than defensive operations, the navy and marines' Maritime Strategy focused on control of the high seas, power projection, operations on the flanks, amphibious warfare, and the ability to build a sea bridge to Europe to bring America's mobilization capability to bear. The army formulated its AirLand Battle doctrine, with multidimensional rear-battle, near-battle, and deep-battle concepts. For its part, the air force concentrated on neutralizing and destroying the enemy's war-fighting capabilities and will to fight.

All of that effort paid off in the Persian Gulf War. The navy's initiative in preparing to build a sea bridge to Europe enabled it to build just such a bridge to the Middle East. The amphibious threat from the marines kept Iraqi divisions pinned down in static defenses. AirLand Battle worked as planned, as the army cut through the Iraqi defenses. And the air force swept the skies, paralyzing the enemy's military, political, and economic bases. Rising phoenix-like from the ashes of Vietnam, the American military had demonstrated convincingly that it was the world's most formidable fighting force.

Force XXI

But the services did not rest on their laurels. After the Persian Gulf War, each reassessed its war-fighting doctrines and organization for combat in preparation for the twenty-first century. Most striking was the navy's abandonment of its traditional blue-water strategy in favor of an emphasis on the world's coastlines, or littorals, as described in *Forward . . . From the Sea.*

The air force similarly underwent a major transformation. Acknowledging that in the post–nuclear age the term "strategic," once a synonym for nuclear weapons, had reverted to its original meaning, the air force discontinued its Strategic Air Command, which had been the very heart of the air force for almost a half-century. It then adopted a new strategy, Global Reach, Global Power, and reorganized its force into "movers" and "shooters" in the new Air Mobility Command and Air Combat Command, the latter with composite squadrons of tankers, bombers, and fighters.

The nation's land forces underwent the least reorientation. Pleased with the performance of its AirLand Battle doctrine in the Persian Gulf War, the army made few immediate changes in either its war-fighting doctrine or its organization for combat. It did, however, set up an experimental force as a test-bed for the digitalization of combat operations.

The U.S. Marine Corps, only slightly affected by the post–Cold War drawdowns, was more than pleased with the navy's new coastal strategy, which seemed tailor-made for the marines' traditional amphibious warfare mission. Prior to the war in the Persian Gulf, the marines had reorganized into marine air-ground task forces, in which units at every level from battalion to corps had an integral land component, air component, and logistics component. From the battalion-level marine expeditionary units to the corps-level First Marine Expeditionary Force, this new structure had been battle tested and validated in the Persian Gulf, and the marines saw no need for major change.

Unlike in previous postwar drawdowns, the military made a major effort in the latest reorganization to adapt its doctrines and structure to new realities. Both the Bush administration's 1991 Base Force model and the Clinton administration's 1993 Bottom-Up Review formulated a military strategy to square the enormous reductions in the size of the force with the dangers of the post–Cold War world. But it soon became obvious that the new strategy had severe deficiencies.

First was the notion that the United States could fight two major regional contingencies nearly simultaneously in Northeast Asia, the Middle East, or Western Europe. Given the cuts in military capabilities, this so-called win-win strategy stretched credibility, for each of the previous wars in Northeast Asia and the Middle East required more divisions than existed in the post–Cold War force, and there was no evidence a new conflict would be any less intense. At best the United States had a "win-hold" capability, and even that was tenuous.

But the real Achilles' heel of the new strategy was that it was seriously underfunded, with estimates of the shortfall ranging from $150 million to $200 billion. But instead of facing that fact, America tried to wish it away and avoid the hard choices that have to be made. One evasion was to assume that historically low inflation rates would make the problem go away. Another, a favorite of the defense contractors, was to argue that high technology could substitute for manpower, enabling further reductions in force size.

Technology versus Manpower

These arguments touch on a basic philosophical difference among the services. In the army and the marines, "machines" serve the man, and force levels are a primary concern. In the navy and air force, man serves the "machine," and technology has the edge, as it does with the American people. The revulsion over the carnage of World War I, where more U.S. soldiers were killed in action in three months on the line than in ten years in Vietnam, encouraged the idea of using "things" rather than people to win wars. On the very eve of Pearl Harbor, for example, columnist Walter Lippman wrote that America would fight World War II with air and naval power, and that there would be little need for land forces. Although events proved him wrong, this thinking led to the enormous postwar cutbacks in ground forces and the hollow army with which the United States entered the Korean War. And these same ideas were at work in the post–Cold War drawdown. Although the army had been cut by more than one-third, that was not good enough for those who believed technology could substitute for soldiers.

"Can we make a trade-off between nine more-modern divisions and ten less-modern divisions?" asked Senator Carl Levin (D-Mich.) during an April 1994 Senate Armed Services Committee meeting. "You could start modernizing tomorrow if you lopped off another two or three divisions," said Senator John Warner (R-Va.).[6] Three years later their notions still persist, and the army today is under pressure to cut 20,000 more soldiers in order to free up funds for new technology. Adding fuel to this debate are the think tanks that preach that high technology renders soldiers obsolete, and that future wars in the Information Age will be fought by computers rather than soldiers. It is no accident, said one panel participant, that many of these think tanks receive a lot of money from the military-industrial complex, whose high-tech systems benefit the contractors instead of the military.

As former army vice chief of staff General Frederick Kroesen pointed out, excessive faith in today's high technology is but the latest manifestation of the "silver bullet" fantasy. Earlier versions included the horse, the phalanx, the crossbow, the iron-clad knight, the cannon, the machine gun, the tank, poison gas, the airplane, and the atomic bomb. Certainly the technology of the Information Age will revolutionize the battlefield, and cyberspace systems and digitalization have already begun to do so. The resulting changes will no doubt be as dramatic as the battlefield changes of the Industrial Age. But as the distinguished military historian Sir Michael Howard noted, the nation must also be prepared to wage war at the level of the Agrarian Age, for old verities about will and courage still apply. Despite the intense debate over technology, the central issue confronting the armed forces has not been faced—whether the United States should maintain a Cold War–type military with a relatively large standing army or whether it should return to the much smaller force of the interwar years.

Instead of using regional contingencies as the criterion for shaping the force, another panelist said, America should plan for

[6]Lisa Burgess, "Congress Wrestles with Technology, Force Cuts," *Defense News*, May 9–15, 1994.

the unforeseeable. U.S. forces should have a more generalized strategy that minimizes the odds that they will get into serious trouble, no matter where they have to fight. But certain vested intellectual, organizational, and industrial interests weigh against such a strategy: planners are wedded to their own ideas and concepts. The services prefer to fight the types of wars for which they are best trained and structured. And industry pushes for scenarios where their weapons systems are optimized.

What America suffers now, asserted another panelist, is a disparity among policy, force posture, and the budget. If, as some argue, war fighting is no longer the primary role of the military and peacekeeping should be the armed forces' principal focus, then the military as it exists today is unnecessary. But since the American people are not anxious to support such a "touchy-feely" military, they are not likely to favor a defense budget geared toward those tasks.

The Military-Industrial Complex and Procurement

Some people assert that the matériel dimension of strategy is the real heart of the "American way of war," by which the enemy is not so much defeated as overwhelmed by the enormous U.S. mobilization capability and matériel superiority. During the April 1951 Chinese spring offensive in Korea, for example, American field artillery fired twenty-seven *Liberty Ship* loads of ammunition to turn back the 250,000-man attack, inflicting 70,000 casualties in the process. *Time* magazine quoted one U.S. officer as saying, "They're spending people the way we spend ammunition."[7] In wartime, that equation suits the American people, who prefer to spend "things" and be the war's "arsenal of democracy" rather than spend the lives of their children and become its charnel house. But in peacetime, many Americans see the "arsenal" as a corrupt "military-industrial complex" that squanders tax money on overpriced toilet seats and $200 hammers. It follows that peacetime defense spending has been a prime target of budget cutters. While the size of the military has been cut by one-third in the wake of the Cold War, the share of the gross domestic product devoted to national defense has been slashed in half, declining by 54 percent in real dollars since 1985 to its lowest level since before World War II.

Moreover, the Defense Department's procurement budget is at

[7]Quoted in Harry G. Summers Jr., "Spring Offensive, 1951," in *Korean War Almanac* (New York: Facts on File, 1990), p. 256.

a fifty-year low. While a crisis is not immediately at hand, such reductions do portend future problems. Technology buys time, and intelligence estimates hold that the U.S. military today has about a fifteen-year edge on its likely opponents. Unless that current technological advantage is maintained, however, a "bow wave" will develop that will reach staggering proportions early in the next century. When the problem becomes apparent then, it will be too late to solve it. To change the military of 2015, one must start now. Except that now there is no vision to initiate those changes.

A case in point is the issue of air dominance. The navy and air force are calling for a $300 billion investment in new jet fighters to replace their aging aircraft. Even though the number of aircraft has been cut by some 35 percent since the Persian Gulf War (from 8,200 to 5,900 planes) to free up dollars for modernization, that is not enough to pay for the new planes. "Getting there by 2001, as planned," notes the *Washington Post*'s Bradley Graham, "assumes future savings from military base closing and more efficient purchasing practices—assumptions that are proving more difficult to achieve than top defense officials had anticipated."[8] Base closings will certainly not compensate for the shortfall. As one panelist pointed out, Washington has already closed some 20 percent of the bases in the United States, but it will be ten years before the government sees any savings.

The other alternative, more efficient purchasing practices, was favored by two panelists whose time in office afforded them substantial experience in promoting competition and second sourcing for military procurement. During their tenure, sole-source and cost-plus procurement fell from 85 percent to 35 percent, with a significant reduction in costs. The cost of an *Aegis* cruiser, for example, went from $1.5 billion to $800 million. But the recent consolidation of defense industries in the name of efficiency has decreased competition. Lockheed-Martin accounts for 60 percent of current procurement. By returning to a Soviet-style monopoly supply system, the United States is in danger of unilateral disarmament.

The Dow Jones industrial index has increased more than 70 percent in the past three years, noted one participant. But during the same period, in an era of declining military budgets, the defense industrial index rose almost 500 percent. Chief executive officers are back in the cost-plus high cotton with $40 million

[8]Bradley Graham, "Pentagon Faces Huge Bill for Jet Fighters," *Washington Post*, Aug. 22, 1996.

bonuses, and none of them can lose money. And a dependence on internal defense industrial facilities is not an answer either. Combined, these large pockets of socialism—such as the army arsenal system, the navy shipyards and weapons stations, and the air force depots—are wasting $40–50 billion a year. A classic example from the Reagan years was the very high speed integrated chip (VHSIC). The Pentagon bureaucracy said Silicon Valley could not be counted on to produce fast enough chips for the integrated circuits of the high-tech weapons system then under development. So Washington taxed each of the services nearly $2 billion a year and sank approximately $12 billion overall into the VHSIC program. When the chip was finally produced in 1989, it was significantly slower and several generations behind the commercial counterpart produced by Silicon Valley companies.

Ironically, America is currently experiencing a golden era of productivity. The U.S. industrial base for high tech, low tech, heavy industry, and manufacturing is the marvel of the world. And this base can still provide the country with an affordable defense if the government tells manufacturers exactly what military capabilities the United States needs. If Washington fails to do that, the industrial base will be in the driver's seat. The U.S. defense posture will then depend on what the industrial complex wants to sell instead of on foreign policy and defense decision makers, leaving the country at the mercy of the American "Krupp."

Although he agreed with that assessment, another panel member pointed out that procurement reform is a second-order issue. Even a 50 percent reduction in the existing $39 billion procurement budget would make only a small dent in the $260 billion defense budget. The big money is in operating and maintenance funds, and cuts there must be accompanied by a clear plan of action. Thus, the armed forces need a new NSC-68, the blueprint that laid out a coherent military policy to guide the Cold War procurement policies.

Conclusion

What was not said by the panelists was as important as what was said. No one forecast any substantial increases in the defense budget in the foreseeable future. Despite some rumblings from the Republicans, defense spending was not a major issue in the 1996 presidential campaign. Perhaps one explanation is that, according to a 1995 public opinion poll, only 9 percent of Americans see foreign policy and defense as America's biggest problem, down from 42 percent in 1982.

But relief may be at hand. On July 17, 1996, the very day the Defense Task Force convened, Chairman of the Joint Chiefs of Staff General John Shalikashvili unveiled his *Joint Vision 2010*, which addressed one of the panel's primary concerns. It was intended to serve as an industry road map for the next fifteen years, said the *Defense Daily*, "by channeling the military services' varied acquisition programs, as well as doctrine and strategy differences, into one common direction."[9]

As the *Defense News* noted,

> Joint Vision 2010 marks the first attempt by a Joint Chiefs chairman to define a strategy for each of the military services to follow in crafting investment and modernization plans. . . . Shalikashvili's plan also will serve as a litmus test for the military services' various weapons programs.[10]

A valiant attempt to apply logic to what has been until now an illogical system, *Joint Vision 2010* was long overdue.

---

[9]Vega Muradian, "New Joint Warfare Plan Also an Industry Road Map," *Defense Daily*, July 18, 1996.
[10]Robert Holzer, "Shali Pushes Future Force Strategy," *Defense News*, Aug. 19–25, 1996.

CIVIL-MILITARY RELATIONS

by Eliot A. Cohen

There is no crisis in American civil-military relations if crisis means the kind of collision between civil and military authority that would breed a coup d'état or other manifestation of a breakdown of civilian control of the military, such as systematic and open disobedience of orders.[1] But, to a remarkable degree, members of the Defense Task Force agreed that deep and pervasive difficulties plague American civil-military relations, that these problems merit attention and exploration, and that dramatic and possibly painful actions are required to resurrect the relationship between the armed forces and civil society that the Founders envisioned and that makes sense for a twenty-first-century democracy. The three core problems discussed at length were the politicization of the military, the growing divide between civil society and those who wear the uniform, and the centralization of military power in the Joint Staff and in the chairman of the Joint Chiefs of Staff (JCS).

A Politicized Military

As one participant put it, when hearing military officers speak about President Bill Clinton, he felt tempted to turn Voltaire's apocryphal defense of free speech on its head: "I agree with everything that you say and am appalled by the fact that you say it." The first two years of the Clinton administration were marked by an extraordinary display of open disdain and hostility by the military for the new president. The ill-advised nature of his manpower policies (particularly his effort to lift the ban on homosexuals serving in uniform), the general disregard for things military that characterized junior staffers in the White House, a proclivity to see the military as a tool of domestic and international social work rather than strategic action, and the president's own evasion of the Vietnam-era draft explained this behavior on the part of officers but in no way made it acceptable. On many occasions sen-

[1]This essay originally appeared in *Orbis*, Spring 1997, and arose from the Foreign Policy Research Institute conference "The Demilitarization of the Military?" Philadelphia, Pa., July 17–18, 1996. This essay is copyright 1997 by Eliot A. Cohen.

ior military officers not only tolerated their subordinates' making contemptuous remarks about the commander in chief—itself an offense subject to court-martial under the Uniform Code of Military Justice—but amplified and reinforced such comments. Military officers also were increasingly willing to announce their political affiliation (almost invariably with the Republican Party) or to display their political beliefs in such ways as driving cars with anti-Clinton bumper stickers onto military bases, in defiance of tradition and the norms of military service.

Yet most conference participants argued that the politicization of the military reflects something more profound than the reaction of the officer corps to a particular politician. As one put it, "There has been a long-term, secular trend towards politicization of the U.S. officer corps." To some extent that mirrors similar trends within other professional groups in American society. The current conception of the military officer still reflects an image drawn from the austere portrait of the "professional" put forward in the 1950s. Professionals, according to the social science literature of the time, were defined by three characteristics: corporateness (that is, a sense of collective identity), responsibility (to society at large and not simply to a particular client or customer), and education (both throughout their careers and at a high intellectual level). Society viewed the professional as someone whose technical expertise and detachment from politics made him both unique and difficult to manage, and much ink was spent on the subject of how professionals defined their relationships with those around them.

Over time, this purist model of the professional has changed and eroded. As doctors and lawyers have become politicized and demythologized, so too have military officers shed the image of pure and apolitical expertise once ascribed to them. Like other interest groups, they lost a sense of uniqueness and learned how to play the game. Indeed, it is not uncommon for officers to describe themselves as a governmental interest group and to justify (if somewhat abashedly) their collective actions in such terms.

Politicization sprang from other sources as well. In the last thirty years, the American military has become remarkably sophisticated regarding politics, in part through a professional military education that stresses the importance of the political dimension of warfare. A revival of the study *On War*, Carl von Clausewitz's classic text examining the relationship between war and politics, followed on the heels of the Vietnam War as officers struggled to understand why they lost a war in which they seemingly held the trump cards of firepower, mobility, and resources. In his introduction to *On Strategy*, one of the earliest critiques of the military's efforts in Vietnam and a major contribution to the Clausewitz revival, Colonel Harry Summers recalled his conversation with a North Vietnamese officer during the final armistice negotiations. When Summers remarked to his counterpart that the Vietnamese never beat the Americans in a single battle, the North Vietnamese colonel paused for a moment and said: "That's true. It's also irrelevant."[2] More than one officer came away from that war convinced of the necessity of entering the next with a far more sophisticated appreciation of policy than that brought to bear in Vietnam. At the same time, the rejection of the military by some segments of American society after the war dismayed members of the officer corps, who consequently came to believe that domestic politics also required their attention.

Yet Vietnam merely accelerated trends that originated during World War II and the early Cold War, when officers found themselves engaged in the murky areas where politics and war overlapped. Programs ranging from courses in American and international politics at the war colleges to internships in government exposed officers to politics in various forms. Today, military officers serve on congressional staffs and are present throughout the federal government, even in such seemingly non-defense-oriented bureaucracies as the Office of Management and Budget (OMB). Indeed, General Colin Powell, perhaps the shrewdest political general since Eisenhower, describes his year as a White House Fellow serving in OMB as his introduction to the bureaucratic politics that he would play so well during his time in Washington.

Seared by its experience in Vietnam, the officer corps reacted by seeking to manipulate political leaders and processes so that any commitment to conflict would be made under circumstances that it approved. An early case in point was General Creighton Abrams's successful creation of the Total Force in the 1970s—in particular, an army dependent on reserve mobilization to conduct any sizable war. With the tacit acquiescence of the civilian leadership, the military in effect created a system that could not go to war without some kind of national mobilization, even though the army's leadership traditionally mistrusted the reserve components.

To some extent, political awareness is desirable in an officer corps. But when military officers lose their self-restraint about

[2]Harry G. Summers Jr., *On Strategy: A Critical Analysis of the Vietnam War* (1982; Novato, Calif.: Presidio Press, 1995), p. 1.

both political identification and actual participation in politics—including behind-the-scenes manipulation of any branch of government—a boundary has been crossed. The military is a unique calling that bears special responsibilities for the security of the nation and poses particular threats when deformed by open partisanship. When officers do not hesitate to refer to themselves as another interest group, when they willingly identify themselves by party affiliation and feel free to comment in public, and in front of their subordinates, about the faults of their civilian superiors, corrective action is needed.

The Gap between Society and the Military

Since 1940, military service has shaped the early careers of millions of American young men, particularly those who have gone on to become business and political leaders. The end of the draft in the early 1970s created a noticeable gap between civilian and military elites. That gap widened with the dramatic shrinkage of the military in the wake of the Cold War, a shrinkage likely to continue. At first glance, this development might not seem terribly important. After all, throughout most of U.S. history the military was small and in many cases unrepresentative of American society. The great difference today is that the United States is, and will remain, a superpower for whom military might is central to national policy. That was not the case in times of peace before World War II.

The gap between the military and society is exacerbated by the military's increasing tendency to recruit from narrower segments of the population. One conference participant reported that some 25 percent of new entrants into the military now come from military families. Of greater concern, in the view of some, is the increased role of the military academies as providers of officer candidates. Whereas West Point, Annapolis, and the Air Force Academy produced only 10 percent of new officers during the Cold War, today they produce roughly one-quarter. In the view of many, the services would be happy not only to restrict as much officer intake as possible to the service academies but to force new officers to serve for extended periods of time. The demands of efficiency, in particular the desire to reduce training expenses and turnover, lead the military to press for long-term service contracts.

Increasingly, some military leaders also see a growing gap

between military and societal values. The U.S. Marine Corps, perhaps the least civilized of all the armed services, has changed its basic training programs to instill values in recruits that it believes American society has failed to provide. Military leaders routinely remark, with more than a little complacency, that the military has coped with problems that still bedevil the rest of American society: drug and alcohol abuse, and even in large measure race relations. As sociologist Charles Moskos has put it, the army is the only institution in which black men routinely give white men orders and no one thinks twice about it. The army's success on issues involving the sexes is less clear. The military has struggled, with varying success, to open to women careers that traditionally embodied masculine qualities. Still, that the military has come to see itself as an organization with better values and more functional social behavior than civil society marks yet another departure from the past, when the armed forces saw themselves more as a reflection of society and less as its superior.

Different issues are inherent on the civilian side of the relationship. Fewer politicians, let alone their staff assistants, have any military experience; yet they will be required to make decisions about the employment and structuring of military forces. Not all conference participants had equal concerns here. Some pointed to political leaders such as Abraham Lincoln who with minimal military experience nonetheless proved to be outstanding strategists and civilian leaders. But all agreed that it would be desirable to improve the military expertise of today's generation of Congress members and journalists. The current ignorance gives rise to two equally problematic trends: a growing number of political elites who have little appreciation for the needs of the military and are inclined to view it in terms of stereotypes of discipline and inflexibility, and, no less troubling, the emergence of a political class that unthinkingly defers to this alone of all public institutions, without subjecting it to critical but informed scrutiny.

The Rise of a Centralized Military Staff

Since the turn of the century, there has been steady movement toward the centralization of military authority in large staffs. The creation of a chief of staff of the army and a chief of naval operations was followed during World War II by the creation and later institutionalization of the Joint Chiefs of Staff. The Defense Department Reorganization Act of 1958 further strengthened the chairman of the JCS and the Joint Staff, and the Goldwater-Nichols legislation of 1986 took another large step in that direction. Today, the chairman of the JCS serves as a de facto commander of the American armed forces, operating under the supervision of either the president or the secretary of defense. The Joint Staff has taken over many of the prerogatives of the service staffs, both civilian and military, and has even strayed into the legitimate territory of the Office of the Secretary of Defense (OSD). These developments have generated several problems:

A reduction of sources of military advice for civilian authority. The president and secretary of defense need more than one senior military adviser. Any one adviser, being human, may have the prejudices and distorted perceptions that naturally can accumulate during a career. While Goldwater-Nichols does not prohibit civilians from seeking advice from the other chiefs, it tacitly discourages such a move. As a result, during the war in the Persian Gulf, the secretary of defense was forced to resort to unusual channels to elicit more options than he was receiving from the Joint Staff.

An attenuation of long-range thinking. The perspective of the Joint Staff and the regional and functional commanders in chief (CINCs) is short term; their understandable concern with immediate operational issues leads them to discount future problems and focus on current activity. In the past, the services provided a long-range perspective, but their weakened bureaucratic clout and exclusion from military planning activities have undercut their ability to make contributions in this area.

A weakening of competition. The United States has benefited greatly from the armed services' competition with one another for resources and missions. In all other walks of life, the United States has traditionally appreciated the merits of competition. Yet in the Pentagon the trend has been towards centralized control and allocation of resources. Particularly as technology allows the services to compete for roles and missions (in the area of deep strike, for example), it makes sense to enhance rather than diminish the competitiveness that has been so valuable in the past.

A diminution of civilian control. Goldwater-Nichols did little to enhance the quality or power of the staff in the Office of the Secretary of Defense, but it tremendously strengthened the roles and career tracks of Joint Staff officers. As a result, the weight of influence within the Pentagon has shifted decidedly in favor of the Joint Staff, which has an increasingly strong hand in bargaining with OSD and sometimes takes positions at variance with it.

To be sure, some of the results of the Goldwater-Nichols legislation have been favorable. "Jointness" is not merely a fad of the moment, but an undeniable trend in military operations brought about by changing technology. When shipboard systems (missiles as well as aircraft) can precisely strike the same targets as land-based ballistic missiles or aircraft, increased coordination of effort is clearly needed. As certain common systems—intelligence-gathering satellites, for example—gain importance, so too does the need for management of them throughout the Department of Defense. Moreover, some of the parochialism and obstructionism of the services conceivably has diminished in the face of the growing power of the chairman of the JCS, the Joint Staff, and the theater CINCs. Nonetheless, like all orthodoxies, that of jointness requires critical examination and a dispassionate review of its impact on long-term strategic thinking and civilian control.

Solutions

The ills besetting civil-military relations in the United States are the deeply rooted product of historical developments dating back several decades or longer. Remedies will take time to have an effect. More important, they will require tough and imaginative civilian leadership, because they will be opposed by important (though by no means all) segments of military opinion and will be relatively unattractive politically. The military opinion will be bolstered by civilian allies, including military retirees (who can speak far more freely than those in uniform) and that large group of civilians who occasionally confuse unthinking support of military traditions and practice with patriotic support for the armed forces.

Reforming the military academies. It should be a basic principle of the American armed forces that the officer corps be as widely recruited as possible. Therefore, for both practical and symbolic reasons, the military academies should be modeled along the lines of Sandhurst. That is, officers would complete their undergraduate educations at any acceptable civilian college or university and then attend a military academy for nine months to a year of military training. This system would preserve the valuable traditions and character-building qualities of the academies, while dispensing with their cliquish and self-absorbed nature. The services would still be pressed to maintain active ROTC presences on campuses, including those that might produce small numbers of high-quality officers.

The service academies currently wrestle with two contradictory missions: the training of young officers and the provision of a liberal education. They cannot be expected to do both well, for the two purposes are somewhat at odds with each other. This proposed reform would allow officers to receive their normal, liberal education elsewhere, leaving the academies free to focus on military training.

Recruitment schemes for the citizen-soldier. Soldiers and civilians alike applaud the concept of the citizen-soldier, but the time has come to reconsider what that term means. It is neither accurate nor adequate to say that professional soldiers have the full rights of all other citizens, thereby making them citizen-soldiers. Rather, citizen-soldiers are best understood to be short-term or temporary service personnel whose primary careers are in the civilian rather than the military world. Ideally, such personnel would comprise a large part of the armed services. The services should therefore be required to develop and advertise programs similar to those operated with some success by the army, which attract young men and women for short (twenty-four-month) stints of service in return for college tuition or other benefits. Similar plans would be designed to attract older men and women to the reserves, which would be revamped to take advantage of the many talents in the civilian sector.

Now more than ever, the National Guard and the reserves embody the concept of the citizen-soldier, whose centrality to the national defense was enshrined in the Constitution and remains important today. The guard and reserves have much to offer the armed services by bringing the maturity and expertise of civilians to bear on military problems, as seen in the notable success of the army reserve civil-affairs units. Moreover, the reserves have a tremendous range of programs, from the extremely successful reliance of the air force on reserve air crew and support personnel to operate the logistics fleet, to the far less successful incorporation of naval reservists into the fleet. Many future units may focus on the realm of information technology, where expertise often commands salaries that the military cannot match. Overall, a general review of reserve policy seems called for, particularly as some reserve units (army civil-affairs units, for example) have begun to be extremely active, to the point of being overstretched, while others (combat divisions in the National Guard) seem to have little function at all.

Professional military education. The conference members also argued for increasing the military educational system's attention to problems in civil-military relations. Too few officers, even at senior levels, have reflected on not only such well-known cases of civil-military friction as Douglas MacArthur's dismissal from command in Korea, but the legislative and philosophical under-pinnings of the U.S. military establishment.

Moreover, as the nature of warfare itself changes, so too does the nature of military professionalism. In an age when the direct-ing of firepower increasingly takes place from a distance, the very concept of officership must be reassessed. To a remarkable degree, current regulations, organizational forms, and rank struc-tures reflect a bygone era, in which the roles and relationships of both commissioned and noncommissioned officers were very dif-ferent from what they are today. A first-order reexamination of what officership means is thus in order. To this end, the curricula of the staff and war colleges need to be reviewed, including the material that deals with civilian control of the military. The clichéd notion that civilian control consists of giving the military unambiguous (and unchanging) goals, providing resources, and stepping aside—a notion particularly prevalent following the Persian Gulf War—needs to be replaced with a more discriminat-ing, if less comfortable, view.

Military familiarization programs. Lastly, it is desirable to institute programs that would improve the quality of civilian lead-ership by educating civilians about military organizations and modern warfare. These programs would be intended for legisla-tors, journalists, and other "opinion leaders" (to include civic leaders and people in business), to help them develop sound crite-ria for evaluating contemporary defense matters. Formats for such an enterprise could include the following:

- lectures on the organization and function of the Department of Defense;
- visits to a variety of facilities, including training installa-tions;
- participation in simulations and exercises; and
- academic work (through case studies, seminars, and site vis-its) in the field of military history.

Currently, the Department of Defense offers many groups vis-its to ships or military facilities, such as the National Training Center at Fort Irwin, California. But these opportunities, though valuable, are episodic (that is, undertaken without a coherent plan of instruction) and are not selectively targeted. A military installation's standard "pitch" for civilian outsiders is generally intended to highlight the sophistication and excellence of its people and machines, not to promote critical evaluation.

A serious program of military instruction would be quite different. It could be a part-time course during two years that would require roughly the same level of participation as reserve duty— say, a weekend a month plus a two-week stint of "active duty." These visitors to military installations would receive more than the standard dog and pony show, and they would be exposed to a variety of opposing views on a range of military matters (for example, the future of the aircraft carrier, or manned aircraft, or women in combat). Innovative use of educational technologies, such as CD-ROM-based instruction like that pioneered by the Air Command and Staff College at Maxwell Air Force Base, would enable participants to absorb quickly many of the basic details of military equipment, organization, and procedure on their own. Participation in such a program would be selective and begun on a small scale.

If Nothing Is Done

No one at the conference suggested that absent these recommendations the republic would be in mortal danger. But it is worth speculating about the direction of American civil-military relations without the kinds of measures indicated above to correct current adverse trends. An ever more inbred military elite would evolve, recruited largely from families of military personnel and increasingly educated at the service academies. Confronted (as appears likely) by a steadily shrinking defense budget, this group would not retire into frosty isolation but would attempt to influence the political process directly. Military officers might, within the bounds of the law (but just barely), attempt to throw support to the political party most favorable to their interests.

At the same time, a political elite generally ignorant of military affairs would divide into three groups. The first, and largest, would simply be indifferent to defense matters and would be inclined to regard military expenditure as wasteful unless proven otherwise. Another group would view the military with suspicion, believing its notions to be both retrograde and at odds with those of society on a variety of issues, most notably homosexuality. And a third group would regard the military with unthinking admiration as the embodiment of virtues shunned by the rest of society.

Oddly enough, this last group could prove to be the most dangerous. Democratic society normally produces a certain amount of healthy suspicion of the military—a distaste for the hierarchy, subordination of self, and adherence to discipline that military life requires. Unrestrained deference to military authority and expertise, on the other hand, can lead to gross errors in both foreign and defense policy. The horrifying experience of World War I, when deference to military authority was at an all-time high, offers an important warning. The generals repeatedly resorted to strategies of appalling bloodshed, not merely out of arrogance, but because of adulation from journalists and politicians who made them into gods of war rather than what they were—fallible men, albeit well-educated, patriotic, and determined. By the end of that conflict, mutual confidence at the top and throughout society had broken down, politicians mistrusted their military subordinates, and more than one military leader was willing to endorse the theory of the "stab in the back."

Healthy civilian control of the military requires a political leadership that understands how uncertain of a business war is and that recognizes that even the best-trained and most dedicated military professionals can err. Such politicians can exert effective civilian control because they appreciate military virtues, can discern which military officers are the best, and can weigh the relative importance of political and military requirements. On the other side of the equation, civil-military relations require officers who understand and accept the preeminence of political considerations in the conduct of war and who can cope with civilian intrusion into their realm whether or not they like it. And at the very top, a dialogue must exist between statesmen and generals, unequal though that dialogue may be. Overall, healthy civil-military relations need a military with standards distinct from those of general society and a society that appreciates the need for the difference, even if it does not always approve of the military's views.

Left uncorrected, the trends in American civil-military relations could breed certain pathologies. The most serious possibility is that of a dramatic civil-military split during a crisis involving the use of force. In the recent past, such tensions did not result in open division. For example, Franklin Roosevelt insisted that the United States invade North Africa in 1942, though the chiefs of both the army and the navy vigorously opposed such a course, favoring instead a buildup in England and an invasion of the continent in 1943. Back then it was inconceivable that a senior military officer would leak word of such a split to the media, where it would have reverberated loudly and destructively. To be sure, from time to time individual officers broke the vow of professional silence to protest a course of action, but in these isolated cases the officers paid the accepted price of termination of their careers.

In the modern environment, such cases might no longer be isolated. Thus, presidents might try to shape U.S. strategy so that it complies with military opinion, and rarely in the annals of statecraft has military opinion alone been an adequate guide to sound foreign policy choices. Had Lincoln followed the advice of his senior military advisers there is a good chance that the Union would have fallen. Had Roosevelt deferred to General George C. Marshall and Admiral Ernest J. King there might well have been a gory debacle on the shores of France in 1943. Had Harry S. Truman heeded the advice of his theater commander in the Far East (and it should be remembered that the Joint Chiefs generally counseled support of the man on the spot) there might have been a third world war.

Throughout much of its history, the U.S. military was remarkably politicized by contemporary standards. One commander of the army, Winfield Scott, even ran for president while in uniform, and others (Leonard Wood, for example) have made no secret of their political views and aspirations. But until 1940, and with the exception of periods of outright warfare, the military was a negligible force in American life, and America was not a central force in international politics. That has changed. Despite the near halving of the defense budget from its high in the 1980s, it remains a significant portion of the federal budget, and the military continues to employ millions of Americans. More important, civil-military relations in the United States now no longer affect merely the closet-room politics of Washington, but the relations of countries around the world. American choices about the use of force, the shrewdness of American strategy, the soundness of American tactics, and the will of American leaders have global consequences. What might have been petty squabbles in bygone years are now magnified into quarrels of a far larger scale, and conceivably with far more grievous consequences. To ignore the problem would neglect one of the cardinal purposes of the federal government: "to provide for the common defense" in a world in which security cannot be taken for granted.

THE U.S. MILITARY MUST FIND ITS VOICE

by Sam C. Sarkesian

To say that the strategic landscape remains unsettled would be an understatement.[1] In the brief period since the end of the Cold War, the U.S. military has fought one major war (Iraq), performed numerous "nontraditional" humanitarian and peacekeeping missions, struggled to adjust to a variety of social demands such as the full integration of women and gays in the ranks, and at the same time attempted to prepare for the twenty-first century. What is more, the armed services have been asked to do all this within the worst budgetary environment in fifty years. As a result, the U.S. military faces a dilemma: how to respond to the uncertainties of the new domestic and strategic landscapes, maintain a healthy relationship with American civil society, and yet retain its core *raison d'être*, which is to deter or win war against the nation's enemies.

The American military faced similar dilemmas after the Civil War and World War I, for a brief time after World War II, and following the Vietnam War.[2] At least one lesson clearly emerged from those experiences: the military profession dare not withdraw into an ethical cocoon and take on a defensive posture. Instead, it must make a prudent and positive response to the travails imposed on it and not shrink from articulating its views in the public square. In short, senior military officers must reshape the very notion of military professionalism by candidly admitting the impact of politics on the military's ability to do its job and daring to practice constructive political engagement. This would appear to violate the sacred code of silence by which the U.S. military is strictly apolitical, offers technical advice only, and goes out of its way to honor the principle of civilian control. But only through constructive

---

[1]This essay originally appeared in slightly different form in *Orbis*, Summer 1998.
[2]See, for example, C. Robert Kemble, *The Image of the Army Officer in America: Background for Current Views* (Westport, Conn.: Greenwood Press, 1973); Allan R. Millett and Peter Maslowski, *For the Common Defense: A Military History of the United States of America*, rev. and enl. (New York: Free Press, 1994); and Peter D. Feaver, "The Civil-Military Problematique: Huntington, Janowitz, and the Question of Civilian Control," *Armed Forces and Society*, Winter 1996, p. 157.

political engagement can military professionals legitimate their role in policy debates, mark a clear boundary between defense policy and merely partisan politics, and provide the American public with a clearer understanding of military life and culture. Nor are constructive political engagement and loyalty to the country, civilian leadership, and the Constitution in any way incongruous. Indeed, such constructive political engagement, far from threatening to make the military an independent actor, presupposes that the military is dependent upon a variety of political actors and the public at large. It is *because* the U.S. military is under such tight civilian control that it needs to make its voice heard in civilian councils.

Any number of issues might fall within the scope of constructive political engagement, but the two most critical are the so-called democratization of the military (the convergence or divergence between the military and society) and the problematical utility of military force in the foreign policy contingencies of the century to come. These issues are interconnected and have a profound impact on the military's operational effectiveness.

To be sure, it has been an article of faith among military professionals and civilians alike that a wall exists in America between the military and politics. But that faith is not only historically invalid, it denies current reality. The American domestic landscape and the international strategic landscape are, and have always been, politically and militarily inextricable, while the use of military force has always been shaped by political considerations. If the skill, wisdom, and experience residing in our officers corps are to be tapped by our national leadership, the military profession itself must be philosophically broadened and encouraged to involve itself judiciously in the policy arena.[3] This would include the development of a more comprehensive view of politics, greater sensitivity to the realities underpinning the American political system, and more assertive presentation of the military viewpoint within the parameters of American democracy.

Nothing makes the point more eloquently than the Vietnam War, the mismanagement of which forced military professionals, especially in the army, to go through an agonizing reappraisal of the meaning of the military profession.[4] In the broader policy

[3]The study of the military profession and civil-military relations addressed here takes its cue from graduate education and military professionalism as reported in Sam C. Sarkesian, John Allen Williams, and Fred B. Bryant, *Soldiers, Society, and National Security* (Boulder, Colo.: Lynne Rienner Publishers, 1995).

[4]See, for example, Sam C. Sarkesian, *Beyond the Battlefield: The New Military Professionalism* (New York: Pergamon Press, 1981).

arena, the failure of senior military leaders to speak out with a realistic military perspective on that war provides an enduring lesson for military professionals.[5] Recently, the role of the chiefs of staff in the decision to go to war in Vietnam and in its conduct has been studied by H. R. McMaster and found wanting, precisely because these "five silent men" did *not* give voice to their professional doubts, but instead submerged themselves under a cloak of political deception.

> As American involvement in Vietnam deepened, the gap between the nature of that commitment and the president's depiction of it to the American people, Congress, and members of his own administration widened. Lyndon Johnson, with the assistance of Robert S. McNamara and the Joint Chiefs of Staff, had set the stage for America's disaster in Vietnam.[6]

Commenting on the internal shadowboxing and cover-ups during the Vietnam War, one member of the Joint Chiefs of Staff remarked, "Maybe we military men were all weak. Maybe we should have stood up and pounded the table. . . . I was part of it and I'm sort of ashamed of myself, too. At times I wonder, 'Why did we go along with this kind of stuff?'"[7]

Whether or not they were weak, the military brass in the 1960s was *not* following an American tradition when they kept their silence and followed the civilians' lead. For as recently as the decade before, General Matthew Ridgway had this to say to his peers in uniform:

> [T]he professional soldier should never pull his punches, should never let himself for one moment be dissuaded from stating honest estimates [of what] his own military experience and judgement tell him will be needed to do the job required of him. No factor of political motivation should excuse, no reason of "party" or political expediency could explain such an action.[8]

Ridgway went on to note that: "Since George Washington's time, no top soldier has forgotten that he is a citizen first and a soldier second, and that the troops under his command are an

[5]There are any number of books on the impact of the Vietnam War on the military, in general, and the ground forces, in particular. An excellent starting point is Lt. Gen. Harold G. Moore (Ret.) and Joseph L. Galloway, *We Were Soldiers Once . . . And Young; Ia Drang: The Battle That Changed the War in Vietnam* (New York: Random House, 1992).

[6]H. R. McMaster, *Dereliction of Duty: Lyndon Johnson, Robert McNamara, the Joint Chiefs of Staff, and the Lies That Led to Vietnam* (New York: HarperCollins, 1997), p. 322. See also Robert S. McNamara with Brian Van DeMark, *In Retrospect: The Tragedy and Lessons of Vietnam* (New York: Random House, 1995).

[7]Adm. David Lamar McDonald, *The Reminiscences of Admiral David Lamar McDonald, U.S. Navy (Retired)* (Annapolis, Md.: U.S. Naval Institute, 1976), pp. 390, 393, as quoted in McMaster, *Dereliction of Duty*, p. 262.

[8]Gen. Matthew B. Ridgway (Ret.), *Soldier: The Memoirs of Matthew B. Ridgway* (New York: Harper and Brothers, 1956), p. 271.

instrument of the people's will."[9]

In the turmoil following Vietnam, General Fred Weyand rediscovered that wisdom. "The American Army," he wrote, "is really a people's Army in the sense that it belongs to the American people who take a jealous proprietary interest in its involvement. . . . The American Army is not so much an arm of the Executive Branch as it as an arm of the American people."[10] Hence, Weyand's advice was:

> As military professionals we must speak out, we must counsel our political leaders and alert the American public that there is no such thing as a "splendid little war." There is no such thing as a war fought on the cheap. . . . The Army must make the price of involvement clear *before* we get involved, so that America can weigh the probable costs of involvement against the degree of noninvolvement.[11]

Most recently, General Colin Powell has echoed the directions laid out by Ridgway and Weyand. He told an audience of military officers at the National Defense University that modern military officers must understand politics and the media and stated that "politics is fundamental."[12] The same account reported the following: "Often accused of being a 'political general,' Powell responded, 'there isn't a general in Washington who isn't political, not if he's going to be successful, because that's the nature of our system.'"[13]

It seems clear that the American military belongs to the American people, and military professionals have the duty and obligation to insure that the public and its political leaders are counseled and alerted to the needs and necessities of military life. This cannot be done by adhering to a notion of the military profession as a silent order of monks isolated from the political realm.

Enlightened Advocacy and Education

Constructive political engagement entails, above all, enlight-

[9]Ibid., p. 269.

[10]Gen. Fred C. Weyand from "Vietnam Myths and American Realities," *CDRS CALL*, July/Aug. 1976, as quoted in Harry G. Summers, *On Strategy: The Vietnam War in Context* (Carlisle Barracks, Pa.: Strategic Studies Institute, U.S. Army War College, 1981), p. 7.

[11]Weyand, "Vietnam Myths," pp. 3, 4, italics in original, as quoted in Summers, *On Strategy*, p. 25.

[12]Bob Woodward, *The Commanders* (New York: Simon and Schuster, 1991), p. 155.

[13]Ibid. See also Colin Powell, John Lehman, William Odom, Samuel Huntington, and Richard H. Kohn, "Exchange on Civil-Military Relations," *National Interest*, Summer 1994, pp. 23–31.

ened advocacy and education.[14] Military professionals must offer intellectually sound advice to inform and instruct those in the policy-making arena about the military implications of specific policies, and, if necessary, recommend and defend the military perspective in public forums. To prepare themselves for these tasks, officers must receive a realistic political education focused on the nature and principles of America's democratic system, its evolution into a modern nation-state and superpower, and the nature of the international landscape. For "it is the man who is both liberally and professionally educated who will be the better soldier."[15]

Civilian graduate education is a key factor in developing the knowledge and acumen needed to engage in enlightened advocacy. Happily, many military professionals have access to formal civilian graduate education, and the latter has been an important consideration for promotion and assignments throughout the military services since the 1970s.[16] In addition, officers should be encouraged to participate in professional associations such as the Inter-University Seminar on Armed Forces and Society, the National Strategy Forum, the Council on Foreign Relations, and the International Institute for Strategic Studies, as well as scholarly organizations in any number of academic disciplines. The purpose of such education would be to raise the political sensitivity of military professionals, broaden their political horizons, expand their political experience, and help them create an informal network of military, academic, and political contacts. At the same time, such networks will enhance the opportunity for civilians to develop a deeper understanding of military professionals and military life in an era when fewer and fewer Americans have any military experience of their own or contact with the uniformed services.

Harold Lasswell's view of politics is "who gets what, when, and how."[17] Although written decades ago, this terminology reflects a realistic view of American politics: The "how" must be within the orbit of the American system and congruent with democratic principles. As one group of scholars observed, "[I]t is important to remember that politics can be conducted in either an

[14]See Sarkesian, Williams, and Bryant, *Soldiers, Society, and National Security*.

[15]Josiah Bunting, "The Humanities in the Education of the Military Professional," in *The System for Educating Military Officers in the U.S.*, ed. Lawrence J. Korb (Pittsburgh, Pa.: International Studies Association, 1976), p. 158.

[16]Sarkesian, Williams, and Bryant, *Soldiers, Society, and National Security*. See also Morris Janowitz, *The Professional Soldier: A Social and Political Portrait* (New York: Free Press, 1971), p. 426.

[17]Harold Lasswell, *Politics: Who Gets What, When, How* (New York: McGraw Hill, 1936).

ethical or unethical way."[18] That is, "playing politics" need not have a negative connotation, but can be a legitimate, credible, and honorable process by which individuals, groups, and institutions advance the national interests of the United States. Such "politics" is, in fact, an essential ingredient of American democracy and a critical aspect of constructive political engagement.

The numerous interconnections that already exist between senior military officers (such as the Joint Chiefs, Service Chiefs, and senior staff officers) and civilians at the national level are well known. These range from linkages with Congress and key members in the national security establishment and the National Command Authority to the Washington press corps. Numerous military professionals are also involved in "politics" in the nation's capital, ranging from linkages with the National Security Council staff and congressional staffs to a variety of think tanks. Likewise, commanders in chief of regional and functional commands have similar contact points that permit them to articulate their views on issues affecting their commands. Military professionals beyond the Beltway and in operating units at local bases and posts have, or should have, linkages with local civilian groups and the media. Equally important, opportunities exist in the normal course of their duties for military professionals to express their views through the chain of command—active espousal of the military perspective, admittedly with a degree of prudence.

Finally, a wide-ranging coalition of political-military networks exists among those that are involved in political activity focused on military issues. For instance, the Military Coalition, an advocacy group of twenty-four associations representing "five million current and former uniformed service members plus their families," includes the Association of the U.S. Army, Air Force Association, Fleet Reserve Association, Navy League of the United States, Marine Corps League, Retired Officers Association, Veterans of Foreign Wars of the United States, Reserve Officers Association, and National Guard Association.[19] In addition, the Federal Reserves and National Guard provide unique linkages between the military profession and the civilian sector. Such networking among military personnel and civilians within various organizations and associations also creates a synergistic effect, multiplying the channels available to the military for

[18]Robert L. Lineberry, George C. Edwards III, and Martin P. Wattenberg, *Government in America: People, Politics, and Policy*, 6th ed. (New York: HarperCollins, 1994), p. 6.
[19]Madilee Wnek, "Team Power," *The Retired Officer*, Nov. 1996, p. 30. For a complete listing of organizations, see pp. 33–34.

effective and legitimate political involvement. Through such channels, military officers can have ample opportunity to offer their perspectives on issues ranging from concerns about present deployments to information-age warfare to the defense budget.

Military views about the involvement in Bosnia are a case in point. At the national level, the Joint Chiefs or Service Chiefs of Staff can and should clarify military concerns about the U.S. peacekeeping mission there and about so-called nontraditional missions in general. At some point, the wise, professional, and patriotic course may be for high-ranking officers to insist that such missions simply cannot be done with the present resources and structure. Indeed, such a view may be a refreshing change from the "can do" syndrome that seems to paralyze open military debate.

Most important, the military brass should feel no hesitancy about providing the commander in chief with its specific and clear opinion on issues such as Bosnia. Disagreements that arise among the military, the president, and members of Congress should not be stifled, as was the case during the Vietnam War, but should be aired honestly and without prejudice to the military's obedience to, and implementation of, civilian directives. Nor should the armed forces wait until a debate occurs before presenting its perspective and objections to a given policy line. Military professionals ought to be as free to make known their technical judgments as engineers, scientists, or doctors without conjuring fears that they are trying to escape civilian control. The alternative, after all, is to perpetuate the timidity, extreme defensiveness, and fear of criticism from the public and Congress that seems to pervade the military today.

Constructive political engagement does not mean that the military can or should embroil itself in partisan politics or engage in media campaigns for political purposes. It merely means that the military must not remain passive and allow misjudgments and misguided policies and strategies to emerge from the political arena absent an airing of the military perspective. For such passivity not only harms the nation at large but can erode the military's own legitimacy and effectiveness. As Fotion and Elfstrom conclude:

> [I]t does not follow that the proper level of involvement by the military in political matters must be total abstinence. The military establishment deserves a fair hearing in the political arena as do other

establishments . . . since each provides services to the community
that need to be explained and funded.[20]

A more salient objection to constructive political engagement
than the bugaboo of military independence is that such advocacy
may lead to heated disputes within the military profession itself,
thus damaging professional unity and cohesion. The military profession is not a monolith, and a diversity of views surely exists.
But the ethos of the military profession itself tends to bind most
officers to a common set of principles and values. As Paul
Christopher observes:

> Military officership is a profession, not simply a vocation. Part of
> what it means to be a member of a profession is having a deep com-
> mitment to a set of abstract values and principles that define the pro-
> fession. This means that members of a profession accept certain val-
> ues that are specific to their profession as being more fundamental
> than other values.[21]

Walter Millis agrees:

> Military service stands by itself. It has some of the qualities of a
> priesthood, of a professional civil servant, of a great bureaucratized
> business organization and of an academic order . . . it has something
> of each of these in it but it corresponds exactly to none. . . . Again
> (the military professional) is set apart, therefore, from those who
> have followed other walks of life.[22]

This is true with respect to not only the officer corps but also the
noncommissioned officer corps throughout the services and down
to the level of small units, whose cohesiveness was poignantly
illustrated during the Gulf War. When ABC correspondent Sam
Donaldson interviewed a young African-American soldier in a
tank platoon on the eve of Desert Storm and repeatedly asked him
to speak to his fear of the impending battle, the young soldier just
as persistently repeated his answer: "This is my family and we'll
take care of each other."[23]

The Civil-Military Cultural Gap

The relationship between the military profession and

---

[20]N. Fotion and G. Elfstrom, *Military Ethics: Guidelines for Peace and War* (Boston: Routledge Kegan Paul, 1986), p. 87.

[21]Paul Christopher, "Unjust War and Moral Obligation: What Should Officers Do?" *Parameters*, Autumn 1995, p. 8.

[22]Walter Millis, "Puzzle of the Military Mind?" *New York Times*, Nov. 18, 1972, p. 144.

[23]Colin L. Powell with Joseph E. Persico, *My American Journey* (New York: Random House, 1995), p. 611. For excellent analyses of social cohesion and the military, see Morris Janowitz and Roger W. Little, *Sociology and the Military Establishment*, rev. ed. (New York: Russell Sage Foundation, 1965); and Wm. Darryl Henderson, *Cohesion: The Human Element in Combat* (Washington, D.C.: National Defense University Press, 1985).

American society can be summarized succinctly:

> The values and beliefs that form the substance of military profes-
> sionalism determine in no small measure the role of the military in
> society, establish the boundaries and criteria for military behavior,
> provide norms for the military subsystem, and establish the profes-
> sional posture vis-à-vis civilian elite. . . . The character of military
> professionalism places the military subsystem in its "orbit" within
> the political system and, in so doing, establishes the reference point
> from which civil-military relations evolve.[24]

Civil-military relations in turn are shaped by four interac-
tions: (a) between the military leadership and the military system; (b) between the military leadership and civilian elites; (c)
between the military leadership and the socio-political system in
general; and (d) between the military system as a whole and the
American socio-political system. The aggregate of these interconnections complicate civil-military relationships and make it
extremely difficult to "fix" a clear civil-military demarcation.[25]

It has always been difficult to discern clearly the relationship
between society and the military.[26] It is even more difficult and
complicated now because the American system is in flux.
Demographic, social, and economic changes, combined with
lowered expectations about major wars, have focused the attention of many Americans on the domestic political-economic environment. At the same time, issues of race, gender, and diversity
have become major concerns in American society. As a result,
questions are raised again about the degree to which the military
should reflect society at large—questions that define a large part
of modern American military history.

A case in point is the hesitancy with which the military profession responded to issues of gender relationships, sexual scan-

[24]Sam C. Sarkesian, "Military Professionalism and Civil-Military Relations in the
West," *International Political Science Review*, vol. 2, no. 3 (1981), p. 285. An excellent
assessment of civil-military relations is Don M. Snider and Miranda A. Carlton-Carew,
eds., *U.S. Civil-Military Relations in Crisis or Transition?* (Washington, D.C.: Center for
Strategic and International Studies, 1995).

[25]See Sam C. Sarkesian, "Civil-Military Relations in a Liberal Society: The United
States in a New Security Era" (unpublished paper presented at the Ohio State Mershon
Center conference on civil-military relations, Dec. 4–6, 1992). See also Don M. Snider
and Miranda A. Carlton-Carew, "The Current State of U.S. Civil-Military Relations: An
Introduction," in *U.S. Civil-Military Relations in Crisis or Transition?* pp. 5–8.

[26]A number of scholars have addressed the issue of civil-military relations, including
Samuel P. Huntington, *The Soldier and the State: The Theory and Politics of Civil-
Military Relations* (New York: Vintage Books, 1964); Janowitz, *The Professional Soldier;*
Franklin D. Margiotta, ed., *The Changing World of the American Military* (Boulder,
Colo.: Westview Press, 1978); Charles Moskos, "Armed Forces and American Society:
Convergence or Divergence?" in *Public Opinion and the Military*, ed. Charles Moskos
(Beverly Hills, Calif.: Sage Publications, 1971), pp. 271–94; and John Allen Williams,
"The New Military Professionals," *U.S. Naval Institute Proceedings*, May 1996, pp.
42–48.

dals, and homosexuality within the ranks, including the navy's Tailhook affair, the air force's Lieutenant Kelly Flinn story, the murder of a presumed homosexual soldier by another soldier at Fort Campbell, Kentucky, and the sexual harassment allegations made in 2000 against Major General Larry Smith by Lieutenant General Claudia Kennedy, the highest-ranking woman in the U.S. Army. Regardless of civilian perspectives and criticisms, the failure of military professionals to articulate clear principles did little to encourage faith in the profession. Only in the first months of the new century has there been some effort by senior Department of Defense officials and military professionals to respond to such matters and articulate clear guidelines.[27] One exception was General Ronald R. Fogelman, who resigned as air force chief of staff in 1997. Being "dedicated to the most basic ideals that forge a coherent force, he found it necessary to explain to U.S. lawmakers why disobedience and lying by a commissioned officer cannot be tolerated."[28] In contrast to the hesitancy displayed by most other senior officers with regard to the Kelly Flinn affair, Fogelman spoke out.

Despite the overwhelming record of obsequiousness on the part of U.S. military professionals, a vocal body of opinion in the civilian sector still believes the military is "out of control" with respect to imposing its views on civilian policymakers.[29] This has its roots in the fear that America may succumb to a "Prussian-style" military that longs to shape the civilian culture and political system. Reinforcing such views are those who believe that the American military has already become politicized, as suggested by the fact that a large majority of military personnel openly

---

[27]See A. J. Bacevich, "The De-Moralization of the Military: Why the Kelly Flinn Story Matters," *Weekly Standard*, June 9, 1997, pp. 24–25; Stephanie Gutmann, "Sex and the Soldier," *New Republic*, Feb. 24, 1997, pp. 18–22; "The Military and the Women," *Wall Street Journal*, Feb. 21, 1997; Walter A. McDougall, "Sex, Lies, and Infantry," *Commentary*, Sept. 1997, pp. 43–47; Charles Moskos, "Smart Rules for Soldiers and Sex," *Washington Post*, June 8, 1997; and Richard J. Newman, "Army Sex Ed. 101," *U.S. News and World Report*, Aug. 11, 1997, pp. 50–52; Department of Defense, Office of the Inspector General, *Report on the Military Environment with Respect to the Homosexual Conduct Policy*, report no. D-2000-101, Mar. 16, 2000 (http://www.dodid.osd.mil/autid/reports/00-101.pdf); and Jane McHugh, "Murder in the Barracks," *Army Times*, Aug. 23, 1999, pp. 12–13.

[28]John G. Roos, "Fogelman's Departure: He's No Tragic Figure," *Armed Forces Journal International*, Sept. 1997, p. 2. Also see Richard J. Neuman, "A General Salutes by Quitting," *U.S. News and World Report*, Aug. 11, 1997, p. 5.

[29]F. G. Hoffman, *Decisive Force: The New American Way of War* (Westport, Conn.: Praeger, 1996), p. 128, in which the author writes, "To some observers, the military is 'out of control' and a scandal exists because the military is vocally reluctant to employ force in pursuit of vague foreign policy objectives." The author refers to Richard Kohn, "Out of Control: The Crisis in Civil-Military Relations," *National Interest*, Spring 1994, pp. 3–17.

identify themselves as Republicans.[30] The fact is that the military has usually been a conservative institution and naturally tends to identify with issues and groups that support the military ethos, regardless of political party. Moreover, "politicization" tends to connote an interest group that is totally absorbed with political issues, is dogmatically focused on political channels to achieve its objectives, and shapes all issues in "political" terms. The U.S. military is not such a group today, and no one proposes it turn into one.

But even if those who fear an "out of control" military are unduly alarmist, few would deny the widening gap between the values of the all-volunteer military and those of American society.[31] Either way, it appears that the armed forces cannot win. If the military is involved in politics, it conjures fears of a politicized military. If the military remains isolated from society, it conjures fears that its own (implicitly dangerous) value system is divorced from the civil society it is meant to protect. Confusing the issue even more are the distinctions that need to be made between career military professionals and those who serve for one hitch, and between those involved in basic and advanced training and those who have gone beyond the recruit phase and are assigned to a line unit. Finally, civil-military relationships are complicated further by the emergence of a new generation of elected government officials, few, if any, of whom have had military experience.[32] While this may not necessarily lead to damaging political-military policies, it may create an environment in which decision makers lack all sensitivity to the realities of military life. As one observer has written, "An uncertain grasp of military affairs is likely to characterize policy making for the foreseeable future."[33] It is also the case that fewer civilians—especially among our "elites"—will have served in the military, creating a large civilian populace with little or no experience with military life.[34]

[30]See Eliot A. Cohen, "Civil-Military Relations," in this volume, p. 85 (from *Orbis*, Spring 1997, p. 178). See also Thomas Ricks, "The Widening Gap Between The Military And Society," *Atlantic Monthly*, July 1997, pp. 66–78.

[31]Ricks, "The Widening Gap"; Amy Waldman, "Military-Civilian Schism Widens, Posing Danger," *USA Today*, Nov. 26, 1996; Clarence Page, "Soldiers vs. Civilians: A Widening Gap," *Chicago Tribune*, Nov. 16, 1997; and Samuel G. Freedman, "The Few, the Proud," review of *Making the Corps*, by Thomas E. Ricks, *Chicago Tribune*, Dec. 14, 1997. See also Cohen, "Civil Military Relations."

[32]See, for example, Waldman, "Military-Civilian Schism"; and Adm. Stanley R. Arthur, "The American Military: Some Thoughts on Who We Are and What We Are," in *Civil-Military Relations and the Not-Quite Wars of the Present and Future*, ed. Vincent Davis (Carlisle Barracks, Pa.: Strategic Studies Institute, U.S. Army War College, Oct. 30, 1996), pp. 15–24.

[33]Ricks, "The Widening Gap," p. 76.

[34]Ibid., pp. 68–69, in which the author writes, "Today's fragmented society is at odds

The wide range of civil-military contacts adumbrated above would seem a basis for challenging the notion of a widening gap between the military and society in the United States. But to the extent the military and society do exist in two worlds, such a "gap" would only seem to underscore the need for a more politically streetwise military, one attuned to certain values and institutions. Indeed, to ensure that the needed equilibrium between the military and society is not thrown out of balance, military professionals must engage the political process. Such engagement would lead to a clearer civilian understanding of military culture and help to correct the distorted views and unrealistic images that currently threaten the effectiveness of the military. For the real danger today is not military dominance of civil government, but rather a civilian policy elite dominating a military of which it has only the most superficial understanding, and thus imposing on the military frivolous "reforms" and imprudent overseas commitments without regard to long-term consequences. As Johnson and Metz observe, civilians are the potters, the armed forces the clay:

> [T]he array of tools held by civilians more than counterbalances the military's more coherent method for cultivating individual skill. Civilians control the military's budget, can fire individual military leaders, and must approve senior-level promotions and assignments. The equilibrium between the military and civilians thus reflects an asymmetry of resources where military acumen is matched by the civilians' wide array of tools.[35]

In terms of civil-military relations, this means that while retaining and reinforcing the notion of civil control and supremacy, the military cannot remain a passive partner. It must move closer to the political system and yet retain enough distance to insure that it preserves the culture and virtues suited to its unique mission. There is no magic formula for determining the proper balance, but the "lifeblood of this equilibrium is constant adjustment shaped by open, informed debate from all segments of the national security community. . . . [I]t is time to 'let a hundred schools of thought contend.'"[36] Once again, General Ridgway may have said it best:

> [C]ivilian authorities must scrupulously respect the integrity, the intellectual honesty, of its officer corps. Any effort to force unanimity of view, to compel adherence to some politico-military "party line" against the honestly expressed views of responsible officers . . .

with the classic military values of sacrifice, unity, self-discipline, and considering the interests of the group before those of the individual."

[35]Douglas Johnson and Steven Metz, "American Civil-Military Relations: A Review of the Recent Literature," in *U.S. Civil-Military Relations in Crisis or Transition?* p. 217.
[36]Ibid.

> is a pernicious practice which jeopardizes rather than protects the
> integrity of the military profession.[37]

Constructive political engagement offers a means by which the realities of military life and the essence of military culture can be presented to the public and elected officials as well as to the mass media. This is particularly important in the information age with the expansive information technology capabilities available to the general public as well as to the military.

Warfighters or Peacekeepers?

The U.S. military is well prepared for conventional wars and wars of a lesser order that are configured in a conventional format. However, the strategic thinking and operational doctrine to respond effectively to conventional conflict may be irrelevant to unconventional conflicts and "operations other than war" (OOTW), for which U.S. forces are not configured or trained.[38] While the superpower era demanded a particular global political-military capacity and strategic thinking, the new strategic landscape demands a different strategic mind-set and operational doctrine. The transition from one to the other has resulted in an ad hoc mixture of strategic and operational guidelines and political-military doctrine. Most troublesome is the phenomenon of wars of conscience in which policy is driven by moral indignation and a "do something" mentality, such as occurred in Somalia, Haiti, and Bosnia. The plethora of peacekeeping missions distracts the military from its primary task, which is preparing for combat, even as budget constraints and domestic priorities shrink the means the U.S. military has at its disposal. It is asked, in short, to do more with less.[39]

There is no denying that the U.S. military cannot dwell solely on its battlefield mission in the post–Cold War environment. As one authority has argued, there is a pressing need today for "diplomat warriors in operations other than war. The unpolitical soldier—the pure warrior—cannot fulfill the requirements for leadership in operations other than war."[40] But there is an underlying fear within the profession that wholesale involvement in OOTW diminishes the effectiveness of the military to perform its

[37]Ridgway, *Soldier*, p. 270.

[38]See *U.S. Intervention Policy for the Post Cold-War Period: New Challenges and New Responses*, final report of the Eighty-Fifth American Assembly (Harriman, N.Y.: American Assembly, Apr. 7–10, 1994), p. 5.

[39]See Les Aspin, *The Bottom-Up Review: Forces for a New Era* (Washington, D.C.: Department of Defense, Sept. 1, 1993).

[40]Rudolph C. Barnes Jr., *Military Legitimacy: Might and Right in the New Millennium*

primary task.[41] Such concerns were well expressed by some in the enlisted ranks. As one private serving in Kosovo said: "You are trained for one thing as an infantryman: war. You are a little bit rougher than most people and you have to come down here and be nice to people. That's not what we are trained for."[42] An enlisted man serving with the 82nd Airborne Division in Kosovo, who spent part of the day guarding Albanian children and another part guarding Serbian children, stated simply, "I wasn't trained to do day care."[43] The concerns of the military about its employment in the new strategic landscape must be spelled out clearly and unequivocally lest the impact of heightened operational tempo and personnel deployments on military readiness and the quality of military life be glanced over or totally ignored.[44] In the case of Bosnia, for example, the changing deadlines for U.S. withdrawal, the clouded political objectives, and the absence of an articulated exit strategy should be a cause for concern within both military and civilian circles.

Some military professionals have indeed warned about the negative impact of OOTW commitments. General Gordon Sullivan and Lieutenant Colonel James Dubik lamented as early as 1993 that the U.S. civilian leadership was requiring the military to

> contract in both size and budget, contribute to domestic recovery, participate in global stability operations, and retain its capability to produce decisive victory in whatever circumstances they are employed—all at the same time. . . . [I]nternational and domestic realities have resulted in the paradox of declining military resources and increasing military missions, a paradox that is stressing our armed forces. The stress is significant. It requires fundamental changes in the way the nation conducts its defense affairs.[45]

Testifying before a congressional subcommittee the same year, a

(London: Frank Cass, 1996), p. 114. But contrast Daniel P. Bolger, *Savage Peace: Americans at War in the 1990s* (Novato, Calif.: Presidio Press, 1995), who argues that "in all their guises, however, OOTW are wars—pure and simple" (p. 381).

[41]See, for example, John G. Roos, "The Perils of Peacekeeping: Tallying the Costs in Blood, Coin, Prestige, and Readiness," *Armed Forces Journal International*, Dec. 1993, p. 17.

[42]Matthew Cox, "You call this soldiering? Walking the beat with KFOR's warrior cops," *Army Times*, Mar. 27, 2000, p. 14. See also the response of Gen. Gordon Sullivan (ret.), "A soldier's work," *Army Times*, Apr. 10, p. 52.

[43]James O'Shea, "Why are we using crack troops on safety patrol?" *Chicago Tribune*, Dec. 5, 1999.

[44]For an excellent study of readiness issues see Richard K. Betts, *Military Readiness: Concepts, Choices, Consequences* (Washington, D.C.: Brookings Institution Press, 1995).

[45]Gen. Gordon R. Sullivan and Lt. Col. James M. Dubik, *Land Warfare in the 21st Century* (Carlisle Barracks, Pa.: Strategic Studies Institute, U.S. Army War College, Feb. 1993), p. 8.

number of retired officers insisted that constant involvement in peacekeeping operations saps combat readiness. The late General Maxwell Thurman complained that "after a peacekeeping mission, soldiers have to go through an extensive training program to regain the level of operational proficiency which they held at the outset of that duty."[46] And in 1995, the chairman of the Joint Chiefs, General John Shalikashvili, made the same point:

> If we are selective and only engage when our interests are very clear, when we have agreement on the limits of our involvement and the conditions of our withdrawal, and we go in when we can make a difference and have the support of an informed public, then maybe in time we will view such missions as supportive of our interests and not as damaging to our security.[47]

In no case, however, were these earnest professional judgments even noticed, much less acted upon, by the civilian government or media, even though they clearly address issues of profound national interest rather than the armed services' narrow self-interest. General Shalikashvili even iterated his concern to several reporters shortly before his retirement, but again his remarks fell on deaf ears.[48]

As the Clinton administration came to an end, it was obvious to many that it had viewed the U.S. military as an arm of the Department of State, that is, as a tool of foreign policy to be employed in peacekeeping operations under the rubric of OOTW. As a result of the controversy surrounding the Clinton administration's military policy, the next administration's handling of the military is sure to come under close scrutiny. The controversy over such missions was aptly described by General Colin Powell:

> My constant, unwelcome message at all meetings on Bosnia was simply that we should not commit military forces until we had a clear political objective. . . . The debate exploded at one session when Madeleine Albright, our ambassador to the UN, asked me in frustration, "What's the point in having this superb military that you're always talking about if we can't use it?" I thought I would have an aneurysm. American GIs were not toy soldiers to be moved around on some sort of global game board. . . . I told Ambassador Albright that the U.S. military would carry out any mission it was handed, but my advice would always be that the tough political goals had to be set first.[49]

For many in the military profession the "Albright syndrome"

[46] Roos, "The Perils of Peacekeeping," p. 17.

[47] Remarks by General John M. Shalikashvili, in the Cantigny Conference Series, "Humanitarian Crises: Meeting the Challenges" (Chicago: Robert R. McCormick Tribune Foundation, 1995), p. 58.

[48] John G. Roos, "Last Call; General 'Shali' Shares His Take on the Past Four Years," *Armed Forces Journal International*, Oct. 1997, p. 2.

[49] Powell, *My American Journey*, pp. 576, 577. Gen. Powell has also spoken about

threatens to undermine military culture and deny the very purpose of the military. It is also the case that no useful purpose is served if military professionals adhere to the "can do" syndrome (regardless of the threat, mission, or contingency) without clearly indicating the likely costs involved, including the impact on combat readiness, quality of military life, and the military's primary purpose. Such matters must be placed in the public arena.[50]

American history offers important lessons about the use of the military in nontraditional missions. For example, during the post–Civil War period between 1870 and 1890, the U.S. Army went through what has been described as the "Dark Ages."[51] During this period, the military officers functioned as governors, police, and judges throughout most of the old Confederacy, suppressed domestic labor strife, and pacified and administered Indian tribes in the West. In reality, wrote a colonel in 1895, "the Army is now a gendarmery—a national police force."[52] Between 1898 and the 1930s, the army and the Marine Corps participated in numerous missions other than conventional conflict in Latin America. Likewise, after World War II, U.S. Army armored units in Germany were reorganized into constabulary squadrons whose purpose was to function as a national gendarmery, taking the place of the German police in the American zone of occupation. These units were trained and equipped to maintain law and order and to deal with the German civilian populace and displaced persons. But such constabulary squadrons quickly lost their preparedness for conventional battle.

Such experiences would seem to supply U.S. military professionals with ample evidence about the costs and consequences of such OOTW. Yet, such evidence has so far had no impact on the prevailing "Albright syndrome."

Conclusion

To adjust to today's uncertain domestic and strategic landscapes, the U.S. officer corps must transcend its purely military

the problems facing the military involvement in Bosnia. See Gen. Colin L. Powell, "U.S. Forces: Challenges Ahead," *Foreign Affairs*, Winter 1992/93, pp. 32–45. His views were not necessarily in accord with those of the Clinton administration, or those of any number of civil-military scholars. See also Harry Summers, "Leave the Military Alone, They Already Have a Full-Time Job," *Army Times*, May 29, 1995, p. 54.

[50]The disagreements over the use of the American military and the various arguments regarding decisive force are well examined in Hoffman, *Decisive Force*.

[51]Kemble, *The Image of the Army Officer in America*, p. 127. See also Russell F. Weigley, *The American Way of War: A History of United States Military Strategy and Policy* (Bloomington, Ind.: Indiana University Press, 1977), pp. 167–71.

[52]Millett and Maslowski, *For Common Defense*, p. 259.

111

notion of professionalism and practice constructive political engagement based on the recognition that the issues it faces have undeniable political dimensions. To be sure, there are limits to constructive political engagement as defined by the military professional ethos and the American democratic system. However, these limits do not proscribe military professionals' airing and articulating their views when policy and strategy (or lack thereof) pose significant dangers to the U.S. military's *raison d'être* and quality of life.

The inescapable fact is that an effective military system must be authoritarian and driven by the need for combat cohesion, unit effectiveness, discipline under a chain of command, subordination of individual rights to the group, and unity of effort. Not least, this unique military culture must be nurtured within the American democratic system. At the same time, within these parameters, individual dignity must be maintained.[53] This was never an easy proposition and it appears even more difficult today, at a time when the reigning ethos of the civilian culture appears increasingly hostile to the professional military ethos, places social agendas above military preparedness on its list of priorities, and embraces the notion that a technological "revolution in military affairs" (push-button warfare) makes possible "clean" wars and a kinder, gentler battlefield. But it has yet to be demonstrated that the information age and smart weapons have eliminated the need for soldiers "on the ground" or will allow killing to be done humanely and nicely.

The task before us should be obvious. It is to reinforce, not undermine, the military culture—a culture that remains rooted in the psychological and physical notions of killing the enemy—while maintaining its loyalty to the principles of democracy and civilian supremacy. At the present time, that task is not advanced by silence. On the contrary, the voice of the military profession must be heard if the military is to serve the nation effectively. It is particularly important for the military profession to respond to those who dogmatically and erroneously associate the U.S. armed forces with a particular political preference, bureaucratic interest group, or subversive conspiracy.

---

[53]This approach attempts to synthesize some elements of Huntington's view of an authoritarian military with those of Janowitz's constabulary concept. See Huntington, *The Soldier and the State*, and Janowitz, *The Professional Soldier*.

In its highly successful program to improve race relations in its ranks, the army adopted what Charles Moskos termed a "race-savvy" approach—that is, an attitude that was neither blind nor preferential, but honest. What the military profession must master today is a mind-set that is equally gender savvy and politically savvy.[54] That means that the armed forces ought not to be blind to the undeniable differences between the sexes, nor obliged to give preferential treatment to women, but instead be free to make their personnel decisions on the basis of unit cohesion, morale, and combat preparedness. This applies as well to the issue of homosexuals serving in the military. The "don't ask, don't tell, don't pursue" policy remains in effect, although much debated. Some people call for major changes that would allow openly homosexual men and women to serve, while others see the current policy as the best way to ensure combat cohesion.[55] Being politically savvy means that the armed forces ought not to pretend that politics do not matter, nor engage in partisanship, but instead be free to counsel national leaders and the American public about the costs of a given policy or deployment in terms of preparedness and to educate them on the inviolable values of military life and culture. To be politically savvy is simply to recognize that the military is an arm of the American people, that military and political objectives are often inextricable, and that a public airing of military perspectives is indispensable to the making of wise policy. Only a politically savvy military profession can remind the public and its elected officials that the military's prime purpose is "to kill and break things" in the defense of their way of life. Perhaps, as so often is the case, John Keegan said it best:

> Soldiers are not as other men—that is the lesson I have learned from a life cast among warriors. The lesson has taught me to view with extreme suspicion all theories and representations of war that equate it with other activity in human affairs. . . . War is fought . . . by men whose values and skills are not those of politicians and diplomats. They are those of a world apart, a very ancient world, which exists in parallel with the everyday world but does not belong to it. Both worlds change over time, and the warrior adapts in step to the civil-

---

[54]David Gergen, "Becoming 'Race Savvy,'" *U.S. News and World Report*, June 2, 1997, p. 78. The notion of race savvy is attributed to Charles Moskos. See Charles Moskos and John Sibley Butler, *Be All That We Can Be: Black Leadership and Racial Integration the Army Way* (New York: Basic Books, 1996). According to Gergen, race savvy "is not race blind" nor "is it racial preferences." Race savvy "demands absolute dedication to ending racial bias, it demands money for more training, and it demands aggressive leadership at the top. Race savvy—surely, an idea whose time is here."

[55]See, for example, Charles Moskos, "Don't Knock 'Don't Ask, Don't Tell,'" *Wall Street Journal*, Dec. 16, 1999; and John Allen Williams and Laura Miller, "Don't Blame 'Don't Ask, Don't Tell,'" *Chicago Tribune*, Mar. 30, 2000.

ian. It follows it, however, at a distance. The distance can never be closed.[56]

[56]John Keegan, *A History of Warfare* (New York: Alfred A. Knopf, 1993), p. xvi.

AN UNINFORMED DEBATE ON MILITARY CULTURE

by Don M. Snider

A decade of debate and legislation in Washington designed to change the "military culture" of our armed forces has not been in vain.[1] The number of African-American and female officers and enlisted persons has increased dramatically, women now hold scores of jobs reserved for men just a few years ago, and President Clinton's "don't ask, don't tell" policy has given homosexuals executive sanction to serve in our armed forces.[2] During the same time, serious failures by the officer corps of two services have focused national attention on isolated incidents of sexual harassment that indicate to many the need for further reform. The most recent example of the continuing attempts to reform military cultures flowed from the celebrated cases of Air Force Lieutenant Kelly Flinn and Army Major General David Hale, and resulted in the attempt by the secretary of defense to standardize across the services the official sanctions imposed for adultery and fraternization.[3]

Various interpretations clash over this ongoing reform of our armed forces. One prominent participant sees the entire debate through political and conspiratorial lenses, positing that it really started in 1975 when women were admitted to the military academies under the feminists' demand for "simple equality," whereas their real purpose was to overthrow the traditional culture. What is more, the effects of such decisions have remained unexamined even today.[4] Another widely read and referenced source holds that the American military is becoming dangerously isolated from the

[1]This essay originally appeared in *Orbis*, Winter 1999, and arose from the Foreign Policy Research Institute conference "The End of American Military Culture," Philadelphia, Pa., July 15–16, 1998. The views expressed here do not represent those of the U.S. Military Academy, the Department of Defense, or the Department of the Army.

[2]Craig Donegan, "New Military Culture," *CQ Researcher*, Apr. 26, 1996, pp. 361–84.

[3]Office of Assistant Secretary of Defense (Public Affairs), "Secretary of Defense Directs More Uniformity and Clarity in Service Policies Pertaining to Good Order and Discipline," News Release no. 404-98, July 29, 1998.

[4]James Webb, "The War on Military Culture," *Weekly Standard*, Jan. 20, 1997, pp. 17–22.

society it protects, and notes the disdain in which some members of the armed forces hold that society. In this view, further changes in military culture are warranted to reconcile the armed forces to civil society.[5]

In my own judgment, it is fair to say that in most of the debate to date, "military culture" has been presented by the progressive advocates as something unacceptably different from the prevailing culture of contemporary American society. Hence they represent military culture as a belief system homogeneous across all services and conforming to a "traditional and exclusionary combat, masculine-warrior paradigm." Counterposed against it is an "evolving model of military culture characterized by egalitarianism and inclusiveness."[6] Clearly, given the author's selection of adjectives, the focus of this representation is on the composition of our armed forces and on issues of gender and sexual preference as they are either included in or excluded from "military culture."

Such attempts to change American military culture no doubt will continue, and they will continue to inspire a largely rhetorical debate focused narrowly on the role of the traditional "warrior" in military culture and on issues of interest to the progressive advocates of identity politics. And insofar as this debate remains centered on the role and treatment of women, minorities, and homosexuals in the military, then uniformed military leaders are clearly not setting the terms.[7] As a result, our national discourse is not really about military culture at all, and is incapable of judging whether the changes it is producing are for the good of America's armed forces and the nation as a whole. I believe that the political discourse leading to these changes has not yet addressed the truly important questions because the debate thus far has been *false* and *misleading*. It has been *false* because it has largely ignored what military culture really is and why it is important. Seldom discussed is the functional, warfighting rationale behind the peculiarities of military culture, what our British colleagues describe as "the right to be different."[8] In fact, the adjective "military" is seldom even defined in the context of military missions and tasks,

[5]Thomas E. Ricks, *Making the Corps* (New York: Scribner, 1997); James Kitfield, "Standing Apart," *National Journal*, June 13, 1998, pp. 1350–58.

[6]Lt. Col. Karen O. Dunivin, "Military Culture: A Paradigm Shift?" Maxwell Paper no. 10 (Maxwell AFB, Ala.: Air War College, 1997), p. iii.

[7]If they had set the terms, the results likely would have been different, as they were in the case of the Weinberger Doctrine. See Cori Dauber, "The Practice of Argument: Reading the Conditions of Civil-Military Relations," *Armed Forces and Society*, Spring 1998, pp. 435–46.

[8]Patrick Mileham, "Military Virtues 1: The Right to be Different," *Defense Analysis*, vol. 14, no. 2 (1998), pp. 169–90.

and perhaps even more important, almost never with the addition-al description as "effective" or "successful." America has, and has had, a very successful military, and to debate policies designed to change its culture without at the same time having an informed discussion of the consequences in terms of military effectiveness is folly.

Secondly, I will argue that the dialogue has been *misleading* largely because of the missing voice of the uniformed military leadership, that is, those charged with representing in a profes-sional manner to the American people the nature, characteristics, and needs of our military forces. Their abdication of this responsi-bility has left others to take it up, albeit with far less effectiveness than they could do themselves.[9] But this goes beyond the issue of who speaks for the military or how vocal they may or should be.[10] Rather it goes to the issue of the very nature and character of the military institution that is being portrayed to the American public. Is it a truly professional institution that the public will continue to legitimize and support as such, or is it a deprofessionalizing mili-tary that will soon lose public support as last occurred after Vietnam? At a time when the press, while reporting on America's newly found "war" on terrorism, is creating moral equivalency between the soldiers of a democracy and international criminals and thugs, this is not a trivial question.

Thus, in the sections that follow, I will synthesize from the various literature and from my own experiences better informed, alternative views of just what military culture is and is not. In con-cluding I shall return to the issue of the missing voices of military professionals.

Military Culture Broadly Defined

Our first understanding of military culture is drawn from the academic disciplines within which it is studied, including organi-zational science, anthropology, sociology, and political science. For the purposes of this discussion, perhaps the most useful start-ing point is the broad definition offered by Edgar Schein for any organizational culture:

---

[9]This is not to denigrate the efforts of those who have filled the void, such as mem-bers of the Pentagon press corps and individuals such as Elaine Donnelly of the Center for Military Readiness. But even Ms. Donnelly admits to the frustration of repeatedly being asked to provide publicly the expertise and nuance that only serving military pro-fessionals possess. (Author's discussions with Ms. Donnelly, July 15, 1998.)

[10]Sam C. Sarkesian, "The U.S. Military Must Find Its Voice," in this volume (from *Orbis*, Summer 1998, pp. 423–37).

> We must first specify that a given set of people has had enough sta-
> bility and common history to have allowed a culture to form. This
> means that some organizations will have no overarching culture
> because they have no common history or have frequent turnover of
> members. Other organizations can be presumed to have strong cul-
> tures because of a long shared history or because they have shared
> important intense experiences (as in a combat unit). But the content
> and strength of a culture have to be empirically determined. They
> cannot be presumed from observing surface cultural phenomena.
> Culture is what a group learns over a period of time as that group
> solves its problems of survival in an external environment and its
> problems of internal integration. Such learning is simultaneously a
> behavioral, cognitive, and an emotional process. . . .

> Culture can now be defined as (a) a pattern of basic assumptions, (b)
> invented, discovered, or developed by a given group, (c) as it learns to
> cope with its problems of external adaptation and internal integration,
> (d) that has worked well enough to be considered valid, and therefore,
> (e) is to be taught to new members as the (f) correct way to perceive,
> think, or feel in relation to these problems.[11]

According to Schein's classic definition, and those of other
theorists, military culture may be said to refer to the deep structure of organizations, rooted in the prevailing assumptions, norms,
values, customs, and traditions which collectively, over time, have
created shared individual expectations among the members.
Meaning is established through socialization to a variety of identity groups that converge in operations of the organization.
Culture includes both attitudes and behavior about what is right,
what is good, and what is important, often manifested in shared
heroes, stories, and rituals that promote bonding among the members. It is, in short, the "glue" that makes organizations a distinctive source of identity and experience.[12] Thus, a strong culture
exists when a clear set of norms and expectations—usually a function of leadership—permeates the entire organization. It is essentially "how we do things around here."[13]

Closely associated with an organization's culture is its climate.
In contrast to culture, organizational climate refers to environmental stimuli rooted in the organization's value system, such as
rewards and punishments, communications flow, and operations
tempo, which determine individual and team perceptions about
the quality of working conditions. It is essentially "how we feel

[11]Edgar Schein, "Organizational Culture," *American Psychologist*, Feb. 1990, p. 110.

[12]Bernard Bass, "A New Paradigm of Leadership: An Inquiry into Transformational
Leadership" (Alexandria, Va.: U.S. Army Research Institute for the Behavioral and
Social Sciences, Feb. 1996).

[13]Walter Ulmer, Joseph Collins, and T. O. Jacobs, *American Military Culture in the
21st Century* (Washington, D.C.: Center for Strategic and International Studies, 2000),
p. xviii.

about this organization."[14] Climate is often considered to be alterable in the near term and largely limited to those aspects of the organizational environment of which members are aware.[15]

Climate and culture are obviously related in complex ways, climate being an observable and measurable artifact of culture and considered by many to be one of the major determinants of organizational effectiveness. More recent research indicates that other cultural traits such as involvement, consistency, adaptability, and mission orientation are positively related not only to members' perceptions of organizational effectiveness, but also to objective measures of the same.[16] Such definitions would seem to establish from the outset that those who tinker with the culture and climate of military organizations may well be, either unknowingly or without concern, modifying the long-term effectiveness of America's armed forces.

The Four Basic Elements of Military Culture

A second view of military culture is functional in its approach. That is, the elements of military culture derive from the purpose or tasks for which societies raise, support, and maintain modern militaries, for instance, waging war on behalf of the nation-state and, if needed, enforcing domestic order. Even though the end of the Cold War has brought a new emphasis on missions such as peacemaking and peacekeeping, James Burk argues, correctly I believe, that "warfighting still determines the central beliefs, values and complex symbolic formations that define military culture."[17]

What makes military culture unique, not surprisingly, is that its central elements derive from "an attempt to deal with (and, if possible, to overcome) the uncertainty of war, to impose some pattern on war, to control war's outcome, and to invest war with meaning and significance." In so saying, scholars are not suggesting that military culture is in any way a mechanistic response to war's horrific environment, nor that the elements are instrumentally rational, thereby "fitting" armed forces to the task of fighting wars. Rather, history abounds with examples of military cultures

[14]Ibid.
[15]Daniel R. Denison, "What IS the Difference Between Organizational Culture and Organizational Climate?" *Academy of Management Review*, July 1996, p. 624.
[16]Daniel Denison and A. Mishra, "Toward a Theory of Organizational Culture and Effectiveness," *Organizational Science*, vol. 6 (1995), pp. 204–23.
[17]Within this section all quotations without footnotes are from James Burk, "Military Culture," in *Encyclopedia of Violence, Peace and Conflict*, ed. Lester Kurtz and Jennifer E. Turpin (San Diego, Calif.: Academic Press, 1999).

that rendered armed forces grossly ineffective at their assigned task, the U.S. Army in Vietnam being a notorious one.[18] These scholars maintain that military culture is "an elaborate social construction, an exercise of creative intelligence, through which we come to imagine war in a particular way and to embrace certain rationalizations about how war should be conducted and for what purposes." While it is a product of war, military culture also influences the likelihood and form of future wars.[19]

The first such element is discipline, "the orderly conduct of military personnel, whether individually or in formation, in battle or in garrison, and most often prescribed by their officers in command." The purpose of discipline, needless to say, is to "minimize the confusion and disintegrative consequences of battle by imposing order on it with a repertoire of patterned actions that they may use on their own initiative, or in coordination with others, quickly to adapt and to prevail in battle." In the Gulf War's celebrated tank battle of 73 Easting, the performance of the Second Armored Cavalry Regiment in combat against the Tawakalna Division of Iraq's Republican Guard convincingly demonstrated the value of individual, team, and unit discipline.[20] A second purpose of discipline, scholars maintain, is to ritualize the violence of war. Following discipline reassures soldiers in combat and defines when and how they are "authorized" to violate the normal societal prohibitions against killing and violence. In my own experience as an infantry company commander in Vietnam, when the enemy was seldom clearly seen and thereby provided few real targets to engage, the discipline of a full rifle team or squad providing covering fire for maneuvering comrades enabled many reluctant soldiers to fire their weapons when they otherwise would not. This reluctance to fire was not new to Vietnam, having been widely documented in previous wars.[21]

Scholars also note historical patterns with respect to the levels of discipline military organizations need and how they are

---

[18]See Andrew Krepinevich, *The Army in Vietnam* (Baltimore, Md.: Johns Hopkins University Press, 1986); and Deborah Avant, *Political Institutions and Military Change* (Ithaca, N.Y.: Cornell University Press, 1994).

[19]Theo Farrell, "Figuring Out Fighting Organizations: The New Organizational Analysis in Strategic Studies," *Journal of Strategic Studies*, March 1996, pp. 122–35.

[20]Stephen Biddle, "Victory Misunderstood: What the Gulf War Tells Us about the Future of Conflict," *International Security*, Fall 1996, pp. 139–79; Stephen Biddle and Robert Zirkle, "Technology, Civil-Military Relations and Warfare in the Developing World," *Journal of Strategic Studies*, June 1996, pp. 171–212.

[21]S. L. A. Marshall, "Americans in Combat," in *The Armed Forces Officer* (Washington, D.C.: American Forces Information Service, Department of Defense, Feb. 1988), p. 80.

achieved. First, since the earliest times discipline within a military culture has been manifest at the individual level, whether as combat among warrior "heroes," charioteers, or individual cavalrymen. It is a tradition carried on today by fighter pilots in aerial dogfights or tank commanders on the desert floor, however distant they may be when they engage the enemy.

A growing pattern in contemporary war, however, is combat based on the crew or team, disciplined units fighting combined-arms battles within joint commands. In such team-based forces the will and needs of the individual must be subordinate to those of the group (in sharp contrast to the trends in our hyperindividualistic society). Such group discipline, military leaders have learned, must be engendered and enforced by other than the primarily punitive means used in earlier eras when the emphasis was on individual discipline. Janowitz hypothesized correctly in 1960 that with the industrialization of war "there has been a change in the basis of authority and discipline in the military establishment, a shift from authoritarian domination to greater reliance on manipulation, persuasion, and group consensus."[22] Today, leadership texts at schools for officers emphasize routinely, almost regardless of the specific theory expounded, the critical role of the team and group to the success of military units.[23]

The second element of military culture is a professional ethos, defined, in the American case, as that "set of normative self-understandings which for the members define the profession's corporate identity, its code of conduct and, for the officers in particular, its social worth." This ethos must also be recognized and accepted by the larger society to provide legitimacy and support to its profession of arms, thus emphasizing again the critical importance of the current debate over military culture. Huntington explains it this way:

> People who act the same way over a long period of time tend to develop distinctive and persistent habits of thought. Their unique relation to the world gives them a unique perspective on the world and leads them to rationalize their behavior and role. This is particularly true where the role is a professional one. A profession is more narrowly defined, more intensively and exclusively pursued, and more clearly isolated from other human activity than are most occupations. *The continuing objective performance of the professional function gives rise to . . . the values, attitudes, and perspectives which inhere in the*

[22]Morris Janowitz, *The Professional Soldier* (New York: Free Press, 1960), pp. 8–9.
[23]Robert L. Hughes, Robert C. Ginnett, and Gordon J. Curphy, *Leadership: Enhancing the Lessons of Experience*, 2nd ed. (Chicago: Irwin Publishing, 1996), particularly chap. 13.

performance of the professional military function and which are deducible from the nature of that function. The military function is performed by a public bureaucratized profession expert in the management of violence and responsible for the military security of the state. *A value or attitude is part of the professional ethic if it is implied by or derived from the peculiar expertise, responsibility, and organization of the military profession.*[24] (italics added)

As Huntington makes quite clear, the professional function—"the management of violence" on behalf of society—is the principal determinant of the military ethos. In General Douglas MacArthur's words, "yours is the profession of arms, the will to win, the sure knowledge that in war there is no substitute for victory; that if you lose the nation will be destroyed, that the very obsession of your public service must be Duty, Honor, Country."[25]

In the American case, however, military ethos is shaped not only by this functional imperative derived from the nature of conflict itself, but also from the society the armed forces serve and from international law, which is accepted as binding on the conduct of this nation's armed forces.[26] Thus, while American military leaders today may share many opinions, values, and professional codes and principles with their counterparts in other countries and eras of history, their military ethos is also uniquely informed by the founding values of our republic, including liberty, equality, and the dignity of the individual. The American ethos holds that military institutions should only exist when and to the extent they are needed for external defense, and that the military establishment is always subordinate to the civilian organs of state. Likewise, the moral character of the international laws of warfare to which the United States ascribes (for example, the humane treatment of prisoners of war) influences the American professional military ethos.

Thus, our military ethos is and likely will remain, in Burk's words, "an amalgam of heroic traditions, technological traditions associated with modern weapons and their use, and managerial traditions of modern bureaucracies that emphasize skilled leadership and coordination of human effort to achieve group goals by rationally efficient means." That said, it is also obvious that there are inherent tensions among these various influences, tensions

---

[24]Samuel P. Huntington, *The Soldier and the State* (Cambridge, Mass.: Harvard University Press, Belknap Press, 1957), p. 61.

[25]Gen. Douglas MacArthur, Address to the Corps of Cadets, West Point, N.Y., May 12, 1962, in William Safire, ed., *Lend Me Your Ears: Great Speeches in History* (New York: W.W. Norton and Company, 1962), pp. 74–78.

[26]Anthony E. Hartle, *Moral Issues in Military Decision Making* (Lawrence, Kans.: University of Kansas Press, 1989), pp. 27–29.

contributing to the debate today over military culture. Members of a society wherein self-serving individualism is extolled will find it difficult to accept the soldier's commitment to unlimited personal liability on behalf of American society, a commitment that presumes personal willingness to kill and to be killed for oneself and for those one commands.

The third element of the military culture, perhaps the most observable in peacetime, consists of the ceremonial displays and etiquette that pervade military life. As Burk writes, "These ceremonies and etiquette make up an elaborate ritual and play the role that ritual typically plays in society: to control or mask our anxieties and ignorance; to affirm our solidarity with one another; and to celebrate our being, usually in conjunction with a larger universe"—in this case the smaller military unit as part of a larger one, and the military as a whole as a part of American society.

Those who have participated in war know only too well the role anxiety plays, both constructively and destructively, in the daily activities of a soldier, sailor, or airman. Thus the reliance on constructed rituals to guide individual conduct and provide a semblance of order to the harsh reality of death and destruction that often threatens to be overwhelming. The salute, the uniform, insignia of rank, ceremonies of induction, promotion, and change of command, all inculcated in training, provide order, hierarchy, and continuity to the life of military units. Burk continues:

> Military weddings, retirements, and funerals mark the life cycle of soldiers just as bugle calls and formations at dawn and dusk mark the passing of the soldiers' working day. Such rituals mark collective identity and group affiliation, forge a common identity and symbolize a common fate. They also serve effectively to connect the unique burdens of military service with the larger society the military serves.

An example of this last function might be when at Andrews Air Force Base political leaders meet the flag-draped coffins of young Americans who "have given the last full measure of devotion" to their comrades and to their country.

As even this brief overview displays, such ceremonialism is not, as many outside the profession of arms contend, an anachronistic persistence of tradition in modern times. Rather, it helps to provide substance and motivation within a culture where one's self-selected and self-abnegating service to country can be sustained, can be deemed sufficiently worthy as to overcome the increasing degradation of the historic career incentives such as income, medical care, and retirement benefits.

The fourth element of military culture is cohesion and esprit de corps, which are the measures of a unit's morale, its willingness to perform a mission and to fight. As discussed earlier, this is a critical element with respect to the connection between military culture and the operational effectiveness of military units. According to Burk,

> Military cohesion refers to the feelings of identity and comradeship that soldiers hold for those in their immediate military unit, the outgrowth of face-to-face or primary (horizontal) group relations. In contrast, esprit de corps refers to the commitment or pride soldiers take in the larger military establishment to which the unit belongs, an outgrowth of secondary (vertical) group relations. Both result to an important degree from structural factors of military organization, but they are primarily matters of belief and emotional attachment.

Behavioral studies since the Second World War have convincingly shown that, in the main, soldiers do not fight cohesively because of ideology or patriotism. Rather, Burk argues that the key factor is loyalty to other members of the unit:

> [It] was the capacity of the soldiers' immediate unit, their company and platoon, to meet their basic needs for food, shelter, affection and esteem. These factors increased in importance as war genuinely threatened soldiers' sense of security and recognition of worth as human beings. So long as these needs were met, soldiers believed themselves part of a powerful group and felt responsible, even empowered, to fight for their group's well being. However, when these needs were not met, soldiers felt alone and unable to protect themselves; the unit disintegrated and stopped fighting.[27]

It should not be concluded from the foregoing, however, that all cohesive military units will be combat effective. Cohesion is a necessary but not sufficient condition for such effectiveness, which depends as well on the technical competence of the individuals and the trust and commitment that link the small unit to the larger command that supplies it with mission, matériel, intelligence, and "the situation specific context within which small unit operations gain or lose meaning and become objects of pride or disgrace." A superb World War II example of the effects of such spirit was the ability of the 101st Airborne Division to fight on at Bastogne, though surrounded, frozen, and badly outnumbered. They had confidence that Patton's Third Army would come to their rescue. These complex relationships between cohesion, com-

---

[27]Indicative of the inadequacy to date of the culture debate is its nearly complete failure to address the implications of this, or subsequent, research on why soldiers fight. What will happen to cohesion and unit effectiveness on the battlefields of the future as units are intentionally more widely dispersed and isolated? See Walter F. Ulmer, "Military Leadership into the 21st Century: Another Bridge Too Far?" *Parameters*, Spring 1998, pp. 4–25.

petence, chain of command, and esprit de corps are seldom noted, much less analyzed, in today's debates on military culture.

The Heterogeneity of Military Culture

A third fruitful approach to the understanding of military culture questions the homogeneity that is seemingly taken for granted in our uninformed public debates. Is there, in fact, such a thing as an American "military culture" that politicians and other advocates should be concerned to preserve, reform, or abolish? Or are there, instead, an identifiable set of subcultures about which the public needs to be educated? I argue that the latter is clearly the case.

To begin with, it should be obvious to any observer, not to mention participant, that the army, navy, air force, and Marine Corps display sharply divergent cultures.[28] Derived over time from their assigned domain of war on land, sea, and in the air, these individual services have developed very different ideals and concepts that in turn strongly influenced their institutional cultures and behavior, particularly their strategic approach to war that establishes their claim on the nation's assets.[29] For example, the air force holds dear to the idea that air power is now the decisive instrument of war.[30] The army has long understood that to be successful in battle, its ground forces must be supported by other branches and services, and cannot even reach battlefields overseas without the aid of the other two services. Thus, historically its strategy has been based on an integrative, joint approach. But where the air force bases its claims to resources on advancing technological development, the army tends to emphasize the human dimension of war and lobbies for resources to meet the needs of the nation's soldiers and their families.

Different from both of the above, the navy emphasizes tradition and independence, as befits a service whose forces are "over the horizon" much of the time and whose personnel remain focused on "going to sea."[31] Hence, the navy's strategic culture has long emphasized America's insularity and reliance on overseas

---

[28]Equally distinct, but beyond the scope of this essay, is the subculture of the reserve components, particularly the Army National Guard with its militia traditions.

[29]Carl H. Builder, *The Masks of War: American Military Styles in Strategy and Analysis*, A RAND Corporation Study (Baltimore, Md.: Johns Hopkins University Press, 1989), pp. 31–43.

[30]Earl H. Tilford Jr., "Halt Phase Strategy: New Wine in Old Wineskins . . . with PowerPoint" (Carlisle Barracks, Pa.: Strategic Studies Institute, U.S. Army War College, July 1998).

[31]David A. Rosenberg, presentation during the conference "The End of Military Culture."

trade, and based its claim to resources on the need to maintain control over (and under) vast oceanic expanses. Thus, "military" culture and "naval" culture have been, of necessity, quite different. Manifestations of these different beliefs and attitudes have been repeatedly documented, most recently in the high-tech aspects of command and control of joint forces.[32]

During the 1980s, the campaign to merge the various services' capabilities in effective joint forces sparked one of the epic battles of inter-service rivalry, resulting in 1986 in the landmark Goldwater-Nichols legislation that reorganized the national military establishment.[33] Of importance to this discussion is the fact that now, more than a decade later, during which America's armed forces have fought several conflicts under unified command, a new joint culture is emerging at the field-grade and senior officer levels, belying yet again any notion of a homogeneous "military culture."[34] Whether this is a good thing is largely unresearched, particularly since it remains to be seen at what level conventional service forces will be integrated into joint formations. If, as it appears, they will not be integrated routinely below battalion or squadron level in the future, then organic units of a single service will still obtain "at the point of the spear." But the fact that an identifiable joint culture is emerging among those officers in permanent joint headquarters suggests the ongoing evolution of multiple military cultures. It also highlights, as will be discussed later, the increasing dominance of the officer subculture.

The myth of a homogeneous military culture is further exposed by easily identifiable sub-subcultures within each uniformed service. Thus, Rosen observes

> that each service is far from monolithic and is not composed of subunits simply pursuing their own organizational self-interest. U.S. Army officers may come from the infantry, armor, artillery, aviation, airborne or special forces. Navy officers may be carrier pilots from the fighter or attack communities, antisubmarine warfare pilots, submariners, surface ship commanders, or from an amphibious force. Each branch has its own culture and distinct way of thinking about the way war should be conducted, not only by its branch, but by the other branches and services with which it would have to interact in wartime. If we start with this perspective we will be inclined to

[32]Kenneth Allard, *Command and Control and the Common Defense*, rev. ed. (Washington, D.C.: National Defense University Press, 1996), pp. 47–88.

[33]James R. Locher III, "Taking Stock of Goldwater-Nichols," *Joint Force Quarterly*, Autumn 1996, pp. 10–17.

[34]Howard D. Graves and Don M. Snider, "Emergence of the Joint Officer," *Joint Force Quarterly*, Autumn 1996, pp. 53–57.

regard military organizations as complex political communities in
which the central concerns are those of any political community: who
should rule, and how the "citizens" should live.[35]

The point here is that identifiable subcultures, and even sub-
subcultures, do exist and are reflective of the domain of war and
applicable warfighting doctrines for which their service, or
branch, is responsible. Good policy analysis and debate should,
indeed must, recognize and account for these differences. It is
doubtful that any single policy change will be equally effective
when applied uniformly to all of the services, as the secretary of
defense is now attempting to do with adultery and fraternization.
Broadly based policy changes applicable to all services and
branches simply fly in the face of a more informed understanding
of military culture. Fortunately, one military leader, the current
commandant of the Marine Corps, understands this and has effectively expressed such views on the issue of standardizing sanctions for the offense of adultery.[36]

Another way to grasp the heterogeneity among military cultures is through the metaphor of the spear. Warrior subcultures
within services, such as the infantry, fighter pilots, and all who do
actual killing, are at the point of the spear. Others farther down the
shaft support those in direct combat through communications and
intelligence. Still others near the base of the spear constitute the
service support and civilian components that provide theater-level
logistical functions such as medical services, matériel logistics,
and mobility operations. Though laid out in operational format,
this metaphor of the spear has its roots in an important body of
sociological research quite relevant to the debate today.

In the late 1970s, after the Vietnam debacle, the armed forces
suffered from an evident malaise, particularly within the officer
corps. Observing this, Moskos theorized in 1977 that the military
seemed to be developing the characteristics of a civilian occupation rather than the profession it had always considered itself. The
basic distinction between these two conceptions of the military lay
in their relation to, and legitimization by, American society.
Moskos noted that society legitimates an institution "in terms of
norms and values, a purpose transcending individual self-interest
in favor of a presumed higher good. Members of a *professional*
institution are often seen as following a calling captured in words

---

[35]Stephen Peter Rosen, *Winning the Next War* (Ithaca, N.Y.: Cornell University Press,
1991), p. 19.
[36]Gen. Charles C. Krulak, "Marines Have to be Held to Higher Standards," *USA
Today*, Aug. 11, 1989.

like *duty, honor, country*."[37] Conversely, an *occupational* model is legitimated in terms of the marketplace where supply and demand are paramount, and self-interest takes priority over communal interests.

Building on this institutional/occupational model (I/O), Moskos cautioned that at least three aspects of the creeping occupationalism should give military leaders concern: mission performance, member motivation, and professional responsibility. Research had already demonstrated that: (1) an institutional identification, rather than occupational, fostered greater organizational commitment and performance by the members; (2) an institutional orientation relied more on intrinsic motivational factors such as social responsibility, as opposed to extrinsic factors such as a soldier's pay; and (3) if an occupational model prevailed, the military function could be falsely quantified for decision-making analysis, severely eroding the value of professional military advice to civilian decision makers. Research conducted over the following decade with the I/O model helped the military make its transition to an all-volunteer force without eroding institutional norms and degrading overall professionalism. In fact, as noted earlier, the 1980s were a period of sharply increased professionalism in all services of our armed forces.

Subsequent research based on Moskos's model shows that soldiers can manifest both orientations and that the career soldier of the post–Cold War era exhibits a "pragmatic military professionalism" reflecting concerns for both individual welfare and collective national security.[38] But where "along the spear" such an orientation has positive results, and where negative, is a question that must be answered by uniformed professionals themselves. Perhaps it is harmless, and even productive, for logistical personnel to "think more like civilians"—but do we really want our combat troops to do so?

The Cultural Dominance of the Officer Corps

The fourth and final perspective on military culture focuses on the stratification of the military by rank, divided as the services are into officer, noncommissioned officer (NCO), and enlisted personnel. This, too, is a distinction seldom addressed, much to

[37]Charles C. Moskos, "Institutional and Occupational Trends in Armed Forces," in *The Military: More Than Just A Job?* ed. Charles C. Moskos and Frank R. Wood (London: Pergamon-Brassey's International Defense Publishers, 1998), p. 16.

[38]David R. Segal, *Recruiting for Uncle Sam: Citizenship and Military Manpower Policy* (Lawrence, Kans.: University of Kansas Press, 1989), p. 72.

the detriment of our current discourse. If it were addressed, then feminists advocating women in combat would recognize, and perhaps even accept, that the vast majority of female soldiers do not rally to their cause since the issue affects for the most part only female officers.[39] The necessary distinctiveness of the officer corps, as well as the nature of the vocation of officership, is perhaps even misunderstood today by members of the profession of arms, including some of the senior officer leaders.

My analysis indicates three reasons for the importance and dominance of the officer subculture. First, officers develop, maintain, and carry through time the unique elements of the profession essential for the military to be accorded high professional status by American society.[40] But it has not always been so, with the profession having to reestablish after the Vietnam War its professional status, both to itself and to the American people. It was a process conceptualized and executed almost exclusively by officers, a process of reintellectualizing, reorganizing, reequipping, and retraining a demoralized and defeated army.[41] And yet this was very similar to the manner in which that same army was, along with the navy, initially professionalized during the decades of 1880–1910.[42]

Why is it that some vocations, particularly military ones, are viewed by our society as true professions? According to Huntington, professional status implies a unique and socially useful expertise (the management of violence), a moral responsibility to provide and use that expertise on behalf of a society that cannot defend itself, and an organic unity and consciousness of itself as a group apart from laymen.[43] Millett, in turn, emphasizes "a life-long calling by the practitioners," and notes that "professions are organized to control performance standards and recruitment," thus using their monopoly of expertise for self-policing of the profession. Such limited autonomy marks all true professions, in his view.[44]

---

[39]Laura Miller, "Feminism and the Exclusion of Army Women from Combat," Working Paper no. 2, Project on Post–Cold War Civil-Military Relations (Cambridge, Mass.: John M. Olin Institute for Strategic Studies, Harvard University, Dec. 1995).

[40]Louis Harris and Associates poll, reported in Rowan Scarborough, "Poll Gives Military Its Top Rating," *Washington Times*, Feb. 17, 1998.

[41]For a very informative and readable current-history review of this process, see James Kitfield, *The Prodigal Soldiers* (New York: Simon and Schuster, 1995).

[42]Allan R. Millett and Peter Maslowski, *A Military History of the United States of America* (New York: Free Press, 1994), particularly chap. 13, pp. 413–49.

[43]Huntington, *The Soldier and the State*, pp. 11–18.

[44]Allen R. Millett, "Military Professionalism and Officership in America," Mershon Center Briefing Paper no. 2 (Ohio State University, May 1977), p. 3.

The point here is that these elements of a profession are almost exclusively the domain of officers, whether it be theorizing about strategy, researching and teaching about war and conflict, crafting the simulations needed to develop new capabilities, writing and controlling the contracts for work done by the private industrial sector, developing the training and evaluation systems, or adjudicating the military legal system to maintain discipline. Very seldom is policy, regulation, doctrine, or personnel action ever promulgated except over the signature of a commanding officer or staff officer. In sum, because of their role, their longevity, and their profession's unique avoidance of lateral entry, officers create and maintain over time those elements that make the military a profession. If you change what the officers think, you will succeed in changing the culture. No wonder that Huntington could confidently conclude decades ago that a military can only be considered professional so long as the vast majority of its officers are loyal to its ethos.[45]

A second argument for the unique dominance of the officer subculture is that officers, through their formal commission as well as their unwritten contract, are the military's connection to American society. It is true that all Americans who have ever served in our armed forces remain connected to their service, if only in memory. But it is also true that officers, particularly while on active duty, fulfill the representative function of the military to civil society. They are the ones who have received a commission, a warrant, from that society to be its agent and to act on its behalf, and it is logical for society to expect individual accountability. As noted decades ago by Marshall, it is the responsibility of the officer corps to serve such that they strengthen the claim of the service on the affections of the American people.[46] Thus, the concern shown by average Americans to the Tailhook and Aberdeen scandals, though exploited by certain lobbyists in Washington, was entirely logical and correct. More surprising to this author is how mild the public reactions were, inasmuch as these instances were egregious examples of officers' betraying their "sacred trust," and significantly diminishing the professionalism of their services. But even this failure points out the dominance of the officer in military subcultures. While the NCOs involved were held accountable to legal standards for their failures, the understandable outrage of Americans was focused on the officer corps, whose unique

---

[45]Huntington, *The Soldier and the State*, pp. 61–62, 74.

[46]S. L. A. Marshall, *The Armed Forces Officer* (Washington, D.C.: U.S. Government Printing Office, 1950).

responsibility it is to shape military subcultures, particularly with regard to discipline and ethos.

The third reason that officers tend to dominate the service subcultures is their responsibility to shape the organizational climate of every operational unit in every armed force every day, wherever deployed. But if officers, and particularly commanding officers, so strongly influence organizational climate and the military's state of professionalism, what is the professional role today of the noncommissioned officers? What is their influence on military culture? The answer is not so clear. Decades ago, Huntington concluded that "enlisted personnel have neither the intellectual skills nor the professional responsibility of the officer. They are specialists in the application of violence, not in the management of violence. Their vocation is a trade, not a profession."[47] But while NCOs do not have the social responsibility of the officer and thus serve without commission, they are today much better educated and trained, particularly in leadership skills. In fact, all services have made significant strides in providing sequential schools for the professional education of their career NCOs, just as they have always had for their officers.[48] The more decentralized military operations become, the more organizational climate will be influenced by the performance of NCOs, thus influencing the overall effectiveness of the unit. This is a key stratum of leadership, but one that has been almost totally ignored in the debates on whether and how to change our military culture.

Conclusions

America can have military cultures different from those that now exist within the services, and in fact further change may be both necessary and desirable. But we will not learn that from the debate as it has been conducted to date. A truly informed debate is called for—one concerned with effective policymaking and focused on all the subcultures and their influences, both positive and negative, on military capabilities and effectiveness. The purposes of the military and its ability to fulfill those purposes should drive the debate, not its racial or gender composition.

At the very least, such a political dialogue should focus on what is distinctively *military* about military culture and why that is

[47]Huntington, *The Soldier and the State*, pp. 17–18.
[48]The army's success in rebuilding its NCO corps by "leadership development" programs that essentially bundled indistinguishably the roles of the officer and NCO, particularly in training soldiers, also had the ironic effect of confusing officers as to their own distinct role under their commission.

so. For example, the changing nature of warfare in each of its domains, as fought by modern Western powers with volunteer soldiers, needs to be injected strongly into the debate. Unlike the generalized discussions of the past, the level of analysis should extend to missions and tasks to be undertaken by the services and the relative priorities of each. As discussed earlier, these are the principle determinants of the professional ethos and the reason there are military cultures in the first place. In particular, the officer subculture should become, for the reasons already presented, a major component of the public dialogue.

Uniformed military professionals must also become much more involved in the political debates over military culture with well-researched analyses and recommendations. Unfortunately, this remains a field of inquiry almost untouched, particularly by historians, and particularly since the inception of the all-volunteer force in the late 1970s.[49] But there is another and more important reason why uniformed professionals within the services must articulate better the needs of their services with respect to potential changes in the culture of the organization they lead. Simply put, they are the professional experts and no one else is! Their expertise is born of decades of training and study and episodic experiences in war and conflict, experiences in which American forces have acquitted themselves superbly. And in addition to their experience from the past, uniformed leaders are charged always with doing the analysis to prepare for the future. In this regard, the current era presents particular problems. In eras between wars, military organizations usually adapt themselves, both intellectually and organizationally, to major changes in the security environment and technologies of the nation they are protecting.[50] The level of professionalism in the armed forces during such periods of peace tends to fall for a number of reasons, but then rises again as the reintellectualization of the profession produces "new theories of victory" and the means to execute them in the campaigns of the future.[51]

Today, it is fair to say that that process of reintellectualization after the Cold War has only just begun, and not evenly across all

[49]Williamson Murray, presentation during conference "The End of Military Culture"; and Andrew J. Bacevich, "Absent History: A Comment on Duaber, Feaver, and Desch," *Armed Forces and Society*, Spring 1998, pp. 447–54.

[50]Williamson Murray and Allen Millett, eds., *Military Innovation in the Interwar Period* (Cambridge: Cambridge University Press, 1996).

[51]Don M. Snider, John A. Nagl, and Tony Pfaff, *Army Professionalism, the Military Ethic and Officership in the 21st Century* (Carlisle Barracks, Pa.: Strategic Studies Institute, U.S. Army War College, 1999), pp. 16–26.

the services. Thus, it is likely that in many areas it is not yet clear just what changes in service cultures are either needed or acceptable. But the responsibility to get on with the necessary research and experimentation to make those determinations rests with no one other than the officer corps itself. To be sure, there will continue to be other voices in the debate, as befits our pluralistic form of government. But none of these other voices speaks with the experience and judgment that derive from the continuous study, experimentation, and refinement of how best to fight our nation's wars.

It is high time, therefore, that our military professionals reread the advice of General Ridgway as he and President Eisenhower faced the mission of "preserving the peace":

> I say that the professional soldier should never pull his punches, should never let himself for one moment be dissuaded from stating the honest estimates his own military experience and judgments tell him will be needed to do the job required of him. No factor of political motivation or political expediency could explain such an action.[52]

---

[52]Gen. Matthew Ridgway, *Soldier: The Memoirs of Matthew B. Ridgway* (New York: Harper and Brothers, 1956), p. 271.

DOES MILITARY CULTURE MATTER?

by Williamson Murray

History, with its grim landscape of defeated armies and shattered nations, would certainly suggest that military culture matters.[1] But how and why that is so is not entirely clear. Unfortunately, historians have done little work on the subject, focusing for the most part on more immediate factors such as leadership, doctrine, or training to explain victory or defeat.[2] Even works specifically examining military effectiveness and innovation tend to discuss military culture as a tangential issue.[3] Yet military culture may be the most important factor not only in military effectiveness, but also in the processes involved in military innovation, which is essential to preparing military organizations for the next war.

If military culture does matter, what might an acceptable definition of it be? Military culture represents the ethos and professional attributes, both in terms of experience and intellectual study, that contribute to a common core understanding of the nature of war within military organizations. As Michael Howard has suggested, no other profession is as demanding in physical or mental terms as the profession of arms.[4] In the latter case this is particularly true because military institutions must spend long periods of time *not* engaged in their fundamental purpose—war.

---

[1]This essay originally appeared in *Orbis*, Winter 1999, and arose from the Foreign Policy Research Institute conference "The End of American Military Culture," Philadelphia, Pa., July 15–16, 1998. The views expressed here do not represent those of the U.S. Army, the Department of Defense, or the U.S. Government.

[2]For a graphic account of the differences between military cultures, and of their resulting effects on the battlefield, see Samuel W. Mitcham Jr., *Rommel's Greatest Victory: The Desert Fox and the Fall of Tobruk, 1942* (Novato, Calif.: Presidio Press, 1998). See also Brian Bond, *British Military Policy Between the Two World Wars* (Oxford: Oxford University Press, 1980); MacGregor Knox, *Mussolini Unleashed: Politics and Strategy in Fascist Italy's Last War* (Cambridge: Cambridge University Press, 1982); and particularly Andrew Gordon, *The Rules of the Game: Jutland and British Naval Command* (London: John Murray, 1997).

[3]See Allan R. Millett and Williamson Murray, eds., *Military Effectiveness*, 3 vols. (London: Unwin Hyman, 1988); and Williamson Murray and Allan R. Millett, eds., *Military Innovation in the Interwar Period* (Cambridge: Cambridge University Press, 1996).

[4]See in particular Michael Howard, "The Use and Abuse of Military History," *Journal of the Royal United Services Institute*, Jan. 1962, pp. 4–10.

Rather, they must estimate the impact of technological, tactical, operational, and societal changes as they apply to war, without fully testing those conceptions until war occurs. Thus, military organizations can never completely evaluate peacetime innovations and preparation until the audit of war itself, in which fear, chaos, ambiguity, and uncertainty dominate. Military culture thus represents the intellectual and spiritual capacity of the armies, naval forces, and air forces to come to grips with the business of preparing for and executing war.

The difficulty in addressing military culture in a scholarly fashion derives not only from the complexity of the subject, but also from the fact that its influence is almost always the result of long-term factors rarely measurable and often obscure even to historians. What is more, military culture obviously changes over time in response to changes in a society's culture, the advance of technology, and the impact of leadership. As one senior marine has noted, military cultures are like great ocean liners or aircraft carriers: they require an enormous effort to change direction.[5] While those making changes in an institution's value system at times have a clear idea of the results they seek, in most cases they do not, and in any case cannot be assured of achieving the desired results.[6]

The purpose of this essay is to suggest some of the complexities involved in military culture, the historical evidence that demonstrates why military culture is so important, the current cultural framework of the U.S. military, and finally some ideas about how we might think about influencing American military culture in positive directions. The larger purpose is not to suggest answers or solutions, but to think more coherently and intelligently about military culture, past, present, and future. There are no short-term solutions to problems in military culture. Those interested in reforming military culture must recognize instead that reforms, changes in emphasis, or even radical surgery will not yield immediate results. An effective change in military culture can only occur over a period of decades, and it is as likely that unintended effects of reforms on the cultural patterns of an organization may be more significant than intended effects.[7]

[5] Lt. Gen. Paul Van Riper, USMC (ret.) to the author in conversation, July 1995.

[6] Changes made in the 1920s to requirements for command positions were intended simply to aid the navy's fledgling aviation community, but as a result, by the late 1930s the navy had become the most aviation-minded in the world. See Barry Watts and Williamson Murray, "Military Innovation in Peacetime," in *Military Innovation*, pp. 383–405.

[7] Along these lines it is the opinion of the author that the efforts at cultural and intel-

The Larger Cultural Framework

As one of the members of this panel suggested, military culture is a coat of many colors. Influencing the culture of military organizations are factors such as history, the professional ethos, geography, the milieu within which that organization operates, recent military experience, and the *Weltanschauung* of the external society. Moreover, even within military organizations there will be separate and distinct subcultures heavily influenced by traditions as well as the mission they perform.[8]

In the largest sense, it is possible to talk about national military styles. The German military possessed a devotion to duty, a seriousness about tactics, and a breathtaking contempt for logistics and intelligence in the two world wars.[9] The reason why German military culture paid so little attention to logistics has much to do with geography. The Germans have always been at the center of military operations throughout the history of European warfare, and Prussia's catastrophe at Jena/Auerstadt in October 1806—whereby a single day's defeat resulted in the collapse of the state—exercised a baleful influence as late as May 1945. The failures of German intelligence are more difficult to understand. They most probably had to do with an overemphasis on tactics and operations, but also with the culture of a society that over the course of two world wars possessed a fundamental belief in the innate racial superiority of the German *Volk*.

On the other hand, the Italian military services, as MacGregor Knox has noted, confronted the fundamental problem of "the Italian general staff tradition: Custoza, Lissa, Adua, Caporetto. On those occasions the military, as yet uncontaminated by contact with Fascism, distinguished itself by the absences of the study, planning, and attention to detail that characterized the Germans. . . ."[10] Admittedly, Italian society at large, particularly the middle class, regarded a military career in the officer corps as worthy of only

lectual change that Gen. Al Gray set in motion when he was commandant of the Marine Corps in the late 1980s (the creation of the Marine Corps University, the Commandant's Reading List, and FMFM 1 [*Warfighting*], among others) are only now beginning to exert their full impact not only on the senior marine leadership, but also on the larger body of the officer corps of that service.

[8]See Don M. Snider's discussion of military heterogeneity in his essay in this volume.

[9]The basic doctrinal manual for the Luftwaffe, *Die Luftkriegführung* [Waging Air War] (Berlin: n.p., 1966), for example, is a brilliant discussion of the operational and tactical framework within which air war has taken place (far superior to anything the U.S. Air Force has ever produced), but it ends with the note that sections on logistics and intelligence had yet to be written. They were never written, and the Luftwaffe's performance in World War II lived up to its sister services' appalling performance in those areas.

[10]MacGregor Knox, *Mussolini Unleashed*, p. 16.

the dumbest—in other words those incapable of supporting them-selves in some other career. The culture of the officer corps lived up to the expectations of the society. As General Ubaldo Soddu, who was largely responsible for the operational and tactical disas-ter in Greece, commented about a career in the Italian military, "when you have a fine plate of pasta guaranteed for life, and a lit-tle music, you don't need anything more." In October 1940, as his troops were suffering a terrible battering from the Greeks, Soddu would spend his evenings composing musical scores for movies.[11] The results spoke for themselves when the Italian officer corps abdicated its responsibilities and military catastrophe followed. Yet Italian soldiers themselves, badly equipped, and ineptly led, fought far better in North Africa and on the plains of Russia than historians have given them credit for.

Thus, a societal rejection of all things military, as well as a governmental emphasis on its military organizations' protecting the regime from revolution, framed Italian military culture.[12] The German military style reflected a national attitude that took war very seriously—a predilection inspired by the numerous invasions that German states had suffered over the course of centuries. The German navy, however, proved in two world wars that there was nothing innately competent about German military organizations; as a result, one should hesitate before ascribing undue influence to national culture in how service cultures develop.

The United States, of course, has had its own military style—one characterized by heavy emphasis on logistics, overwhelming material superiority, and an inclination to avoid military or politi-cal conflict until late in the game. To a great extent this culture also reflects the impact of geography. The United States is a great island nation protected by oceans. Thus, the projection of military power has demanded an emphasis on logistics. Even in the American Civil War, which has exercised such great influence over the general military culture of the U.S. services, Union forces waged a continental war on a scale equivalent to the distances in Europe from Paris to Moscow.[13]

Another major factor in military culture is the generational change that occurs in military organizations as the collective experiences of the senior officer corps evolve with the passage of

[11]Ibid., p. 57.

[12]The *Carabinieri*, Italy's militarized police, have been regarded as the elite formation of the Italian military, a sure indication of the emphasis on the military's internal role over its external one.

[13]See Williamson Murray, "Why Did It Take the North So Long?" *Military History Quarterly*, Summer 1989, pp. 24–33.

time. Such a change has been occurring in the American military over the past decade, as the Vietnam War generation has reached retirement.[14] When such change in the collective experiences of the officer corps occurs, officers come to view the world differently. Similarly, the U.S. Army, which so heavily focused on defense of West Germany's Fulda Gap from 1973 through the end of the Cold War, will only fully adapt to the military problems raised by the new strategic environment when those officers whose Weltanschauung was so heavily framed by European experience have retired.

It is almost impossible to change the larger cultural and geographic framework within which military organizations operate.[15] The United States will always confront the problem of projecting military power across the world's oceans, hence a focus on logistics will remain a dominant theme in the culture of U.S. services. Nevertheless, if one cannot change this larger framework, except perhaps as societal and political changes work their influence over decades, one certainly needs to remain aware of the peculiar circumstances that frame the larger military culture—particularly if one is interested in the issue of military reform.

Military Cultures in the Past

Historians have correctly judged the German victory on the banks of the Meuse in May 1940 as one of the crucial events in the history of the twentieth century. That victory enabled the Germans to overcome their considerable strategic weaknesses and in effect to fight the great world war that lasted until 1945.[16] That war, in turn, terminated the period of European imperialism and led inevitably to the Cold War. Yet the military capabilities that enabled the Germans to win in 1940 resulted not from revolutionary changes occurring in the 1930s, but rather from fundamental changes in the German military's organizational culture that had occurred during the early 1920s, when Hans von Seeckt, the first chief of staff and in 1920 commander in chief of the Reichswehr, altered the cultural patterns of the German officer corps as a whole. Faced with the task of reducing the German army's officer

[14]See Williamson Murray, "Computers In, Clausewitz Out," *National Interest*, Summer 1997, pp. 57–64.

[15]Perhaps an experience such as catastrophe can result in great change in the culture of military organizations, as occurred in Germany in 1945, but one suspects such a change reflected the changes in the larger political culture of German society after the war.

[16]See Williamson Murray, *The Change in the European Balance of Power, 1938–1939: The Path to Ruin* (Princeton, N.J.: Princeton University Press, 1984), chap. 1.

corps from more than 20,000 officers to the limit set by the Treaty of Versailles, Seeckt turned the officer corps over to the control of the great general staff.[17] By so doing he deselected important constituencies, namely the Junker aristocracy and *Frontsoldaten*. The effect was to infuse the whole army with the cultural attributes of the general staff: the hallmarks of the new German army were systematic, thorough analysis; a willingness to grapple with what was really happening on the battlefield; and a rigorous selection process that emphasized officers' intellectual attainments—in a professional sense—as well as their performance in leadership positions.

Along with this emphasis, Seeckt appointed no fewer than fifty-seven different committees to study the lessons of World War I. This thorough, complete study of the last war stands in stark contrast to the experience of the British army, which failed to establish a single committee to study the lessons of that war until 1932, more than a decade after the Germans. Even then, the chief of the British imperial general staff had the report rewritten to cast a more favorable light on the army's wartime performance. The Germans built on the work of Seeckt's committees to fashion a coherent, combined arms doctrine; by 1923 the German army was well on the way to inventing the Blitzkrieg.[18]

In 1932 two of the Reichswehr's most respected generals, Werner von Fritsch and Ludwig Beck, rewrote the German army's basic doctrinal manual, *Die Truppenführung* (Troop Leadership), which served as the basis for the combined-arms battle doctrine with which the Germans fought the Second World War. The opening paragraphs of that manual encompassed the fundamental cultural assumptions of the German army:

1. The conduct of war is an art, depending upon free, creative activity, scientifically grounded. It makes the highest demands on individuals.

2. The conduct of war is based on continuous development. New means of warfare call forth ever changing employment. . . .

3. Situations in war are of unlimited variety. They change often and suddenly and are rarely discernible at an early point. Incalculable ele-

[17]While the general staff tradition had played a major role in the German army's inventing of modern war between 1916 and 1918, it remained a subculture within the army until 1920. See Timothy Lupfer, *The Dynamics of Doctrine: The Changes in German Tactical Doctrine During the First World War* (Fort Leavenworth, Kans.: Government Printing Office, 1981); and Martin Samuels, *Command or Control? Command, Training and Tactics in the British and German Armies, 1888–1918* (London: Frank Cass, 1995).

[18]James S. Corum, *The Roots of Blitzkrieg: Hans von Seeckt and German Military Reform* (Lawrence, Kans.: University of Kansas Press, 1992), especially chap. 4; Williamson Murray, "Armored Warfare," in *Military Innovation*, p. 20.

ments are often of great influence. The independent will of the enemy is pitted against ours. Frictions and mistakes are an every day occurrence.[19]

Fritsch and Beck would assume control of the German army soon after Hitler came to power, and held responsibility for developing the qualities that made that army such a formidable fighting instrument in the coming war.

Throughout the 1920s and 1930s, German army culture demanded not only high standards in terms of troop leadership but also serious study of the profession of arms. The case of Erwin Rommel suggests how widespread was this culture of serious intellectual preparation of the officer corps. If ever there was a "muddy boots combat soldier," it was Rommel, yet he not only avidly devoured books, he wrote them. His *Infantrie Greift An* (Infantry Attacks) is one of the great classics in the literature of war.[20]

Historians have often suggested that armies study only the last war and that is why they do badly in the next. In fact, as the above suggests, there are few military organizations that possess a culture that encourages the study of even the recent past with any thoroughness. Most military organizations quickly develop myths that allow escape from unpleasant truths; such was the case with the French army in the immediate aftermath of World War I.[21] And in some cases military cultures reject the past as having no relevance to the future of war. Air forces have been particularly attracted to a technological culture that holds that even the study of recent military experience is of limited use in preparing for a revolutionary technological future.[22]

Such military cultures tend to mold the evidence to support the view of those at the top. The French army in the interwar years, along with the U.S. Army Air Corps and the Royal Air Force during the same period, was particularly prone to making evidence fit

[19]*Troop Leadership*, trans. of *Die Truppenführung* (Washington, D.C.: U.S. War Department, 1936 [1933]), p. 1.

[20]A recent biography of Rommel, Sir David Fraser's *Knights Cross: A Life of Field Marshal Erwin Rommel* (London: Harper Collins, 1993), underlines the extraordinary interest and effort that Rommel devoted to the study of military history and his profession.

[21]See in particular Robert Doughty, *Seeds of Disaster: The Development of French Army Doctrine, 1919–1939* (Hamden, Conn.: Shoe String Press, 1985).

[22]The Royal Air Force's air staff explicitly stated in 1924 that an air force can "either bomb military objectives in populated areas from the beginning of the war, with the objective of obtaining a decision by moral effect . . . or, alternatively, they can be used in the first instance to attack enemy aerodromes with the aim to gain some measure of air superiority. . . . The latter alternative is the method which the lessons of military history seem to recommend, but the air staff are convinced that the former is the correct one." Public Record Office AIR 20/40, Air Staff Memorandum no. 11A, Mar. 1924.

its theory. Such cultures are also intolerant of any kind of dissent from the "official" view. Moreover, with a hard, unyielding view of war, such military cultures have proven resistant to adapting to the actual conditions of war.[23] In peacetime they tend to follow a preconceived trail that will even reject technological possibilities as impossible if they do not fit dogmatic notions of what war will look like.[24]

In other words it has often taken defeat to force substantive adaptation to the actual conditions of war. The less willing a culture is to display flexibility in peacetime, the more likely it is to have difficulty in adapting to the real conditions of war. There is a consistent historical pattern of military organizations' attempting to impose their prewar concepts of future combat on the actual conditions of war instead of adapting to those conditions. In the case of the French army in World War II, the resulting defeat could only be reversed by the intervention of other powers. The serious losses suffered by the Eighth Air Force in summer 1943 were not sufficient to derail the Combined Bomber Offensive. But it is worth noting that it took catastrophic losses on two missions against the ball bearing factories in Schweinfurt (August and October 1943) before the Eighth Air Force leadership finally recognized that unescorted bomber formations, as prescribed in prewar doctrine, were simply incapable of fighting their way through the ferocious opposition of the fighter planes thrown up by the Luftwaffe.[25]

The history of the U.S. military services likewise suggests the strengths and weaknesses of a democratic system of civil-military relations. Accustomed usually to minimal civilian support, the American military endured a glacial promotion system that kept officers in the same grade for interminable periods of time. On the other hand, the performance of U.S. military institutions in World War II suggests that Martin van Creveld's view that the American officer system was entirely deficient in comparison to the German

[23]Andrew Krepinevich's *The Army in Vietnam* (Baltimore, Md.: Johns Hopkins University Press, 1986) underlines the unwillingness of the U.S. Army to change its paradigm in accordance with the actual conditions of war in Southeast Asia. Timothy Travers, in his *The Killing Ground: The British Army, the Western Front and the Emergence of Modern Warfare, 1900–1918* (London: Allen and Unwin, 1987), is also particularly good on the similar inability of the British high command in World War I to adapt to the real conditions of war.

[24]Even as late as 1941 the senior leadership of the RAF was arguing that a long-range escort fighter was technologically impossible. Sir Charles Webster and Noble Frankland, *The Strategic Air Offensive Against Germany*, vol. 1, *Preparations* (London: HMSO, 1961), p. 177.

[25]For a discussion of the air battles of 1943, see Williamson Murray, *Luftwaffe* (Baltimore, Md.: Nautical and Aviation Press, 1985), chaps. 5 and 6.

one has considerable flaws.[26] Thus, recent historical works have judged the U.S. Army's performance in World War II, particularly against the Germans, far more favorably than was the case a decade ago.[27] U.S. Army formations proved adaptable, flexible, and increasingly combat effective from 1943 on.[28] Moreover, whatever the difficulties in 1942 and early 1943, one needs to remember that American rearmament began late in comparison to that of Nazi Germany, while U.S. forces were committed to battle almost immediately. Rearmament of the U.S. Navy began in 1938, but that of the army only in July 1940 in response to the catastrophe in France. Thus, hastily prepared U.S. ground forces found themselves in combat with the Japanese in the Pacific in summer 1942 and with German forces in North Africa in November 1942. In contrast, the German army did not find itself in combat until September 1939—six and a half years after Hitler had embarked on a massive program of rearmament. The desperate fears the German army's leadership felt about the remilitarization of the Rhineland in March 1936 suggest how little prepared that army was after its first three years of rearmament.

Throughout the interwar period, the culture of the American military appears to have been open to serious thinking about the profession of arms. In the aftermath of World War I the American Expeditionary Force (AEF) headquarters established twenty separate boards to examine the lessons of the last war. Then a group led by some of the army's most respected officers produced a final report drawing from the reports of the twenty boards.[29] That analysis played a major role in the codification of a new basic doctrinal manual, *Field Service Regulations*, in 1923. Far more than was the case with the British, the Americans made a considerable effort to come to grips with the harsh lessons of the Western Front. The new doctrine displayed some influence of the French top-down approach to war, but German experiences also influenced American thinking.[30] In fact, both influences are still evident today, in the form of a top-down mechanistic emphasis on distant

---

[26]See Martin Van Creveld, *Fighting Power: German and U.S. Army Performance, 1939–1945* (Westport, Conn.: Greenwood Press, 1982).

[27]See in particular Michael D. Dobler, *Closing with the Enemy: How GIs Fought the War in Europe, 1944–1945* (Lawrence, Kans.: University of Kansas Press, 1994).

[28]To compare that with the performance of the British army in World War II, see Williamson Murray, "British Military Effectiveness," in *Military Effectiveness*, vol. 3, chap. 3.

[29]William Odom, *After the Trenches: The Transformation of U.S. Army Doctrine, 1918–1939* (College Station, Tex.: Texas A&M University Press, 1999).

[30]As James Corum pointed out in a paper presented at the Dueling Doctrines conference sponsored by the Center for Strategic and International Studies (Washington,

firepower (the French influence) and the emphasis on maneuver warfare (the German approach).

The emphasis that professional military education received throughout the interwar period in the United States also suggests a military culture that placed considerable emphasis on the preparation of officers for the serious business of war. Unlike its German and British counterparts, the U.S. Army developed a two-tier approach to professional military education, the Command and General Staff College at Fort Leavenworth, Kansas, and the Army War College in Washington, D.C.[31] The navy had its own war college, while the marines' school at Quantico, Virginia, and the Air Corps Tactical School at Maxwell Air Force Base, Alabama, provided substantial input into the innovations that contributed so much to the American victory in World War II. Equally important from the army's point of view were the branch schools, particularly the Infantry School at Fort Benning, Georgia. Under the leadership of George C. Marshall a whole generation of army officers received a first-rate education in thinking about war, as well as being judged by the cold blue eyes of the army's future chief of staff.

The respect with which the U.S. military's leadership regarded tours on the faculty of such schools suggests how seriously it took professional military education. The future admiral Raymond Spruance served not one but two tours on the faculty of the Naval War College at Newport, Rhode Island.[32] Richmond Kelly Turner, who played a commanding role in amphibious warfare in the Pacific, and John Reeves, a key aviation pioneer, also served on the Newport faculty. After the war Admiral Chester Nimitz went so far as to suggest that "I credit the Naval War College for such success [as] I achieved in strategy and tactics in the war."[33] As for the army, out of its seven members, the faculty of the Army War College for the 1939–40 academic year counted Colonel W. H. Simpson and Major J. Lawton Collins; the former would be a three-star commander within four years, while the latter eventually ended his career as the army's chief of staff. The following year Alexander Patch, also to become an army commander in World

D.C., June 1998), there was a strong French influence on the American military since the 1840s and strong German influence since the 1870s.

[31]After World War II, the Army War College moved to Carlisle Barracks, Pa., while the National War College took over its buildings at Fort McNair.

[32]Over the past thirty years there has apparently been only one admiral who served on the faculty at Newport. Since it is hard enough for the navy to justify sending its best officers as *students* to Newport, this is not surprising.

[33]E. B. Potter, *Nimitz* (Annapolis, Md.: U.S. Naval Institute Press, 1976), p. 136.

War II, reported for duty on the faculty.

The contribution of the schools at Quantico in writing the basic doctrine for amphibious warfare is well known. Similarly, the Naval War College and its president in the early 1920s, Admiral William S. Sims, were experimenting with possible uses for aircraft carriers before the U.S. Navy possessed a single one. Significantly, Sims had chosen to return from his position as commander of U.S. naval forces in Europe during World War I to become the president of the Naval War College.[34]

The history of the first half of this century would suggest that military culture was a crucial determinant in how well military organizations adapted to war. But an examination of the historical record also suggests that there are no easy ways to change the cultural patterns by which officers judge themselves and their environment. In fact, the history of the interwar period suggests that cultural patterns were set almost immediately after the First World War and, for better or worse, remained fixed throughout the run-up to the Second.[35]

Military Cultures, Present and Future

If military culture has mattered in the past, then it is surely important to judge the current cultural climate in the U.S. military services. As suggested earlier, there is no monolithic American military culture. Rather, the four services, reflecting their differing historical antecedents and the differences in the environments in which they operate, have evolved cultures that are extraordinarily different. The environmental influences are particularly important to any understanding of the peculiar cultures that the services have developed. Even with the best will in the world to make the American military "joint," those differences will continue to shape how airmen, sailors, soldiers, and marines view war. The air force will remain a technologically driven organization. Moreover, the nature of air war, with hundreds if not thousands of aircraft launched against targets on the ground and in the air, will demand a degree of top-down organization that ground operations do not. The demands for tanker support, suppression of enemy air defens-

[34]Barry Watts and Williamson Murray, "Military Innovation in Peacetime," in *Military Innovation*, pp. 383–405. Similarly, Admiral Spruance chose to come back from command in the Pacific to become president of the Naval War College.

[35]The one exception to this might be the German military, where Nazi ideology came to have a greater influence over the officer corps as the war approached, and over German military effectiveness throughout World War II. In particular, see Omer Bartov, *Hitler's Army: Soldiers, Nazis, and War in the Third Reich* (Oxford: Oxford University Press, 1991).

es, and the interplay between air-to-air fighters and bomb-droppers inevitably requires a mechanistic approach to military operations in the air.[36] Similarly, the highly technical nature of surface, submarine, and aviation combat in the navy push that service towards a technological, engineering-based approach to warfare.[37] On the other hand, both the army and Marine Corps, influenced by the nature of land combat, will be driven to a more Clausewitzian view of war.

Yet whatever the environmental differences, service cultures also possess beliefs and traditions that play crucial roles in how they think about and prepare for war. Here, there are worrisome signs, not only within the services themselves, but within the "joint" community as well. First, as suggested above, there has been a generational change in all the services as those with experience in the Vietnam War retire. The Vietnam generation returned from Southeast Asia skeptical that technological solutions offered a means to simplify the complexities and ambiguities of war. In a profound sense, they were Clausewitzian in their outlook on the utility and conduct of war. As the 1986 edition of the army's basic doctrinal manual, FM 100-5, underlined, "Friction—the accumulation of chance errors, unexpected difficulties, and the confusion of battle—will impede both sides. To overcome it, leaders . . . must be prepared to risk commitment without complete information, recognizing that waiting for such information will invariably forfeit the opportunity to act."[38]

The new generation of officers, with the exception of the Marine Corps, has proven far more attracted by technological, mechanistic solutions to the complex problems raised by war. In fact, a considerable number of senior officers have been arguing that advances in computer technology and communication systems will allow the U.S. military to see and destroy everything in the wide expanses of a battle. Others have gone so far as to suggest that these advances will eliminate friction by allowing commanders absolute knowledge about what the enemy is doing: "The emerging system . . . promises the capacity to use military force without the same risks as before—it suggests we will dissipate the

---

[36]See the discussion of the third day's mission against Baghdad flown during the Gulf War, in Williamson Murray, *The Air Campaign in the Persian Gulf* (Baltimore, Md.: Nautical and Aviation Press, 1996), pp. 86–96.

[37]Only the shattering experience of major fleet combat in the Solomons forced the navy toward a broader, less mechanistic view of fleet operations.

[38]Field Manual 100-5, *U.S. Army Blueprint for Air/Land Battle*, 1986, p. 16. The Marine Corps Manual FMFM 1, *Warfighting*, represented an even more emphatic statement of such a point of view.

'fog of war.'"[39]

Indeed, what appears to be occurring—especially in the air force—is a reprise of the sort of mechanistic, engineering, systems-analysis approach that contributed so much to failure in Vietnam. As the air force's *New World Vistas* suggests: "The power of the new information systems will lie in their ability to correlate data automatically and rapidly from many sources to form a *complete* picture of the operational area, whether it be a battlefield or the site of a mobility operation" (italics added). Such claims betray a general disinterest and ignorance of basic science.[40] But the navy, too, has displayed a considerable penchant for believing that technology is a "silver bullet," and its thinkers argue for something called "network-centric warfare," according to which integrated information systems can grasp everything that is happening in a vast battlespace and destroy the crucial targets on which the enemy depends. As the chief proponent of this view, Admiral Arthur Cebrowski, recently argued:

> Network-centric operations . . . create a higher awareness, and allow it to be maintained [in combat]. Such awareness will improve our ability to deter conflict, or to prevail if conflict becomes unavoidable. . . . The structural or logical model for network-centric warfare has emerged. The entry fee is a high-performance information grid that provides a backplane for computing and communications. The information grid enables the operational architectures of sensor grids and engagement grids. Sensor grids rapidly generate high levels of battlespace awareness and synchronize awareness of military operations. Engagement grids exploit this awareness and translate it into increased combat power.[41]

This summer's war game at Newport indicated that some in the navy believe that "the great data base in the sky" will provide U.S. commanders with absolute knowledge of everything that happens in an enemy nation in the next war. Clearly, they believe that the theater commander will fight a future war the way a ship commander runs his combat center. Fog, friction, ambiguities, and

---

[39]Adm. William Owens (former vice chairman of the Joint Chiefs), "System of systems," *Armed Forces Journal*, Jan. 1996, p. 47. See also, Thomas Duffy, "Breakthrough Could Give Forces Total Command of Future Battlefield," *Inside the Navy*, Jan. 23, 1995; and Peter Grier, "Preparing for 21st-Century Information War," *Government Executive*, Aug. 1995, pp. 130–32.

[40]Department of the Air Force, *New World Vistas: Air and Space Power for the 21st Century* (Washington, D.C.: U.S. Government Printing Office, 1995).

[41]Vice Adm. Arthur K. Cebrowski, USN, and John J. Garstka, "Network-Centric Warfare, Its Origin and Future," *Proceedings of the U.S. Naval Institute*, Jan. 1998, p. 33. In Cebrowski's defense, he does at least argue for a bottom-up rather than a top-down approach to command and control. But in the world of economics, where he draws his examples, no one is trying to kill, maim, or mutilate his opponents. For a devastating reply, see Col. T. X. Hammes, USMC, "War Isn't A Rational Business," *Proceedings of the U.S. Naval Institute*, July 1998, pp. 22–25.

uncertainties will ostensibly disappear under the searching eye and superior capabilities of technology that provides U.S. forces with an ever greater flow of data and information.[42]

Finally, even some senior army officers display such faith in technology. Two years ago a senior army general announced to the students of the Marine War College that "the digitization of the battlefield means the end of Clausewitz"—in other words, computer technology and modern communications will remove fog and friction from the future battlefield, at least for American military forces. There is clearly a major struggle within the army at present between those who follow the technological line and those who adhere to a less mechanistic view of the world.

What makes this techno-craze so dangerous is that it flies in the face of 2,500 years of history, not to mention modern science. Friction, ambiguity, chance, and uncertainty are not merely manifestations of inadequate communications and technology that U.S. military organizations in the next century may overcome, but rather manifestations of the fundamental nature of the world, where if something can go wrong, it will.

> Consider, after all, how much would have to be overturned or rejected to conclude otherwise. Among other things, one would need to overthrow nonlinear dynamics, the second law of thermodynamics, the fundamental tenets of neo-Darwinian evolutionary biology, and all the limiting metatheorems of mathematical logic. . . . No small task indeed![43]

Another apparent weakness in the current military cultural climate—and one that certainly did not obtain in the interwar period—is the decline of professional military education, the subject of a devastating House Armed Services Committee report of the late 1980s. To be sure, the Naval War College remains the finest institution of its kind in the world, but unfortunately the navy still resolutely refuses to send its officers to school. Elsewhere, the fact that the National Defense University seriously considered getting rid of its entire civilian faculty so that it could finance the buying of sophisticated computers suggests a general disdain for serious military education among those heading such institutions. In fact, the inclinations within the world of professional military educa-

---

[42]Yet at the end of that war game, the navy's campaign had entirely failed to achieve the national objectives: despite massive bombardment by U.S. air power that destroyed the enemy's military forces and wrecked its country, the enemy remained defiant and unbroken. To learn how close to replicating the real world the war game was, see Anatol Lieven, *Chechnya, Tombstone of Russian Power* (New Haven, Conn.: Yale University Press, 1998).

[43]Barry D. Watts, *Clausewitzian Friction and Future War* (Washington, D.C.: National Defense University Press, 1996), p. 132.

tion reflect the attitudes of both the larger military culture and society: profoundly anti-intellectual and ahistorical.[44]

Only the Marine Corps has made a major, across-the-board effort to upgrade its entire educational system, with particular emphasis on the intellectual vitality of its officer corps outside the classroom. The commandant's professional reading list represents the most coherent and consistent effort to provide an intellectual compass that any service has ever possessed. Moreover, the marines take pains to insure that the books on the list are available in exchanges and libraries. Not surprisingly, the navy does not have a professional reading list, the air force's list is remarkable for its shortness and superficiality, and the army's list remains largely unavailable to its officer corps.

The area of military doctrine underlines to an even greater extent the disparity between the service cultures, and has proven a crucial enabler for military forces engaged in combat throughout this century. It has provided the basic framework for thinking seriously about the business of preparing for and conducting war. The navy has only recently created a doctrine command and until this summer it was led by a one-star admiral. In contrast, a four-star general has headed the army's Training and Doctrine Command since the 1970s. The air force has also devoted considerable resources to doctrine, but the results reflect a service with few interests outside of technology (and certainly not the study of war). Its new *Air Force Basic Doctrine* is long on pictures and short on content. In the doctrinal world its approach is close to that of "See Spot fly; see Jane bomb." And in case the reader is incapable of picking out the key points, they are italicized in blue.[45]

The army represents the most important service in terms of determining where the U.S. military will go in coming decades. The mid-1980s version of manual FM 100-5 was at the time the most realistic, Clausewitzian doctrine ever written by the American military. But a subsequent version published in the early 1990s was a far less satisfactory examination of war and

[44]See Williamson Murray, "Grading the War Colleges," *National Interest*, Winter 1986/1987, pp. 12–19; and Williamson Murray, "How Not to Advance Professional Military Education," *Strategic Review*, Summer 1997, pp. 73–77. For the current state of U.S. professional military education, see Lt. Gen. Leonard D. Holder Jr. and Williamson Murray, "Prospects for Military Education," *Joint Force Quarterly*, Spring 1998, pp. 81–90.

[45]U.S. Air Force, *Air Force Basic Doctrine, Air Force Doctrine Document 1*, Sept. 1997. Among the astonishing statements made in the manual is that decentralized command has not withstood the test of time.

military operations. There is now a very good new draft of FM 100-5 being considered and reviewed by the army, but there are indications that the draft, which represents a return to the serious-ness and focus of the 1986 version, has been withdrawn. How the debate within the army plays out will say a great deal about where its culture is headed.

Perhaps the most worrisome indications that all is not well with U.S. military culture are the publications that pass for the thinking done by the joint staff. Over the past decade the joint staff has published a whole set of doctrinal publications. For the most part these publications are harmless, except to those con-demned to read them. In their mind-numbing prose, their lack of any significant intellectual content, and their interminable laundry lists of bureaucratic concerns, they are best suited to insomniacs. They certainly do not provide much guidance to warfighters.[46] But more insidious has been the appearance of a "blueprint" for the U.S. military in the twenty-first century, published under the guid-ance of the joint staff. *Joint Vision 2010* supposedly provides "an operationally based template for the evolution of the armed forces for a challenging and uncertain future." Its intellectual value is virtually zero. One marine general accurately described it as a "collection of bumper stickers and advertising slogans."[47] The doc-ument posits four "emerging operational concepts: dominant maneuver, precision engagement, focused logistics, and full-dimension protection." These concepts are then tied together by information superiority to achieve "massed effects—full spectrum dominance." Not surprisingly, given the current civilian bosses in the Pentagon, the document is completely politically correct.[48] But what is really dangerous is that *JV2010* possesses a strong empha-sis on the top-down, mechanistic approach to war of the McNamara era. In effect, it represents the worst aspects of the French army's culture of the 1930s without the underpinnings of serious study that characterized the French in that period.

The one oasis in the desert that is military doctrine remains the Marine Corps. Its doctrinal manuals connect with the real world and to the fact that the American military is supposed to be

---

[46]To gain a sense of the joint doctrine, consult "Joint Doctrine, Capstone and Keystone Primer," July 15, 1997; Joint Pub 0-2, "Unified Action, Armed Forces," Feb. 24, 1995; and Joint Pub 3-0, "Doctrine for Joint Operations," Feb. 1, 1995.

[47]*Joint Vision 2010* (Washington, D.C., 1996), p. ii. Lt. Gen. Paul Van Riper, USMC (ret.), to the author in July 1997.

[48]For instance, "Commanders will be expected to reduce the cost of military opera-tions, from environmental disruption in training to collateral damage in combat." *JV2010*, p. 8. "Full spectrum" quote on p. 19.

preparing and thinking seriously about war.

> The essence of war is a violent struggle between two hostile, inde-
> pendent, and irreconcilable wills, each trying to impose itself on the
> other. . . . It is critical to keep in mind that the enemy is not an inani-
> mate object to be acted upon but an independent and animate force
> with its own objectives and plans.[49]

In every respect the series of common-sense, historically based publications that have followed *Warfighting* aim to give marines a realistic and intelligent understanding of war's uncertainties, ambiguities, and horror. They could provide a model for the other services and joint staff to think about war in the century ahead. Unfortunately, they will not—at least not as long as the dominant cultures in those services remain unchallenged and unchanged.

One of the dangerous aspects of the current cultures has been the growing propensity to shut down debate. The air force has traditionally been a service that aimed to speak with one voice and demanded that its officers submit their writings for policy review. The current situation with regards to the army is even more disturbing. The current draft of AR 600-20, "Army Command Guidance," clearly aims to shut off any hint of debate within the army. As a recent editorial in *Strategic Review* has noted, "in effect it proscribes an officer from even holding certain views which contravene official policy, much less from espousing them; it would cast those who even think of dissenting as belonging to extremist organizations."[50] It is well to remember that in the mid-1930s the French army commander in chief, General Maurice Gamelin, demanded that all officers submit their writings for review by the high command. "Everyone got the message," a junior officer later wrote, "and a profound silence reigned until the awakening of 1940."[51]

Conclusions

In a recent edition of *Army*, a senior officer commented about his service:

> As an institution, the Army finds itself so comfortable without
> debate, unconcerned that . . . "the Army goes rolling along." We

---

[49]*Warfighting*, pp. 1–2.
[50]Benjamin F. Schemmer, "Principled Disobedience," editorial, *Strategic Review*, Summer 1998, p. 3.
[51]André Beaufre, *1940: The Fall of France*, trans. Desmond Flower (New York: Alfred A. Knopf, 1968), p. 47.

should remember, however, that rolling along works best in one direction: downhill.[52]

The greatest danger for the United States in the coming century is that the American military will possess self-satisfied, intellectually stagnant cultures that believe they have found the technological lodestone.

Military cultures that remain enmeshed in the day-to-day tasks of administration, that ignore history and serious study, and allow themselves to believe that the enemy will possess no asymmetric responses are military organizations headed for defeat. Certainly in comparison to the thinking and atmosphere of the U.S. military in the last interwar period, the present picture suggests that there are major weaknesses in the current cultures. Consequently, any major efforts at military reform will founder unless they address fundamental problems to which there are no simple solutions. Moreover, any serious reforms can only have long-term results over decades, not months or even years. At least the United States is presently in a period of strategic quiescence and consequently possesses some time, that most precious of factors. But how much time, and how that time will be used, remain very much open to question.

Above all, the services need to practice some profound introspection, for unless they understand themselves and how different their world views are from those of the country's opponents in the next century, the United States is headed for a major crack-up that could prove even more disastrous than the Vietnam War. For at a minimum, notes an eminent military historian, American strategists

> must see clearly both themselves and potential adversaries, their strengths, weaknesses, preconceptions, and limits—through humility, relentless and historically informed critical analysis, and restless dissatisfaction even in victory. They must weigh imponderables through structured debates that pare away personal, organizational, and national illusions and conceits. They must unerringly discern and prepare to strike the enemy's jugular—whether by surprise attack or attrition, in war or in political and economic struggle. And in the end, makers of strategy must cheerfully face the uncertainties of decision and the dangers of action.[53]

There are few indications that the American military is capable at present of engaging the world in such terms.

[52]Col. David Fastebend, "Toning Down the Silence," letter to the editor, *Army*, July 1998, pp. 5–6.

[53]MacGregor Knox, "Continuity and Revolution in Strategy," in *The Making of Strategy, Rulers, States, and War*, ed. Williamson Murray and MacGregor Knox (Cambridge: Cambridge University Press, 1994), p. 645.

Must U.S. Military Culture Reform?

by John Hillen

Change is characteristic of military culture because of the many influences that constantly affect the values, behavior, and beliefs that together define it.[1] The proper question for debate is therefore not whether American military culture will change but rather *how* it should change in response to such pressures. To be more precise: What are the central tasks of the military? What legitimacy does it draw from founding documents and national laws? How does it reflect the culture of the society it serves? The answers to these questions form the context in which military culture evolves.

At the present time, a confluence of powerful and diverse imperatives is at work. Contemporary social mores and the end of the Cold War have combined to change the military's roles and missions, budgeting, organization, legal foundation, and internal disciplinary code, even as it is pushed and pulled according to political advocates' judgments as to the extent to which it should or should not reflect American society in general. (Table 1 illustrates the most important of these, listed in comparison to those of the Cold War era.) Yet within what General Douglas MacArthur once called "a welter of change and development," certain constants always apply lest U.S. military culture: (1) no longer effectively provide for the common defense; (2) lose the institutional "soul" rooted, as Don Snider suggests, in "warfighting"; or (3) accommodate demands for social change at the expense of the military's functional or legal imperatives.[2]

This panel examined all these pressures, and this report will explore all the challenges likely to shape American military culture in the future. But for several reasons the main focus here will be the social imperatives. That is because functional pressures, as

---

[1] This essay originally appeared in *Orbis*, Winter 1999, and arose from the Foreign Policy Research Institute conference "The End of American Military Culture," Philadelphia, Pa., July 15–16, 1998.

[2] See Nora Kinzer Stewart's fascinating sociological analysis of the dichotomy between the Argentine and British military cultures operating in the 1982 Falklands War, *Mates and Muchachos: Unit Cohesion in the Falklands/Malvinas War* (Washington, D.C.: Brassey's, 1991).

Williamson Murray demonstrates, can be generally understood through historical or strategic analysis, and are adapted to in "the light of day"—in clear cognizance of the strategic environment in which major policy decisions are taken. To be sure, policy decisions driving functional imperatives are always hotly debated, but all parties share a common determination to maximize U.S. security. Similarly, Congress may alter the legal imperatives of military culture at times, but it does so in order to provide better for the common defense. Social imperatives, conversely, can be profoundly "anti-functional" because they are not derived from security needs and can even at times be entirely divorced from them. Moreover, the imposition of certain social imperatives can undermine the ability of the military to carry out the tasks that alone justify its existence. At the same time, it must be said that armed forces in the service of a democracy must reflect to some degree the culture of the society they are sworn to defend. Therein lies the critical nexus of the debate. Exactly how does a military protect the professional culture necessary to perform its missions in the unnatural stresses of war within the legal prerogatives of its government, and yet remain responsive to and reflective of the civilian culture it serves?

Functional Imperatives

Edgar Schein, the eminent MIT organizational psychologist, states that "culture is what a group learns over a period of time as that group solves its problems of survival in an external environment and its problems of internal integration." The result of this process can ultimately be seen in the "three fundamental levels at which culture manifests itself: observable artifacts, values, and basic underlying assumptions."[3] It is useful in a discussion of changing military culture to focus on values, given the vogue in government and corporate worlds in the 1990s to define an organization's "core values." Military culture, or cultures, cannot be centered on values invented in the abstract.[4] All of the conference's contributors noted how the values underpinning the world's military cultures evolved throughout history in response to the needs of men attempting to succeed in combat, that is, as a result of occupational necessity. Quite simply, soldiers need codes of conduct, values, methods, procedures, and organizations characterized by what we might quaintly term the "military virtues,"

---

[3]Edgar H. Schein, "Organizational Culture," *American Psychologist*, Feb. 1990, p. 111.
[4]See Don M. Snider's essay "An Uninformed Debate on Military Culture" in this volume.

Table 1
Changing Pressures on Military Culture

	Cold War Military	Post–Cold War Military
FUNCTIONAL IMPERATIVES		
• **Strategic Focus**	• Major wars; emphasis on Soviet threat	• All manner of operations, especially peacekeeping; no overarching threat
• **Financial resources**	• Large (1960-90 average 7 percent of GDP)	• Small (by 2002, projected at less than 3 percent of GDP)
• **Personnel structure**	• Large conscript/ professional force, emphasizing ground troops	• Small professional force, far fewer ground troops
• **Technological orientation**	• Emphasis on ground operations, heavy firepower	• Emphasis on air and space operations, precision, computerization
• **Institutional icon**	• "Heroic" warrior (infantryman, fighter pilot)	• Peacekeeper, hacker, information manager?
LEGAL IMPERATIVES		
• **Documents defining and legitimizing roles**	• Constitution, statutes (Posse Comitatus Act)	• Constitution, statutes (Military Cooperation with Civilian Law Enforcement Agencies Act)
• **Legal code governing military personnel**	• Uniformed Code of Military Justice, etc., as changed by Congress or the Supreme Court	• Uniformed Code of Military Justice, etc., as "reshaped" by Executive Order
SOCIAL IMPERATIVES		
• **Women in combat**	• Rigid combat exclusion	• Almost all military specialties opened
• **Homosexuals in military**	• Not tolerated	• "Don't ask, don't tell"
• **Gender-integrated basic training**	• Air Force only (after 1974)	• Army, Navy, and Air Force
• **Interaction between civilian and military cultures**	• Cultures not as distinct; little pressure for complete uniformity	• Gap widens; pressure increases to bring military in line with civilian culture

including Duty, Honor, Patriotism, Courage, Discipline, Commitment, Strength, Integrity, Trust, and Resolve. While many other social, legal, psychological, and historical factors influenced the development of particular military cultures, for the most part the values of the military have been shaped by the unique requirements of its workplace, and the best test of a given military culture was whether its recruits could train and fight effectively, especially when they first came under fire.

It follows, therefore, that if you change the principal task for which the military prepares, you are bound to change the culture. Snider tells us rightly that "warfighting still determines the central beliefs, values, and complex symbolic formations that define military culture," raising the question of how our services might change if warfighting is no longer the primary mission. But in fact, the U.S. military throughout its history has been involved in many more Military Operations Other Than War (MOOTW) than in war itself.[5] Granted, many of these MOOTW had the general characteristics of war (as the old soldier's dictum goes, "there is no such thing as a low-intensity conflict if you're the guy on the ground"), but the post–Cold War shift in U.S. policy toward preparing for peacekeeping missions such as in Bosnia, Somalia, Haiti, and Rwanda will challenge a traditional military culture rooted in the heroic efforts of past wars.[6] Even the much ballyhooed "war on terrorism" shares more characteristics with law enforcement than traditional war. In this respect, the manifest cultural change in the Israeli Defense Force from that of 1948–82 (focused on external wars to defend the state) versus 1988–98 (focused on internal policing of the *intifada* and other security challenges within the state) is instructive.

The Kelly Flinn affair of 1997 and other sexual scandals revealed that many Americans seemed neither to understand nor to appreciate how and why military culture was special. Editorials and opinion columns ridiculed the military ethos as an archaic manifestation of a patriarchal institution. Civilian elites (including the conservative Senate majority leader) seemed not to grasp that the military is the way it is because of what it does and where and under what circumstances it does it. As Schein has noted, what you do forms who you are, what you value, and in what you

[5]There are over 250 instances of the use of U.S. armed forces abroad since 1798 and only five declared wars. Congressional Research Service Report no. 96-119F, "Instances of Use of U.S. Armed Forces Abroad, 1798–1995," Feb. 6, 1996.

[6]Panelist Deborah Avant competently explores many of these issues in *Political Institutions and Military Change: Lessons from Peripheral Wars* (Ithaca, N.Y.: Cornell University Press, 1994).

believe, and in Lieutenant Flinn's case the "what you do" entailed the dropping of bombs and missiles, possibly nuclear, in time of war. Despite the gravity of her profession, many letter writers to the *New York Times* and *Washington Post* appeared mystified that the U.S. Air Force would make a crime of widely accepted societal trespasses such as adultery, lying, and disobeying orders. This phenomenon represents the convergence of changing functional and social imperatives that challenge military culture today.

A second powerful functional imperative that determines military culture is the resources devoted to national defense. In 1998 the U.S. military establishment was funded at the lowest levels (as a percentage of both gross domestic product and the federal budget) since before Pearl Harbor. Social security, Medicare, other entitlement programs, and interest on the national debt all have a higher priority in the federal budget. Once the premier instrument of the state, the military has shrunk so considerably that in some ways its culture may revert to that of the small frontier forces of the nineteenth century. Moreover, personnel policy aims at just such a small professional force. Between 1940 and 1973 personnel policy was based on a large conscript force, and between 1973 and 1991 on a fairly large professional force. But the post–Cold War shrinkage not only alters U.S. military culture on its own account, it exacerbates the friction born of the new social imperatives.

Thirdly, the way in which a military is organized and conducts its missions has a profound influence on culture. Williamson Murray noted that traditionally the United States "has had its own military style" that emphasizes logistics, overwhelming superiority, and the application of technology to problems that other states might approach differently. In particular, technology has been a singularly seductive approach for the United States since the advent of the industrial age, and this cultural trait is even more prevalent today, not least due to the military's shrinking personnel base.[7]

It is helpful to understand this in the context of the institutional icon, that figure who seems to represent the beating heart of military culture. In the early industrial age, it was the infantryman or the fighter pilot—the heroic leader. In the nuclear age, with total war unthinkable, some military sociologists predicted a shift away from the heroic leader and toward the "modern military

[7]See also Williamson Murray, "Computers In, Clausewitz Out," *National Interest*, Summer 1997, pp. 57–69.

manager." Morris Janowitz, in his seminal work *The Professional Soldier*, wrote that the complex and largely bureaucratic nature of warfare in the nuclear age would require a sophisticated knowledge of strategic deterrence, military, industrial, and economic alliances, and political warfare designed to avoid absolute conflict. Janowitz saw a narrowing skill differential between military and civilian elites and noted that a complex and bureaucratic nuclear-age military would display an increasingly "civilian character."[8] But Janowitz's icon of the sophisticated manager was so tarnished by Robert McNamara's "whiz kids" and the failure of their systems-analysis approach in the jungles of Vietnam that the army and marines, especially, spent the 1970s and 1980s initiating programs to reinculcate "the warrior spirit" into their services' cultures.[9]

Who or what will be the institutional icon of the twenty-first century American military? Author James Adams, one of many who have written on the military implications of the digital age, sees the computer wizard as the new icon. He writes in his book *The Next World War* that "in the new world, the soldier will be the young geek in uniform who can insert a virus into Teheran's electricity supply to plunge the city into darkness."[10] As the "revolution in military affairs" seems to replace troops, tanks, ships, and planes with computers, unmanned aircraft, and satellites in the calculations of strategists, what Eliot Cohen has called "the geek-to-warrior ratio" will rise dramatically. Similarly, in the peacekeeping missions that have occupied America's military in the past few years, the most sought-after military specialists have been military policemen and civil-affairs officers, formerly peripheral players in supporting the institutional icons of the past. Rapid change in all these functional arenas—strategy, policy, resources, organization, and technology—will profoundly affect military culture.

Legal Imperatives

Though not discussed at length during the conference, legal imperatives are critical to military culture in that they establish the legitimacy for the existence and missions of the armed forces. Legal imperatives are rooted principally in the Constitution and

---

[8]Morris Janowitz, *The Professional Soldier: A Social and Political Portrait* (New York: Free Press, 1960), pp. 21–78.

[9]James Kitfield, *Prodigal Soldiers* (New York: Simon and Schuster, 1995); and Thomas Ricks, *Making the Corps* (New York: Simon and Schuster, 1997), chap. 4.

[10]James Adams, *The Next World War: Computers Are the Weapons and the Front Line is Everywhere* (New York: Simon and Schuster, 1998), p. 14.

various U.S. statutes that spell out the roles and missions of the military, as well as the separate legal codes by which the military governs itself. While the Constitution changes little, U.S. statutes concerning military missions have recently been amended. For instance, in the aftermath of the Gulf War, with global military threats much reduced, a movement arose on Capitol Hill, led by Senator Sam Nunn (D-Ga.) among others, to have the active-duty military assist in such domestic activities as the "war on drugs," civil order (as regular troops did during the Los Angeles riots of 1992), patrolling the border, and disaster relief. Some of these activities were in direct contravention of the Posse Comitatus Act that prohibits regular armed forces from assisting in civilian law enforcement. Momentum to amend that act began when Congress passed the Military Cooperation with Civilian Law Enforcement Agencies Act in 1981 to allow the military a much greater role in drug interdiction.

Nunn justified his proposals to use the military more in domestic missions by stating that the nation needed to take advantage of "the hardworking, disciplined men and women" of the armed forces. Similarly, Republican presidential candidates Robert Dole, Lamar Alexander, and Patrick Buchanan proposed in 1996 to use the military to seal porous U.S. borders and assist civilian agencies in drug interdiction. These proposals threatened in many ways the core function of the military, which in Huntington's words is "successful armed combat." Further attempts to amend legal imperatives face two challenges. First, they could well be counterproductive. The military is "hardworking and disciplined" precisely because it prepares with an uncommon sense of urgency for battlefield tasks that require those very attributes. If you remove the task, you remove the need for the culture underpinning those missions. There is a reason civilian law-enforcement agencies do not have the culture of the military—it is because of what they do (or, more precisely, what they do not do). Using the military to correct the failings of other institutions would cause military culture to atrophy, denying politicians the very instrument they hoped to use for domestic tasks.[11] More dangerous perhaps, as Charles Dunlap writes, is the possibility that the changing of legal imperatives toward domestic missions will undermine the civil-military balance and thrust the armed forces

---

[11]See John Hillen, "Don't Misuse the Armed Forces," *Investor's Business Daily*, Feb. 28, 1996.

into internal affairs in a corrosive way.[12]

Legal imperatives affecting military culture have also been under challenge as a result of the recent sexual episodes. In 1997–98, the secretary of defense convened a panel to investigate whether legal provisions concerning adultery and other offenses covered by the Uniformed Code of Military Justice should be revised in "recognition that, at least in some ways—the military world should not really be so different from the civilian."[13] The impetus for these sorts of legal proposals is discussed below. What should be recognized here is that the legal imperatives shaping what the military does and how it does it are subject to change and amendment through political intervention that may be very short-sighted.

Social Imperatives

Three distinct types of social imperatives have an impact on military culture. First, there are pressures from small but vocal constituencies seeking to use the military as a vehicle for social change, or even what Charles Moskos and others have called "social experimentation." Some observers believe that these activists seek not only to further their agendas via the military, but to destroy its prevailing culture in the process.[14] One is reminded of the gleeful pronouncement of Congresswoman Patricia Schroeder (D-Colo.) during the Tailhook investigation that the troubles of the navy represented "the sound of a culture cracking." Secondly, there are those military and public officials who abet the activists in the belief that functional imperatives have so changed the nature of war that the military can and perhaps should accommodate seemingly contradictory social imperatives. Other "accommodators" simply believe that many of the vestiges of military culture are overly authoritarian, masculine, or otherwise out of step with the times. Thirdly, some reformers stress social imperatives on the military in the belief that any severe gap between civilian and military culture bodes ill for a democracy. They would push the military to adopt contemporary values, patterns of behavior, and social mores on race, class, gender, and sexual orientation so as to close the gap. While the panel spent much time discussing all these issues, the last is the most recent and

---

[12]See Charles Dunlap, "The Origins of the American Military Coup of 2012," *Parameters*, Winter 1992–93, pp. 2–20.

[13]Steven Lee Myers, "Military Weighing Changes in Policy towards Adultery," *New York Times*, July 19, 1998.

[14]James Webb, "The War on the Military Culture," *Weekly Standard*, Jan. 20, 1997.

most potentially far reaching, and it is to that heated topic that this paper devotes the greatest attention.

The "Agenda Pushers"

The military, being a "top-down" institution driven by authoritarian dictates, is viewed by many as an ideal vehicle for imposing social change. President Truman recognized this when he fully integrated the armed forces in 1948 while much of the United States was still locked in a pattern of legal, systemic racial discrimination. The social imperatives pressuring the military today also derive from demands for equal opportunity—in this case, for women and homosexuals. Many of their advocates make no secret of their radical politics and aggressive agendas. Dr. Madeleine Morris, a Duke University law professor officially advising former secretary of the army Togo West on gender issues, wrote a 130-page law review article putting forward an "ungendered vision" of the military based in part on the model of Communist Party cells and proposed a plan for dismantling the "masculinist military construct" that encourages a "proclivity for rape."[15] This sort of unsubstantiated deconstructionist agitprop is taken seriously in much of the academic world and in activist circles, but had not previously penetrated the sober world of military policymaking.

By 1994, however, the equal opportunity agenda, informed by "analysis" such as that from Dr. Morris, had begun to have an impact on policy. Within eighteen months of President Clinton's election, several steps were taken that seriously challenged traditional military culture. In January 1994 Secretary of Defense Les Aspin announced that he was lifting long-standing exclusion rules and opening some 15,000 to 20,000 combat and near-combat positions to women.[16] By that time Clinton had acted on his long-standing campaign pledge to eliminate the prohibition against avowed homosexuals in the armed services. This controversial move was resisted by Chairman of the Joint Chiefs Colin Powell, among others, and resulted in the enigmatic and legally ambiguous "don't ask, don't tell" compromise. Finally, although it had been tried and deemed to have failed in the 1980s, the army and navy reintroduced sexually integrated basic training. A series of embarrassing and highly publicized incidents soon occurred,

[15]Elaine Donnelly, "Social Fiction in the Ungendered Military," *Washington Times*, Apr. 7, 1997.
[16]See Eric Schmitt, "Aspin Moves to Open Many Military Jobs to Women," *New York Times*, Jan. 14, 1994.

sparking a national scandal worthy of investigation by two blue-ribbon congressional panels in 1997 and 1998.[17]

While the military conference panel discussed these issues at length, some participants took the position that the equal-opportunity changes thrust on the military do not constitute the greater problem. To them, the pressing worry is that the military might accommodate these changes by compromising its standards and the cultural values it thought necessary to meet its functional challenges. In other words, the cultural angst experienced by the military in accommodating these imperatives was somewhat self-inflicted.

The "Accommodators"

If women in combat, homosexuals in the military, or coeducational basic training damage traditional military culture, that damage would most likely be manifested in lesser cohesion in combat units (traditionally based on small-group dynamics among males), privacy concerns, and increased incidences of sexual misbehavior. As Mackubin Owens has written, these phenomena represent friction in the classic Clausewitzian sense. Both he and Don Snider note that military culture is formed precisely to overcome friction, especially in times of greatest stress.[18] However, the sources of friction normally cited in critiques of these social experiments are the double standards, reduced standards, less rigorous training, indiscipline, and reduced readiness derived from the need to accommodate females in the ranks. For instance, the report of the Commission on Gender Integrated Training led by former senator Nancy Kassebaum Baker focused most of its criticisms of gender-integrated basic training on the latter category of problems. That being the case, the panel suspected that the disingenuous way in which the military was accommodating the social imperatives was more problematic than the imperatives themselves. For instance, the army has known for a decade that women tend to quit basic training at a rate almost twice that of men. But rather than accepting that as the price of maintaining high standards in a demanding environment, the army lowered its standards so as to "gender-norm" the numbers. Panel members provided numerous other examples of this sort of appeasement, drawn from the Kassebaum

[17]See James Anderson, "Boot Camp or Summer Camp? Restoring Rigorous Standards to Basic Training," *Heritage Foundation Backgrounder*, no. 1147 (Nov. 6, 1997).

[18]See Mackubin Thomas Owens, "It's Time to Face the Gender Parodox," *Naval Institute Proceedings*, July 1998, pp. 43–49.

Baker commission and other official studies.[19]

Clearly the pressure on the military to make these social experiments "work" reveals that the U.S. military and America's political system are not mature enough to handle "gender and sexual orientation issues" honestly and in ways that are fair to the institution as well as the individuals involved. Political and military leaders seem convinced that American society, and therefore its military, must inevitably progress on a path leading to a social order in which gender is physically and behaviorally irrelevant, in which sex and sexual orientation have no impact, and in which teenagers view each other according to a benign and respectful androgyny. This new orthodoxy is a purely social construct without any functional imperative and was justified, in the words of accommodationist Les Aspin, simply because it "is the right thing to do."[20] Three years after Aspin's decisions, when independent commissions and numerous reports found the military compromised and suffering from the way in which these changes were imposed, the majority of uniformed and political leaders continue to support social imperatives at the clear expense of functional ones and resort to Orwellian phraseology in their attempts to defend their new regime against the truth.[21] While many uniformed leaders showed great courage in their battlefield exploits to turn back the nation's enemies, they seem petrified before activists who might accuse them of "turning back the clock."

To say that the battlefield imposes its own timeless logic, including a viciously impartial meritocracy, would seem to be a simple enough proposition. But in times of peace it can be overwhelmed by social imperatives pressed by activists with a larger agenda, which accommodators in turn accept as "the will of the people."[22] Thus, a recent statement from the army's leadership that "any proposal that calls for gender segregation of both trainees and cadre violates the very foundation of the Army" led one incredulous observer to ask, "Which foundation is that? Winning wars for our nation; the will to win; 'Duty, Honor, Country'; 'There is no substitute for victory'? What specific foundation was the Army leadership referring to?"[23]

[19]Elaine Donnelly, Testimony to the House National Security Subcommittee on Personnel, Mar. 17, 1998 (http://www.house.gov/hasc/testimony/105thcongress/3-17-98donnelly.htm).

[20]Schmitt, "Aspin Moves."

[21]Rowan Scarborough, "Did the Army Tell House to Buzz Off?" *Washington Times*, Aug. 31, 1998.

[22]In fact, all these recent changes were imposed by executive order, not congressional statutes.

[23]Col. (ret.) Michael D. Mahler, "Has the Army Lost Its Way?" *Army*, May 1998, p. 57.

The "Close the Gappers"

In the past few years, it has become accepted and widely reported that a gap is growing between American society and the U.S. military. For the most part, however, these warnings pertained to those official relationships between political leaders making defense policy and uniformed military leaders in the Pentagon.[24] The civil-military gap as then portrayed was manifest only within the government, and mostly at its highest levels. However, since 1996, the focus of concern over this gap has broadened, and public conversation has recently magnified the gap into a "nearly unbridgeable cultural divide" between American society in general and the U.S. military establishment.[25] Dire warnings over the consequences of this gap have caused many policymakers automatically to assume that its very existence is fundamentally unhealthy in a democracy. Hence, their alarmist cries to close the gap.[26] Civilian defense officials such as Secretary of Defense William Cohen have made "reconnecting the military to society" a top priority, and prominent veterans such as Senator John McCain have publicly worried about a professional U.S. military estranged from society.[27]

Whether politically motivated by the "agenda pushers" or not, there is now an inexorable momentum to close the gap between the military and society without clearly identifying the nature of the gap, the extent to which it might in fact be healthy and desirable, or how such a gap might be narrowed. So instead of reasoned study and judgment, we witness a series of *a priori* assumptions to the effect that there is a fundamental, corrosive gap between the military and society, and that no democracy can tolerate a military whose culture does not mirror that of civil society. Moreover, it goes without saying that under the new dispensation, if society or the military must move to accommodate the cultural norms of the other, it will be the military that is pressured to lower its standards, not society to raise civilian behavior. Finally, since no criteria establishing an "acceptable" gap have been articulated, the military will likely be under pressure to close the gap entirely, what-

---

[24]See, for instance, Richard Kohn, "Out of Control: The Crisis in Civil-Military Relations," *National Interest*, Spring 1994, pp. 3–17, and the responses to his essay in the following issue of that journal.

[25]James Kitfield, "Standing Apart," *National Journal*, June 13, 1998, pp. 1350–58. See also Thomas Ricks, "The Widening Gap Between the Military and Society," *Atlantic Monthly*, July 1997, pp. 66–78.

[26]See Congressman Ike Skelton, "Close the Gap between Military and Civilian America," *Association of the United States Army News*, July 1996, p. 7.

[27]Kitfield, "Standing Apart," pp. 1355, 1357.

ever ruin this may visit on the culture, ethos, and value system that justify its existence.

A gap between civilian and military culture does exist. It always has and always will so long as American society remains as it has been since 1865: a relatively unthreatened polity focused almost exclusively on the "pursuit of happiness" while its military is responsible for acting outside America's borders to preserve that basic condition.[28] The cultural gap between the two entities is not necessarily dangerous to American democracy in and of itself, but can and should exist so the military can accommodate both the society it protects and the battlefield on which it must perform. On the one hand, closing the gap for the sole sake of accommodating social imperatives can only betray the military's ability to meet the uncompromising needs of its mission. On the other hand, the gap can become problematic for civil-military relations if the military swings in the other direction and answers solely to the battlefield without being cognizant of and responsive to the mores and values of society at large.

To many observers, the values and social mores of 1990s America—narcissistic, morally relativist, self-indulgent, hedonistic, consumerist, individualistic, victim-centered, nihilistic, and soft—seem hopelessly at odds with those of traditional military culture.[29] Critics ranging from Soviet dissident Aleksandr Solzhenitsyn to pollster Daniel Yankelovich have warned of what William Bennett calls a "palpable culture decline" and "marked shift in the public's beliefs, attitudes, and priorities."[30] Even Garry Trudeau's characters in the comic strip *Doonesbury* poke fun at the nihilism of *Seinfeld*, saying the television show was "the last gasp of a self-centered, dysfunctional, arrested generation choking on the banal, irony-soaked detritus of its own popular culture . . . not that there's anything wrong with that."[31]

Clearly, American society today finds classic military values increasingly foreign. The Marine Corps instituted an extra week of recruit training focused on values precisely because the "raw

[28]See Benjamin R. Barber, *Jihad vs. McWorld* (New York: Ballantine Books, 1995) for an interesting extrapolation of this phenomenon. As writer Ralph Peters has said, in the twenty-first century America is likely to be "fat, smart, and happy" while its soldiers police the fringes of its empire to keep the conflicts that have plagued Africa, the Balkans, and the Middle East as far from public concern as possible (comment to conference audience, U.S. Army War College, Carlisle Barracks, Pa., April 1998).

[29]See especially Robert Hughes, *Culture of Complaint* (New York: Warner Books, 1993); and Robert Bork, *Slouching Towards Gomorrah* (New York: HarperCollins, 1996).

[30]William J. Bennett, *The Index of Leading Cultural Indicators* (New York: Simon and Schuster, 1994), p. 9.

[31]Garry Trudeau, *Doonesbury*, Universal Press Synicate, Apr. 29, 1998.

product" the corps was getting from society was of a different (read: lower) standard insofar as values were concerned.[32] The gap is a recurring theme in the recent book *Making the Corps*, by conference panelist Thomas Ricks.[33] As Ricks notes throughout his story of Marine Corps basic training, the values of contemporary society are the opposite of those needed to succeed in the unequivocal business of war: "Parris Island is the first place many of them encounter absolute and impersonal standards of right and wrong, of success and failure." The cultural juxtaposition of values in American society at large versus those in the Marine Corps manifests itself almost every day in the training of Ricks's platoon. One drill instructor, a former gang member from Los Angeles, testifies that "the Marine Corps taught me values—not just words. Honor, courage, commitment. Fidelity. Integrity. Not just using them, but actually practicing them. Out in the civilian world, those words don't even get mentioned. I'll say, 'Integrity,' and they'll say 'What kind of shit you talking? You done got brainwashed in the Marine Corps.'"

Do these and similar vignettes prove an "unbridgeable cultural divide"? Ricks believes that in a democratic society it is dangerous for a professional military to differ sharply from the society it defends, since a military that holds civil society in contempt might cease to behave as its servant. Former assistant secretary of the army Sarah Lister publicly called the marines "extremists" for standing out so differently from society. But where Ricks intimates that it would be better for society to adopt some Marine Corps values, Lister clearly wants the marines to move toward civilian values.

Gap-closing, however, is a false game. We should accept the fact that military and society can coexist and complement each other despite different values. For, elite opinion and advocacy groups notwithstanding, the American people as a whole appreciate traditional military culture.[34] To the extent that there is a worrisome gap between civilian and military cultures, it is one of shared experience, understanding, and appreciation—especially among elite segments of American society and the military. The House of Representatives had 320 veterans in 1970, but fewer than 130 in 1994. Moreover, in 1997, for the first time ever, nei-

---

[32]See John Hillen, "Teaching Values to Beavis and Butthead," *Navy Times*, Dec. 15, 1997.

[33]All of the following quotes are from Ricks, *Making the Corps*.

[34]John Hillen, "They'll Leave the Farm Once They've Seen Parris," *American Enterprise*, May/June 1998, pp. 82–83.

ther the secretary of defense, the national security advisor, the secretary of state, nor any of their deputies had ever been in uniform.[35] As Senator Charles Robb noted, "with less interaction between the civilian and military cultures, we're going to have progressively less understanding of one another."[36] This gap is a function of demographics, strategy, defense spending, and military policy. Changes in any of those variables (such as the end of the draft in 1973 or the decline in post–Cold War defense spending) will profoundly affect the magnitude and nature of civil-military interaction. There certainly is a cultural gap, but it is not one of diametrically opposed values. Much as many other professional cultures differ from each other (imagine, for instance, lawyers and doctors), military culture will differ from that of society at large.

The Danger in Closing the Gap

There are, of course, profound dangers for civil-military relations if the military is so different from society that it holds itself above society and unaccountable to those it serves. The symptoms, pointed out by Richard Kohn and others, are disrespect and unresponsiveness on the part of the military to civilian leaders, elements that in other countries have led to military coups. No panelists felt there was a threat of that in America, however. More likely, the gap in shared experience, understanding, and appreciation could result at the political level in an "over or under propensity to use force, civilian operational meddling, inadequate support of the military, or the imposition of policies destructive of military culture."[37] At the societal level, it could result in a sense among soldiers and civilians that they have separate fortunes, as when Prussian citizens in 1806 considered that the army, not Prussia, much less themselves, had been "defeated" by Napoleon, whereupon Prussian leaders recognized that a "gulf existed between the state machine and the . . . people."[38] However, if the military socializes its culture at the expense of functional imperatives, it can fail in the most critical way—in war. Both the initial failure of American troops in Korea in 1950 and the sorry state of

---

[35]*VFW Magazine*, Feb. 1997, p. 15. See also Mark Shields, "When Heroes Were Ordinary Men," *Washington Post*, Aug. 3, 1998.

[36]Kitfield, "Standing Apart," p. 1354.

[37]See Peter Feaver, "Officers as Citizens: Politically Insulated? Politically Diverse?" presentation to the McCormick Tribune Foundation's Soldiers and Citizens Conference, Chicago, May 1, 1998.

[38]See Gordon A. Craig, *Politics of the Prussian Army* (London: Oxford University Press, 1955).

the military in the mid-1970s have been traced in part to attempts by the military to mirror prevailing civilian culture too closely. Regarding the Korean debacle, which he blamed on the social imperatives behind the Doolittle reforms of 1945, historian T. R. Fehrenbach wrote that "in 1945, somehow confusing the plumbers with the men who pulled the chain, the public demanded that the Army be changed to conform with decent, liberal society."[39] The changes did not appear to have detrimental effects on the U.S. military forces because "the troops looked good. Their appearance made the generals smile. What they lacked couldn't be seen, not until the guns sounded."

In the aftermath of the disaster, Fehrenbach angrily wrote that "liberal society, in its heart, wants not only domination of the military, but acquiescence of the military toward the liberal view of life. But acquiescence society may not have, if it wants an army worth a damn. . . . Society's purpose is to live; the military's is to stand ready, if need be, to die." Similarly, attempts by the military in the mid-1970s to recruit an all-volunteer force from a society still nursing the counterculture and Vietnam syndrome led to a dramatic weakening of standards.[40] General Walter "Dutch" Kerwin was one who resisted, writing in the 1970s that "the values necessary to defend the society are often at odds with the values of the society itself. To be an effective servant of the people, the Army must concentrate not on the values of our liberal society, but on the hard values of the battlefield." Kerwin made headway: the army dropped the accommodating "We Want the Army to Join YOU!" in favor of the challenge "Be All That You Can Be." But today, several panelists think, American society has come full circle, displaying another identity crisis, while the military, facing recruiting and retention problems, is again trying hard to look like society. Political leaders of both parties press the military to "get with it" and conform to prevailing civilian values. Thus, the army, in its never-ending effort to sell itself in the absence of conscription, stresses such incentives as financial benefits, training, and job security, as if the army were a sort of high school with a salary and fresh air. Nevertheless, enlistments decline and the army is having to accept enlistees who would have been turned away five years ago. And thanks to the trend toward feminization, the army is losing Hispanic recruits to the Marine Corps, which alone satis-

---

[39]T. R. Fehrenbach, *This Kind of War: Korea, a Study in Unpreparedness* (New York: Macmillan, 1963), p. 467.

[40]See John Hillen, "The Military Culture Wars," *Weekly Standard*, Jan. 12, 1998.

fies their pursuit of *machismo*.[41] Indeed, the Marine Corps still sells itself not as a place to work, but as a place to grow in honor, courage, and commitment—values little taught or even respected in much of civilian society. Small wonder that Thomas Ricks found some new marines contemptuous of the society whence they came after meeting the uncompromised standards of boot camp. They had achieved genuine self-actualization, not the feel-good therapy of victimhood.

The perceived importance of answering to social imperatives often leads to the compromise of proven military standards. In those cases, as Mackubin Owens has suggested, "the danger to the republic does not arise from any military threat to liberal American society, but from the reverse: the civilianization of the U.S. military ethos."[42] One wonders whether the Marine Corps and the shrinking combat elements of the other services can hold out against the relentless onslaught of social-advocacy groups. And as Fehrenbach noted in his day, modern proponents of traditional military culture cannot even look with certainty to the Pentagon or Capitol Hill for allies.

Conclusion

Social and functional imperatives are often inherently contradictory. The civil culture of a liberal democracy pulls the military one way, while the hierarchy of values needed to succeed in the unnatural stresses of war pulls it another way. The gap between the military and American society varies according to the balance between these imperatives. Currently, many people think that the gap is too large and needs to be closed. I argue instead that the gap is a fact of life: it should not be closed, indeed it cannot be closed, but managed. Such management is difficult and takes political courage of a high order, especially in a liberal society during peacetime. Unfortunately, the peacetime "default solution," the path of least resistance for the military, is just to abandon many tenets of its traditional culture and surrender to society at large. The result is that social imperatives are imposed at the expense of functional imperatives, introducing a possibly calamitous confusion between means and ends. If the purpose of having a military establishment in the first place is to promote cozy civil-military

---

[41]Thomas E. Ricks, "Army Faces Recruiting Obstacle: Less Macho Image," *Wall Street Journal*, July 15, 1997.

[42]Mackubin Thomas Owens, "American Society and the Military: Is There a Gap?" *Providence Journal*, Mar. 27, 1998.

relations, then military culture should be forcibly brought into line with civilian culture. If, however, the purpose of having a military is to provide for the common defense, then the military must nurture the unique culture developed for that purpose. "Different, but not separate" must be the slogan guiding an effort that keeps the military responsive to society without ruining its functionally unique culture. In the 1950s, '60s, and '70s, military sociologists such as Huntington, Janowitz, Finer, and others helped to delineate the boundaries that make for healthy relations between the military and society. But they were addressing the challenges of a large conscript army during the Cold War, a genuine national emergency. In the absence of up-to-date and reasoned criteria for maintaining healthy civil-military relations in a time of peace, we are confronted by the simple demand to "Close the gap!" Thus, Senator McCain has said, "It's a fundamental principle that armed services can truly serve a democracy only if they are a reflection of that society and are impacted by the same social trends."[43] But what exactly does that mean? If society is "slouching towards Gomorrah," must the military slouch along with it? Should it go just part of the way—softening rigid codes of conduct but maintaining enough discipline and order to keep the problems that infect greater society at bay? It would be hard to imagine the ex-POW McCain approving of a military shaped by the same narcissism, relativism, and "culture of complaint" that social critics tell us characterize American society today. And yet Secretary of the Navy John Dalton said in July 1994 that "as American society changes, the Naval service changes with it. That's not bad—that's the way it's supposed to be."

The question policymakers should be asking is not "How can we close the gap?" but rather "What is the cost of closing the gap?" And the answer is that sooner or later the cost will be measured in the security and well-being of the *civilian* culture which the military is mustered to defend. The military cannot, of course, violate the legal imperatives that influence its culture—they are nonnegotiable. Likewise, the military dare not violate its functional imperatives lest it lose its country's wars. Therefore, if contradictions exist among the various imperatives that shape military culture, it is the social ones that the brass must find the courage to "stiff-arm." There are many today who insist that America fix the "gap" problem by abandoning the military's functional and legal imperatives in order to accommodate societal pressures. But for anyone with the least historical sensibilities, that notion is simply preposterous.

THE CASE FOR NATIONAL MISSILE DEFENSE

by Keith B. Payne

After spending more than $70 billion over three decades on more or less urgent research and development, the United States appears finally to be moving toward the deployment of a ballistic missile defense (BMD) system.[1] It will consist of interceptor missiles and sensors designed to protect all fifty states from a small long-range ballistic missile attack. Such a system, now called National Missile Defense (NMD), has been the subject of fierce debate in Washington in three distinct periods: first in the late 1960s and early 1970s, again in the latter half of the 1980s, and finally since the mid-1990s.

Of these three debates, the most heated polemics followed Ronald Reagan's 1983 announcement of the Strategic Defense Initiative (or SDI, pejoratively dubbed "Star Wars" by Senator Edward Kennedy). The SDI debate, however, did little more than restate the positions for and against NMD that had first been raised during the earlier debate of the 1960s, and both those debates concluded with decisive policy decisions against NMD deployment. Although a decision for NMD appeared plausible at various points during those years, the political consensus necessary for deployment could not be sustained. Throughout this thirty-year period, therefore, the United States consciously chose not to deploy NMD, preferring instead to rely almost exclusively on deterrence to protect the American people against the threat of intercontinental missile attack.

In contrast, the current NMD debate, ongoing since the mid-1990s, contains many important new elements and appears to be concluding with a political consensus in favor of deployment. The 1999 National Missile Defense Act, backed by majorities in the Senate and the House and signed by President Clinton, states that it is U.S. policy to deploy NMD "as soon as technologically possible." As a reflection of this new political consensus, President

[1]This essay originally appeared in *Orbis*, Spring 2000, and arose from the Foreign Policy Research Institute conference "America the Vulnerable: Three Threats and What to Do about Them," Philadelphia, Pa., Oct. 7–8, 1999.

Clinton or his successor is likely to move forward with a decision for NMD deployment.

The defeat of NMD proponents in the past was self-inflicted to a considerable extent. They continually fought the fiercest battles against one another and frequently failed even to rebut the standard and by now tired ideological arguments against NMD. The modus operandi of NMD proponents was, and largely remains, to pour their energies into political battle against any but their own favored NMD concept—oblivious to the fact that the policy war for any sort of NMD deployment was yet to be won. The result was that no NMD program could survive the gauntlet of critics.

Why is it that NMD finally seems ready to become a reality, and why is it happening now? Neither the Reagan nor Bush administration was able to establish the necessary consensus, and the Clinton administration clearly has shown little sympathy for NMD deployment, giving ground to Congress only grudgingly. Indeed, opposition to NMD has been a core element of the Clinton administration's ideology. In 1993, for example, it shut down discussions with Russia on the subject of cooperative NMD deployment that had made rapid progress during the final year of the Bush administration (the Ross-Mamedov talks). It then proceeded to cut, revise, and rename SDI, shifting it away from NMD and toward theater missile defense (TMD, the defense of overseas allies and U.S. expeditionary forces sent abroad). How could it happen, then, that during the final months of the Clinton administration a political consensus in favor of NMD deployment emerged, and that Washington is close to a decision for at least some protection of American cities?

Several developments converged at the end of the century to create momentum in favor of NMD sufficiently strong to gain the support of the majority in Congress and to overcome the Clinton administration's ideological opposition. These developments include the changed nature of the ballistic missile threat, corresponding changes in American goals and technical requirements, changes in thinking about the effectiveness of deterrence, and a serious reconsideration of the 1972 Antiballistic Missile (ABM) Treaty that severely constrained BMD deployments. Together, these interrelated developments have produced a working consensus in favor of NMD deployment where, alone, none would have sufficed, a fact illustrated by a comparison of the present NMD debate with those of the past.

Offense Is Defense and Vice Versa

Previous NMD debates occurred during the Cold War and understandably focused on the U.S.-Soviet balance. To risk understatement, the Soviet long-range missile arsenal constituted a formidable technical challenge for NMD. Armed with over 9,000 strategic nuclear warheads by the late 1980s, the Soviet Union posed an enormous threat. Effective NMD protection for American cities against a deliberate Soviet attack, if feasible, would have required a huge and expensive NMD system. That in itself was sufficient to limit support for the program, particularly within the military and Congress.

Given the cost and technical challenges confronting a system intended to protect cities from Soviet missile attack, most NMD proponents, including Reagan administration officials, quickly retreated to the less ambitious goal of protecting not the population, but U.S. strategic retaliatory capabilities against a Soviet nuclear first strike. This goal certainly appeared affordable and technically feasible, and made sense from the perspective of strategy. But it lacked the necessary political appeal to galvanize support, and there was no obvious and immediate need for missile defense to protect U.S. strategic forces. According to critics, U.S. strategic forces already were protected adequately, and arms control was the preferred method for further reducing the Soviet first-strike threat. In short, given the nature of the Soviet threat, President Reagan's goal of protecting people was undercut politically by the apparent expense and technical challenge, while the more obviously attainable NMD goal of protecting strategic forces appeared to lack urgency.

In addition, Washington had come to rely quite comfortably on nuclear deterrence as the proper way to address the Soviet missile threat. Over the decades of the Cold War, prominent military and civilian officials had generally come to believe that deterrence, if managed properly, was a reliable tool for preventing Soviet missile attack. Why pay more for missile defense if deterrence provides protection? NMD was contrary to the prevailing theory of deterrence, commonly known as Mutual Assured Destruction (MAD), which positively relied on the mutual vulnerability of the United States and Soviet Union to prevent a nuclear holocaust. Washington had become accustomed to spending considerable resources on offensive forces to maintain its side of the mutual vulnerability stalemate. Any threat to mutual vulnerability, but particularly that posed by NMD, was considered "destabilizing."

Indeed, the ABM Treaty, the "crown jewel of arms control," was presented to the Senate for ratification as the codification of the "stability" supposedly guaranteed via mutual vulnerability.

As a result, NMD for the purpose of defending American cities faced a triple challenge: prevailing wisdom about the effectiveness of deterrence suggested that NMD was unnecessary; the particular approach to deterrence that dominated U.S. thought specifically identified NMD as a threat to "stability"; and after 1972, U.S. NMD programs came up against the ABM Treaty and thus the vested interests of Washington's arms-control lobby. Consequently, NMD proponents not only had to battle politically with the usual arms controllers and opponents of military spending, they were also frequently at odds with the proponents of America's strategic nuclear deterrent. In short, NMD faced severe critics on the Left and the Right, hardly a favorable position from which to build a political consensus supporting NMD deployment. The changed circumstances attending the end of the Cold War, however, have made the rationale for NMD deployment persuasive to many past foes, and all but the most doctrinaire critics now acknowledge, at least in principle, a potentially useful role for NMD.

What factors have led to this dramatic change in the prospects for NMD? First, the ballistic missile threat against which NMD now is expected to play is not remotely comparable to that of the Soviet Union. The Soviet Union is mercifully gone and the probability of a deliberate missile attack from Russia generally is considered to be very low. The sources of concern today are "rogue states" such as North Korea, Iraq, and Iran, which are openly hostile to the United States and intent on acquiring long-range missiles to deliver weapons of mass destruction (WMD). Their prospective arsenals of long-range missiles, however, are likely to remain relatively modest for decades, so U.S. NMD programs need only to neutralize missiles numbering in the dozens as opposed to the thousands. This reduction in threat has gone far to ease concerns over cost and technical feasibility. Even organizations that in the past argued vociferously against SDI, such as the Arms Control Association, have acknowledged that defending against a limited rogue missile threat is practicable. Likewise, where cost estimates for an NMD addressing the Soviet missile threat ranged in the hundreds of billions of dollars, systems designed to counter the rogue missile threat run at most to the few tens of billions as projected by the Congressional Budget Office (never known for having sympathies for NMD). Finally, several successful interceptor tests have recently provided some empirical evidence that defense against a small missile threat is well within America's technical and financial reach.

Even the controversy surrounding the pace of the emerging rogue missile threat to the United States has contributed to the consensus in favor of NMD. At first, National Intelligence Estimate 95-19 appeared to place a serious obstacle in NMD's path. In the midst of the 1996 congressional and White House wrangling over missile defense, the intelligence community publicly released to NMD opponents in the Senate its conclusions concerning the missile threat to the United States: there would be no new missile threats to the continental United States for at least fifteen years. Curiously, this intelligence estimate ignored the two states, Alaska and Hawaii, closest to North Korea, but its conclusion nevertheless dampened any sense of urgency for NMD deployment. Senior military and civilian leaders disposed to view NMD unfavorably now could point to the absence of any threat in their arguments against it.[2] Russian officials, always eager to steer Washington away from NMD, similarly pointed to America's own intelligence estimate to challenge the officially declared "rogue rationale" for NMD and to charge that renewed interest in it was part of an American conspiracy to destroy Russia. In this context, President Clinton and Senate Democrats were able to head off serious movement toward NMD deployment in 1996–97.

However, the congressional response to this intelligence estimate was to establish a bipartisan, blue-ribbon commission to reexamine the emerging missile threat to the United States. The commission's mandate was simply to assess potential threats, not to make any recommendations on how they might be addressed. Chaired by Donald Rumsfeld, the widely respected former secretary of defense, the commission issued its public report in July 1998. The "Rumsfeld Report" was a dramatic rebuke to the intelligence community's earlier benign forecast. It identified several potential near-term rogue missile threats and pointed to serious methodological problems with the previous sanguine forecasts. As if on cue, on August 31, 1998, the North Koreans tested a three-stage missile reportedly with enough potential range to target portions of the United States. The fact that the North Korean test came as an admitted surprise to the intelligence community effec-

---

[2]See, for example, Gen. Henry Shelton's statements in Rowan Scarborough, "Chiefs Defend Stand on Missiles," *Washington Times*, Aug. 27, 1998.

tively underscored the Rumsfeld Commission's rebuke and left some senior military and civilian leaders embarrassed.

The intelligence community quickly revised its earlier "fifteen-year rule." Indeed, most recently the National Intelligence Council released an unclassified report forecasting that North Korea would indeed pose a near-term missile threat to the United States, and that within fifteen years Iran (probably) and Iraq (possibly) would also pose missile threats.

It is difficult to exaggerate the impact that the Rumsfeld Commission had on the NMD debate in Washington. It validated beyond reasonable doubt the new threat that NMD was to address. North Korea's missile test led even a member of the commission to remark that its conclusions had been overly optimistic. The subsequent change in the tone of the debate was immediate and dramatic. Prior to the commission's report, NMD opponents, including senior political appointees in the Department of Defense, could and did tar as naive or extremist those who expressed concern about a near-term rogue missile threat. After the report and the North Korean test, it was the opponents of NMD who appeared naive.

Deterrence Theory Dethroned

A new perspective on the reliability of deterrence also helped to move Washington toward a consensus on NMD. It may appear that a subject as seemingly esoteric as deterrence theory could have little impact on Washington's rough-and-tumble NMD debates. And, in fact, most theoretical discussions of deterrence will frighten away any audience, military or civilian, whatever its view of NMD. Nevertheless, there has always been a significant link between confidence in deterrence and opposition to NMD. Unfortunately for NMD prospects, part of American strategic culture for decades has been great overconfidence in Washington's mastery of deterrence theory, particularly nuclear deterrence. During debates in the 1960s and 1980s, for example, the assumed effectiveness of deterrence was presented as reason enough for rejecting NMD. In short, it is better to deter than to defend, particularly when we know how to deter but not how to defend. Although such confidence in deterrence is folly, it has until recently been a matter of conventional wisdom in Washington.[3]

---

[3]See, for example, George Lewis, Lisbeth Gronlund, and David Wright, "National Missile Defense: An Indefensible System," *Foreign Policy*, Winter 1999–2000, pp. 120–37.

This faith in deterrence was again trotted out to shoot down NMD during the debate of the 1990s. NMD opponents argued that since deterrence never failed throughout the entire Cold War, Washington's mastery of that approach was proven, hence the absence of any compelling need for missile defense. For example, Jan Lodal, a senior Clinton appointee in the Pentagon, made the following claim in 1995: "Nuclear deterrence worked throughout the Cold War, it continues to work now, it will work into the future. . . . The exact same kinds of nuclear deterrence calculations that have always worked will continue to work."[4] Some opponents of NMD took the theology of deterrence to an absurd level in their efforts to denigrate the rationale for NMD. For example, Spurgeon Keeny, executive director of the Arms Control Association, claimed, "Even fanatical, paranoid regimes are deterred by the prospect of catastrophic consequences."[5]

Such vain assertions, however, make the mistake of viewing the practice (as opposed to the theory) of deterrence as relatively simple and predictable. In fact, deterrence frequently is difficult or impossible in practice.[6] Beyond the presence of a fearsome threat, its success requires a variety of contextual conditions that generally pertained to U.S.-Soviet relations during much of the Cold War but are far from ubiquitous. These include well-informed decision makers, a prevalent rationality on both sides, a degree of mutual familiarity, effective channels of communication, and leaders who are sensitive to cost and risk. Because these conditions did generally obtain in U.S.-Soviet relations, Cold War–vintage discussions of deterrence simply came to assume their presence. Consequently, deterrence calculations became a deceptively simple matter of posing a severe enough threat to stay the hand of the Kremlin leadership. The simplistic notion that deterrence was ensured by a fearsome threat was even blessed with the term of art "existential deterrence," meaning that because nuclear weapons exist, they will deter. Such confidence was misplaced even during the Cold War, and it certainly has no place now that the challengers confronting Washington are so various, unfamiliar, and possibly fanatical, at least by Washington's standards.

Fortunately, the Gulf War and the various post–Cold War crises with Iraq, Serbia, North Korea, and China have encouraged

---

[4]Jan Lodal, principal deputy under secretary of defense, with selected reporters, July 31, 1995, Washington, D.C., news conference transcript, pp. 9–10.

[5]Spurgeon Keeny, "Inventing an Enemy," *New York Times*, June 18, 1994.

[6]See Keith B. Payne, *Deterrence in the Second Nuclear Age* (Lexington, Ky.: University Press of Kentucky, 1996).

a more sober assessment of what may reasonably be expected from deterrence. Defense Department, White House, and congressional reports increasingly acknowledge that the deterrence of regional challengers may not follow Cold War patterns. Given the rogues' relatively unfamiliar goals and values, deterrence cannot be predictable and indeed may simply fail.

For example, the U.S. Commission on National Security, chaired by former senators Gary Hart and Warren Rudman, stated the point succinctly in its recent report on the emerging international security environment: "Deterrence will not work as it once did; in many cases it may not work at all."[7] This markedly reduced confidence in the reliability of deterrence has led to an increased appreciation of the need for NMD in the post–Cold War period—to provide a hedge of protection for the United States in the event deterrence fails. In short, a generally accepted proposition now is that because the deterrence of missile attack cannot be considered reliable, the United States must have some defense. What is more, NMD is also viewed widely as necessary if regional challengers are to be denied the capability to deter or coerce the United States. That is, a principal and oft-expressed reason why some regional powers seek long-range missiles and WMD is to dissuade the United States from intervening against whatever aggressive designs they have within their region. Their logic is simple and possibly accurate: if by acquiring long-range missiles and WMD a regional power can easily threaten American cities, then American leaders (well known to be highly sensitive even to military, let alone civilian, casualties) are not likely to risk military intervention against that regional power. For second-tier military powers that could not hope to compete with U.S. conventional force projection capabilities, long-range missiles and WMD are effective tools of deterrence and coercion.

The potential for such "asymmetrical responses" to U.S. conventional force projection has highlighted the potential value of NMD in the post–Cold War period. It is increasingly understood in Washington that for the United States to have the freedom to act globally it must be able to limit its vulnerability to threats against the American homeland. The question can be posed starkly: if Saddam Hussein had posed a nuclear-armed missile threat to Washington and New York in 1991, would President Bush have been able to rally sufficient support to wage the Gulf War? The

---

[7]*New World Coming: American Security in the 21st Century*, U.S. Commission on National Security/21st Century, Sept. 15, 1999, p. 8.

tenuous political support he did receive (based on the fear of significant casualties, and reflected in the very close Senate vote affirming the use of force) suggests strongly that the answer is no.

There are, of course, other suggested approaches to addressing rogue threats, including arms control and preemptive strikes, and these measures should be exploited where practicable.[8] The Gulf War and its aftermath, however, have provided graphic demonstrations of the limited effectiveness of arms control (even with unprecedented international inspections) and preemptive strikes for dealing with rogue missile or WMD threats. Consequently, NMD increasingly is recognized as a necessary ingredient in any effort to counter the emerging rogue missile or WMD threat and correspondingly to limit the prospects for the deterrence and coercion of Washington by regional challengers.

Why NMD and why now? In large measure the answer is that few today still challenge the fact of an emerging rogue missile danger, the fact that a sufficiently modest NMD system is practicable and affordable, the fact that deterrence is just not reliable, or the fact that NMD can help to maintain American freedom of action even in the face of coercive missile threats from otherwise second-rate regional powers.

It is important to note here that these NMD roles and the resultant new consensus for NMD have been driven by the practical realities of emerging threats, which themselves stem from the seemingly unstoppable process of proliferation. NMD is not, as some of the remaining critics contend, a program in search of a mission. The consensus behind NMD exists largely because wishful thinking about deterrence and missile/WMD proliferation has been corrected by cold reality in such persuasive ways that even Washington has had to pay attention.

Moscow's Objections

A final significant factor concerns the ABM Treaty, originally a reflection of orthodox deterrence theory. As noted above, U.S. strategic thought posited that stability was the fruit of mutual vulnerability, which the ABM Treaty was intended to cast in iron. Even to the present day, the Clinton administration regards it as "a cornerstone of strategic stability," hence any consideration of NMD deployment has been marginalized by arms control advo-

[8]Paul Nitze, for example, suggests conventional preemption of rogue nuclear capabilities upon "unambiguous indication" of their intended use. See "A Threat Mostly to Ourselves," *New York Times*, Oct. 28, 1999.

cates and government lawyers on the grounds that it would threaten the ABM Treaty. However, the logic of continued, willful U.S. vulnerability to missile attack, along with the treaty designed to ensure that vulnerability, has not fared well in the post–Cold War environment. With Washington's new appreciation of the need for a limited NMD, assaults on the previously sacrosanct ABM Treaty have mounted.

For example, some legal scholars challenge the validity of the treaty altogether, since one of the two parties (the Soviet Union) no longer exists and the collapse of the Soviet Union into more than a dozen successor states involves material changes to the treaty.[9] Republican presidential candidate George W. Bush has expressed a position regarding the treaty that would have been considered extreme just a few years ago, but now is wholly mainstream: the treaty must be amended promptly to permit the type of NMD America needs for its security, in cooperation with the Russians if possible, but without their cooperation if necessary.

Even President Clinton's State Department appointees who are strongly committed to the ABM Treaty have stated that the administration will pursue negotiations with Russia to modify it if the NMD system to be deployed so requires. Clearly, therefore, the entire direction of discussion concerning NMD and the ABM Treaty has radically shifted, and the treaty is no longer considered sacrosanct in Washington. To observe that the United States must either modify it or withdraw from it is now more or less commonplace, and the question is only one of optimal means: to negotiate with Russia, withdraw upon six months' notice as provided by Article 15 of the treaty, or negotiate in the context of an announced U.S. intention to withdraw? Debate will continue with regard to how to get out from under the ABM Treaty, but the principle of so doing is now widely accepted.

How Moscow plays out its own hand regarding the ABM Treaty will be critical to the future of NMD. The official Russian position is one of implacable opposition to any American NMD and to any modification of existing treaties. This position is largely a reflection of the ideological rigidity and ignorance of the Russian leadership and Duma on the subject: to oppose anything proposed by Washington is seen as a sign of patriotism and strength in Moscow at this point. If the United States honestly offered to put a chicken in every Russian pot and a car in every

[9]See, for example, Robert Turner, *The ABM Treaty and the Senate: Issues of International and Constitutional Law*, report, Center for National Security Law, University of Virginia School of Law, Charlottesville, Va., May 14, 1999.

driveway, the Communists and nationalists in Moscow would see in that a dark conspiracy to destroy Russia.

Nevertheless, more reasonable and pragmatic Russian leaders recognize that rigidity regarding the treaty could compel Washington to choose between withdrawing from it in order to deploy limited NMD and continuing to remain vulnerable to *all* missile threats, whatever their source. If Russia were to force that choice on Washington, it would be shooting itself in the foot, because Americans would almost certainly opt for withdrawal and unconstrained NMD, the worst possible outcome for Moscow. Consequently, it is possible and even likely that Moscow ultimately will decide to engage the United States on the matter.

In sum, the answer to the question of why a consensus for NMD deployment has been established after so many years of intense debate and opposition involves a complex mixture of changes in the international security environment and domestic opinion about strategy. While that consensus appears relatively stable, the prospect for limited NMD deployment could still be derailed for a season by an overly solicitous attitude toward Moscow (or Beijing) or by some spectacular failures in the testing of NMD technology. Even so, the variety of factors driving the political consensus in favor of NMD, most notably the continuing pace of missile and WMD proliferation, are beyond the control of the Clinton administration and NMD critics. In short, the "objective conditions" (to borrow a Marxist expression) that have been the dynamic behind the creation of an NMD consensus show no sign of abating and ultimately point to a decision by Clinton or his successor in favor of limited NMD deployment. Ronald Reagan should take a bow.

RETHINKING BIO-CHEMICAL DANGERS

by Henry Sokolski

Well before the Aum Shinrikyo sarin gas subway attack of 1995, the Defense Department was forced to consider the implications of a biological weapons attack directed against the Pentagon.[1] It was not a real threat, but rather a scenario posed by a leading biological weapons expert to a meeting of senior Defense Department officials shortly after President Bush had committed U.S. forces to defend Saudi Arabia. What, this expert asked, was the Defense Department doing to protect against the possibility of an anthrax letter-bomb being sent to the Pentagon by Saddam Hussein? All the officials at the meeting shifted uncomfortably in their chairs. There was some discussion of the difficulty of searching over 25,000 briefcases and purses carried into the building daily. This was followed by a somewhat lengthier discussion about the need to be in touch with the Centers for Disease Control and the local fire department.

The awkwardness continued until one of the junior officials present was asked what could be done. Not much, was his answer. However, he was not sure that there was much of a threat. An anthrax letter-bomb might kill officials in the Pentagon, but was unlikely to paralyze U.S. armed forces (most of whom were housed elsewhere). And in any case, he explained, such an attack would solve the White House's key problem, which was to win public support for a ground attack on Iraq. The only real worry was that Saddam could not be counted on to be so stupid. With this, the meeting ended and no action was taken.

Although Operation Desert Shield is now nearly a decade past, the relevance of this story could not be more immediate to today's popular assessment of the chemical and biological weapons threat and what our government should do. In fact, since Desert Storm and the Aum Shinrikyo attack, Americans' concern about these threats has only grown. The essential difference now, however, is

[1]This essay originally appeared in *Orbis*, Spring 2000, and arose from the Foreign Policy Research Institute conference "America the Vulnerable: Three Threats and What to Do about Them," Philadelphia, Pa., Oct. 7–8, 1999.

that unlike the Pentagon of 1990, Washington has reacted with energy.

Thus, in January 1999 the president announced his intention to spend $10 billion on countering terrorism, including biological and chemical threats, for fiscal year 2000. In addition, ten National Guard response units of twenty-two men each have been created along with fifty smaller state guard units to help local authorities respond to chemical and biological attacks. Then the secretary of defense announced in the fall of 1999 that the U.S. Preparedness Command would be in charge of Homeland Defense.

The presumption in all this seems to be that what happened in Japan in 1995 is likely to happen here, and on a much grander scale. Consider the comments of high officials and the press. ABC-TV's *Nightline*, in one of the most lavish efforts to cover the chemical and biological threat, ran a week-long series in which experts commented on a hypothetical anthrax terrorist attack against the New York subway system. The pace and tragedy of the scenario are driven by the central frightening fact that most of the anthrax spread in the attack is presumed to have been inhaled on day one. Given that anthrax has an incubation period of only three to seven days, the scenario did not allow public officials to get help to those exposed. By the end of the seven-day scenario, 65,000 New Yorkers had become ill and 80 percent were expected to die.[2]

A Future Unlike Our Past?

Although gruesome, this coverage hardly seems like hyperbole when compared to the views of other top U.S. officials. Perhaps the most famous of these was the one offered by the secretary of defense on ABC's *This Week*. Holding a five-pound Domino sugar bag, the secretary explained how little anthrax would be needed to kill half the residents of Washington. In a subsequent, syndicated

[2]In fact, there is a vaccine for anthrax. If diagnosed early, anthrax victims can be treated with antibiotics for several weeks to keep the anthrax from taking over and to allow the vaccine to kick in. See Donald A. Henderson, "Dangerous Fictions about Bioterrorism," *Washington Post*, Nov. 8, 1999. Dr. Henderson, a public health physician and director of the Johns Hopkins Center for Civilian Biodefense Studies, points out that the critical period "would extend far longer than the seven days portrayed" along with the "window of opportunity for carrying out life-saving medical interventions beyond a week." *Nightline*'s story, however, ended at day seven, "implying—incorrectly—that no further interventions would be useful." As Dr. Henderson notes, one of the largest anthrax outbreaks in recent history took place in Sverdlovsk, Russia, in 1979, and some infections occurred as early as two days after the anthrax's release and some as late as 47 days later.

column, the secretary cited the Aum Shinrikyo attack of 1995 (which killed twelve) and declared that "the race is on between our preparations [against domestic chemical or biological attacks] and those of our adversaries. . . . There is not a moment to lose."[3] And then there was the impetus for President Clinton's first briefing on bioterrorism—a novel called *The Cobra Event*. Written to scare, the novel describes an act of domestic terrorism in which a disease that involves self-cannibalism is hatched in New York.[4] The president wanted to know from the Central Intelligence Agency: was this plausible?

Not so long as our future is unlike our past. As David C. Rapoport, editor of *Terrorism and Political Violence*, documents in his path-breaking analysis, "Terrorism and Weapons of the Apocalypse," the threat of biological and chemical domestic terrorism has so far been fairly remote. In fact, the CIA reports that between 1960 and 1980 there were 40,000 international terror incidents. Of these, twenty-two, or one in 2,000, had chemical or biological elements.

Going back a full century, the relative numbers are even lower. Since 1900 there have only been seventy-one known terrorist acts worldwide involving the use of chemical or biological agents. Of the 123 fatalities these attacks caused, only one was American—a California school superintendent targeted by a Symbionese Liberation Army cyanide-laced bullet. Of the 3,774 nonfatal injuries these attacks caused, no more than 784 involved Americans. Almost all of these—751—were the result of a salmonella food poisoning incident perpetrated in 1985 by an Oregon-based religious sect. As for biological attacks worldwide, seventy have occurred in the last century, causing nine deaths, but only eighteen of these seventy attacks were made by terrorists.[5]

These are not large numbers. What is perhaps worrisome (and largely a function of the media's recent coverage and so many

[3]See William S. Cohen, "Preparing for a Grave New World," *Washington Post*, July 26, 1999. For an earlier similar view, see William S. Cohen, "In the Age of Terror Weapons," *Washington Post*, Nov. 26, 1997.

[4]See Richard Preston, *The Cobra Event* (New York: Random House, 1997) and the author's own review of his book (http://www.amazon.com/exec/obidos/ts/book-reviews), in which he explains, "The story of the bioterror event in New York City is fiction. But a lot of the background is totally real. The disease, which involves self-cannibalism, is real, though in reality it is not contagious."

[5]See Jonathan B. Tucker and Amy Sands, "An Unlikely Threat," *Bulletin of the Atomic Scientists*, July/Aug. 1999, pp. 46–52; David Rapoport, "Terrorism and Weapons of the Apocalypse," *National Security Studies Quarterly*, Summer 1999, p. 59; and Seth Carus, *Bioterrorism and Biocrimes: The Illicit Use of Biological Agents in the Twentieth Century* (Washington, D.C.: Center for Counterproliferation Research, July 1999).

officials' pronouncements) is that forty-five of the seventy attacks reported this century occurred within the last ten years.[6] Yet, so far, none has been very effective. The increased number of incidents, however, does make it both politically and substantively imprudent to dismiss such threats.

Downside Risks

That said, how much should one make of the threats? There are, after all, risks not only in underestimating the chemical and biological domestic terrorist threat, but in overestimating it as well. So far, such downside risks have received scant attention. The most prominent of these include:

• Raising public consciousness about the possible threat in a manner that emboldens and empowers criminals and terrorists to attempt precisely what the government and public want to avoid.

• Reassuring the public about the preparedness of government such that any government shortcoming is likely to be magnified to politically fatal levels (i.e., to levels perhaps desired by the perpetrators).

• Preemptively undermining significant U.S. civil liberties in the name of enhanced homeland defense by encouraging overreaction on the part of law enforcement agencies. What we do not need are scenarios similar to Ruby Ridge and Waco, Texas, that inspire chemical or biological "Oklahoma City" incidents in retaliation.

• Expanding the role of the U.S. military (and of martial law) into the domestic realms of law enforcement by making the response to domestic chemical and biological attacks a core military mission.

• Distracting the military from chemical, biological, and conventional threats to U.S. bases and embassies overseas.

• Encouraging an "America first" siege mentality and a retreat from foreign commitments critical to our nation's security.

Most of these risks, of course, are far from immediate. The White House and Defense Department are sensitive to military intrusions into domestic law enforcement and are just as concerned about

---

[6]For one of the only quantitative analyses of the relationships among press coverage, terrorism involving weapons of mass destruction, and the threat perceptions of the U.S. government and public, see Martha Crenshaw, "Threat Perception in Democracies: 'WMD' Terrorism in the U.S. Policy Debate," presented before the 22nd Annual Scientific Meeting of the International Society for Political Psychology, Amsterdam, July 18–21, 1999.

preserving the fullest enjoyment of civil liberties.

This, however, could change. Some of the nation's most respected security experts, after all, want to make responding to domestic terrorism a high-priority mission for our military. Others are just as convinced that it is critical to "resolve the tension" between judicial rules of due-process discovery with the demands of national security and the need to protect intelligence sources and methods.[7]

The point is that ultimately the downside risks listed are at least as likely as the domestic biological and chemical terrorism threats that might generate them. Either set of threats, if realized, could jeopardize our way of life. If we are serious about one, then we need to be serious about the other. The question is how? Part of the difficulty in balancing these concerns is that it is easier to speculate on what terrorists may be able to do and design programs to mitigate such threats than it is to know when and why to *stop* speculating and designing. Focusing on two broad considerations, however, should help. The first of these is determining just how practical current chemical and biological agents are for military and terrorist use. The second is identifying what defensive strengths the United States can exploit to mitigate these threats.

Technical Considerations

About traditional chemical agents, history suggests that in military settings they injure far more than they kill. This makes sense if only because it takes massive amounts of chemical agent to produce military casualties with any reliability, and maximizing their military dissemination is no easy task. If the agent is released too high in the atmosphere, it will be too diluted to do much harm when it comes to the ground. If it is released too close to the ground, the lethal area of the attack will be small. Wind can blow agents off their intended path, and sun and heat can evaporate volatile ones such as sarin.[8]

If one is aiming to kill massive numbers of troops or residents with chemicals, then quantity matters. In the case of a terrorist sarin attack against Washington, D.C., terrorists would need more

[7]See, e.g., Richard A. Falkenrath, Robert D. Newman, and Bradley A. Thayer, *America's Achilles Heel: Nuclear, Biological, and Chemical Terrorism and Covert Attack* (Cambridge, Mass.: MIT Press, 1998), pp. 261–336; and Ashton B. Carter, John M. Deutch, and Philip D. Zelikow, *Catastrophic Terrorism: Elements of a National Policy* (Stanford, Calif.: Stanford-Harvard Preventive Defense Project, Oct. 1998), pp. 6–10.

[8]See Brian Chow et al., *Air Force Operations in a Chemical and Biological Environment*, DB-189/1-AF (Santa Monica, Calif.: RAND, 1998), pp. 12–37.

than a vial or a tall building to deliver much of a punch. In fact, the Congressional Office of Technology Assessment estimated that terrorists would need a ton of sarin disseminated by airplane under ideal weather conditions to produce 3,000 to 8,000 deaths. Under breezy conditions, the same attack might only kill 300 to 800. With nerve gas, which is much more lethal, the amount needed to produce heavy casualties among an unprotected population in an open area of one kilometer square would still be measured in tons.[9]

Given these facts, it is not surprising that, even in total wars, chemical weapons have not been the absolute weapon. On the Western Front in World War I it took an average of just over a ton of agent to kill a single soldier. Only two or three percent of those exposed to gas on the Western Front actually died, and gas was responsible for no more than 5 percent of the war's total casualties. In Iraq's war against Iran, the story was much the same. Of the 27,000 Iranians reported to have been exposed to Iraqi gas through March 1987, only 265 died. Over the entire war, Iraqi chemical weapons killed 5,000 Iranians. This constituted less than one percent of the 600,000 Iranians who died from all causes during the war.[10]

These facts should not be used to denigrate any loss of life or suffering caused by chemical weapons. They are, however, directly relevant to how seriously we should view the chemical threat. First, they help to explain why traditional chemical agents have been used so rarely even in war. It is not merely that it takes so much agent to kill. It is that any military hoping to injure the enemy or force him into donning protective gear must be able to defend against possible chemical counterstrikes.

Having anything less than this is an invitation to trouble unless (1) one's opponent lacks nuclear, chemical, or biological weapons to strike back or sufficient passive protection to survive an attack; or (2) one is fighting a desperate war of attrition along a relatively fixed front and requires a tactical means to support an offensive breakthrough or to defend against one. On several occasions, these military criteria have been met, and in these instances chemical agents have been used. At no time, however, has such use produced strategic results.

[9]See U.S. Congress, Office of Technology Assessment, *Proliferation of Weapons of Mass Destruction: Assessing the Risks* (Washington, D.C.: U.S. Government Printing Office, Aug. 1993), pp. 52–56.

[10]For more complete reviews of this historical data, see John and Karl Mueller, "Sanctions of Mass Destruction," *Foreign Affairs*, May/June 1999, pp. 46–48; and Rapoport, "Terrorism and Weapons of the Apocalypse," pp. 52–55.

This may be different in the American case, however, where the toleration for casualties within the military (if not the public) is still quite low. Certainly, to the extent that the United States depends on access to overseas ports, airfields, and command centers to project force, protecting these assets against chemical and biological attack will be critical. The American military and its allies must have enough warning to don protection soon enough to avoid the worst, and since our chemical and biological sensors are quite crude, more needs to be done in this area.[11]

If military use of chemical and biological agents has been historically rare, domestic criminal and terrorist use of them has been rarer still. Part of the reason for that fact is technical and part operational. Technically, dissemination of chemicals to produce massive casualties is difficult, as demonstrated by the Aum Shinrikyo experience. In an attack in Matsumoto, Japan, a year before the famous Tokyo subway strike, things went awry. The intended targets—three judges—failed to receive fatal doses. Instead, wind blew the agent in the wrong direction and killed seven innocents.[12]

Nor are the perpetrators themselves immune. One of the Aum terrorists was overwhelmed by the agent he tried to deliver, after which the group decided to dilute the agent, rendering it less lethal. Also, in the case of the most successful of the subway attacks, the sarin was not optimized for the widest possible dissemination, i.e., as a gas. All twelve of the deaths caused by the attack were due to the victims' direct contact with liquid sarin. Optimizing effectiveness via gas delivery, however, would have increased the risk of killing the carriers. Likewise, more lethal aerosol dispensers and airplanes might have been employed, but that would have also increased the operation's complexity and the likelihood of its early detection by law enforcement officials. Finally, the production of chemical agents runs the risk of killing the producers.

The technical challenges of terrorists using traditional biological agents to produce massive fatalities are no less daunting. Effectively disseminating these agents is particularly difficult

[11]Biological agents are inhaled. Protection against them is a face mask. Chemical agents, on the other hand, can enter the body through the skin as well. As such, a suit covering the entire body must be donned as protection. Inoculations and vaccines are also available for a variety of agents. However, given the inability to anticipate what agent might be used, protective gear is the first and main line of defense.

[12]See Senate Committee on Governmental Affairs, *Global Proliferation of Weapons of Mass Destruction, Part I, Hearings before the Subcommittee on Investigations*, 104th Cong., 1st sess., 1995, pp. 15–103; and Rapoport, "Terrorism and Weapons of the Apocalypse," pp. 56–58.

since traditional biological agents are lethal only if inhaled, and particles larger than ten microns are likely to be blocked before they reach the lungs. On the other hand, agent particles approaching one micron are likely to be exhaled and so will not remain in the lungs. Operationally, particles sized between five and ten microns are optimal.

Spreading biological agent in particles of that precise size, however, is difficult. Indeed, the Federal Bureau of Investigation has yet to find a terrorist organization that has built an effective delivery system for mass-casualty biological agents; the only organizations that have done so are states. But dispersal of correctly sized biological particles still does not guarantee an effective attack. Sunlight kills or denatures most biological agents (making nighttime dispersal imperative), and wind patterns and humidity matter. An anthrax attack under optimal conditions, for example, would be at least a thousand times more lethal than one made during a sunny day in light winds.[13]

Operational Issues

For soldiers and terrorists alike, these facts have operational consequences. First, biological and chemical agents would be most attractive to desperate nations and military commanders anxious to threaten opposing expeditionary forces and their use of local ports or airfields, or to test an invading nation's political will to continue operations. Secondly, while traditional biological agents would be potentially most effective in killing enemy forces, their delayed effect would not be anywhere near as telling as chemical agents in disrupting ongoing military operations. Thirdly, given the volatility of many chemical agents and the uncertainties associated with biological agent dissemination and their delayed and varied incubation periods, a military decision to use such agents would be complicated. At a minimum, it might turn as much on an assessment of these agents' likely physical impact as their impact on the enemy's will to continue to fight or to escalate the conflict.

As for terrorist use of traditional agents, the technical facts noted above would make their use to inflict massive casualties even less likely. First, the difficulties of acquiring and deploying chemical and biological agents and their poor past performance as compared to high explosives would weigh heavily against their

[13]On these points, see Tucker and Sands, "An Unlikely Threat," p. 51; and Chow et al., *Air Force Operations*, pp. 27–37.

initial selection. Secondly, given these difficulties (particularly with biological agents), state sponsorship or assistance would seem useful. Osama bin Laden may not have had a direct link to the Khartoum pharmaceutical plant the United States bombed in 1998, but if he wanted chemical agents, he had a clear interest in seeking Sudanese help. The problem with asking for such assistance (as bin Laden and the Sudanese learned) is that it increases the risks of being discovered and targeted.

Thirdly, foreign entities seeking asymmetric advantage in hopes of persuading the United States to withdraw from their part of the world would probably want to avoid the complications of using chemical or biological agents on American soil. As the recent arrest of the Algerian Ahmed Ressam in Washington State clearly demonstrates, merely attempting an attack with conventional explosives is risky enough.[14] Indeed, mounting terrorist operations with chemical or biological agents would only increase the likelihood that U.S. authorities might discover the affair and disrupt it or retaliate. Finally, the more indiscriminate and identifiable a foreign terrorist attack is, the more likely would be an American overseas counterstrike.

Emerging Agents

All of the above observations pertain to the use of traditional chemical and biological agents to produce massive casualties. To date, most analyses have focused on the most horrific domestic terrorist scenarios. Two new developments, however, suggest that greater attention should be paid to how the United States might be threatened by more discriminate military agent attacks overseas. The first is Russia's development in the late 1980s and early 1990s of a far more lethal and persistent family of binary chemical substances known as *Novichok* (Russian for "newcomer") agents. The second is the possible development of a new class of biological agents known as bioregulators.

The earliest information on Russia's *Novichok* chemical weapons program came just prior to Moscow's signing of the Chemical Weapons Convention (CWC) from two Russian chemists, Vil Mirzayanov and Lev Fedorov.[15] In the late 1980s and

---

[14]See Vernon Loeb and Steven Perlstein, "U.S. Puts Borders on High Alert," *Washington Post*, Dec. 19, 1999.

[15]See "Mirzayanov, Fedorov Detail Russian CW Production," from *Novoye Vremya*, Oct. 27, 1992; and "Mirzayanov, Fedorov Article on CW 'War Against Environment,'" from *Nezavisimaya Gazeta*, Oct. 24, 1992, both in Joint Publication Research Service, Commonwealth of Independent States (JPRS-TAC-92-033), Nov. 14, 1992, pp. 44–60. See also Vil Mirzayanov, "Free to Develop Chemical Weapons," *Wall Street Journal*, May 25, 1994.

early 1990s, Russia produced several new agents that were made of chemicals not controlled by the CWC. These agents, referenced by a variety of code names (including Substance 33, A-230, A-232, A-234, Novichok-5, and Novichok-7), are geared for the deployment of binaries, that is, munitions using two agents that are benign when kept separate, but lethal when mixed.

Indeed, they were extremely lethal—at least as toxic and persistent as the most lethal nerve agent, VX, and some are reported to be ten times as toxic. At the same time, they are far more difficult to detect and far easier to manufacture covertly using common chemicals and relatively simple pesticide factories. In addition, unlike VX, which can be defeated quickly with injectable antidotes, Novichok agents are at least as resistant to treatment as Soman.[16]

As of late 1993, Mirzayanov believed that Russia had only produced a few tens of tons of *Novichok* agents for experimental use. Still, there is cause for concern because *Novichok* agents are made of benign industrial and agricultural chemicals and can be made quickly in quantity. There is far less need to produce and stockpile vast quantities of agent or controlled precursors in advance. In addition, despite several defectors' public revelations, the Russian government has never formally admitted developing these agents, and Russian expert opinion remains disturbingly divided over the utility of retaining chemical weapons. Many Russian military experts see chemical agents as yesterday's weapon, but others believe that chemical weapons, especially the new *Novichok* agents, are a needed additional deterrent. What is more, there is reason to fear that Russia might export its *Novichok* data to its traditional clients in Libya, Syria, Iran, or Iraq.[17]

One thing is certain. Given their relative ease of manufacture for chemical-producing nations and these agents' persistence, novelty, and lethality, the *Novichok* family of chemical weapons would be much more attractive for a military to use than traditional agents. At the very least, current chemical detector devices are unlikely to be set off by their use. This alone could prove to be fatal. If delivery were accomplished covertly with special forces,

---

[16]See Center for Security Policy, "Russia's Covert Chemical Weapons Program," Decision Brief no. 97-D19, Feb. 4, 1997; Vil S. Mirzayanov, "Dismantling the Soviet/Russian Chemical Weapons Complex: An Insider's View," in *Chemical Weapons Disarmament in Russia: Problems and Prospects*, Amy E. Smithson et al., report no. 17 (Washington, D.C.: Henry L. Stimson Center, Oct. 1995), pp. 23–26; and Igor Khripunov and Derek Averre, "Russia's CBW Closet Poses Ongoing Threat," *Jane's Intelligence Review*, May 1999, pp. 20–23.

[17]See Khripunov and Averre, "Russia's CBW Closet."

there might not be any warning at all and targeted troops would be unable to don protective gear before lethal exposure. Also, given these agents' persistence and lethality, far less would be needed to accomplish any given mission.

More remote than *Novichok* agents, but still worrisome, is the prospect that incapacitants known as bioregulators might be developed in a form that could be weaponized. Bioregulators are present in our bodies in small amounts. They determine hormone release, control of body temperature, sleep, mood, consciousness, and emotions. Using the latest recombinant-DNA techniques, scientists might modify bioregulators to enhance their potency and effect. So far, the key obstacle to weaponizing such agents has been dissemination. In one of its last reports, the Congressional Office of Technology Assessment reported that although the small peptide hormone ADH (antidiuretic hormone) had been introduced into the blood stream with a nasal aerosol, similar attempts to do so with insulin failed because of the molecule's large size.[18]

Assuming further research overcomes these problems, such bioregulator agents would be militarily attractive for three reasons: their novelty would almost guarantee their ability to evade current biological agent detectors; they would, unlike other biological agents, have immediate effects and thus could be used to disrupt military operations at key ports, airfields, and command centers; and they could function without losing the key advantage of biological agents, which is their potency as compared to chemical agents.[19]

What We Can Do at Home

Given their rarity and complexity, worrying about imminent use of bioregulators or *Novichok* agents by terrorists would be a mistake. However, given all the attention chemical and biological terrorism has received, the possible use of traditional agents by criminals or terrorists, if only to cause panic through minor attacks, cannot be dismissed.

---

[18]See U.S. Congress, Office of Technology Assessment, *Technologies Underlying Weapons of Mass Destruction*, OTA-BP-115 (Washington, D.C.: U.S. Government Printing Office, Dec. 1993), pp. 116–17.

[19]There is good reason to believe that the obstacles to weaponizing bioregulators may fall in the next five to ten years. For a projection of what biotechnology has in store regarding agent development, see House Committee on Government Reform, Subcommittee on National Security, Veterans Affairs, and International Relations, "Assessing the Threat of Bioterrorism," testimony of Dr. Raymond Zilinskas, senior scientist at the Center for Nonproliferation Studies at the Monterey Institute of International Studies, Oct. 20, 1999 (http://www.cns.miis.edu/pubs/reports/zilin.htm).

Fortunately, the United States has considerable resources already in place to address such threats. As Virginia governor James S. Gilmore II, chairman of a presidential terrorism commission, recently explained, "We do not need to create a new mechanism to deal with [chemical and biological terrorism]. . . . We simply need to build on what we have."[20] All told, there are 32,000 fire departments, 8,000 emergency medical services, and 17,000 law-enforcement agencies in the United States, constituting a force of over 2 million first-responders. A good number of fire departments located in industrial areas are already trained to deal with hazardous chemicals. With additional training and equipment, chemical agents could be addressed by these and other departments merely as additional hazardous materials.[21]

As for dealing with domestic biological terrorism, the United States is blessed with a massive health-care system. The country spends nearly four times as much on its public health and medical system as it does on its entire military. The government plans to spend nearly $400 million conducting research on all aspects of chemical and biological weapons defense, but the budget of the National Institutes of Health alone approaches $20 billion. Factor in the fire-fighting services and police, and it is clear that these civilian institutions (and the Centers for Disease Control) are the ones best positioned to respond to domestic terrorism.

Indeed, relying more heavily on these institutions than on the military has several advantages. First, they are already locally deployed. The newly created Rapid Assessment and Initial Detection (RAID) teams actually are unlikely to detect or respond to terrorist attacks first, and in some cases they will not have much training to pass on. As Jerome Hauer, director of emergency planning in New York City's mayor's office, recently explained, with 40,000 police officers, 15,000 firefighters and emergency medical teams, New York already has the "ninth biggest army in the world." Hauer insists, "I don't need RAID teams because my guys are probably better trained than RAIDs." New York firefighters already deal with more than a thousand hazardous-materials accidents a year.[22]

Secondly, in comparison with what is required of the national health-care system to deal with natural diseases, domestic bioter-

[20]See Chuck McCutcheon, "'Homeland Defense': Mobilizing against Terrorism," *Congressional Quarterly Weekly*, Mar. 6, 1999, pp. 522.
[21]See Ron Laurenzo, "Front Line Is Weak Link in Homeland Defense," *Defense Week*, Mar. 15, 1999, p. 1.
[22]Ibid.

rorism is likely to long remain the lesser-included case. Efforts to improve the health-care system's ability to deal with natural incidents should only improve its ability to cope with terrorist incidents and vice versa. As one expert put it, "Our society's response to a natural versus deliberately caused disease outbreak would differ only after there are clear signs that the disease of concern might be the result of a terrorist or criminal attack." What is critical to treating both is early detection, and there are far more natural disease outbreaks to monitor and report than terrorist acts.[23]

Finally, using civilian institutions avoids the downside risks of relying too much on the military. Not only are civil liberties likely to be safer, but the military's ability to focus on its own self-defense requirements will be improved. As it is, the military needs to concentrate on bringing its chemical and biological protection and decontamination units to bear overseas, where the likelihood of use is highest. Yet none of the newly created Reserve and National Guard RAID units is a part of the active military. Given that the most threatening use of chemical and biological agents against Americans is likely to occur abroad, it is critical that our military focus as much as it can on addressing these dangers.

Also, as argued above, our military cannot simply focus on domestic terrorist threats, which have to do with the possible use of traditional agents, without running even greater military risks overseas. In specific, it must do more to tackle the difficult task of developing detection and protection capabilities (especially against new agents, such as the *Novichok* family) and to stay ahead of whatever other agents hostile biotechnologists might develop.

Rethinking the Thinkable

In its first annual report of December 1999, a congressionally mandated advisory panel on domestic nuclear, chemical, and biological terrorism quietly criticized the government's emphasis on massive worst-case scenarios. "As serious and potentially catastrophic as a domestic terrorist attack might prove," the panel reported, "it is highly unlikely that it could ever completely undermine the national security, much less threaten the survival of the United States as a nation."[24]

---

[23]Of the $10 billion the federal government will spend combating terrorism next year, something less than 2 percent is earmarked for public health surveillance and reporting. See Zilinskas, "Assessing the Threat."
[24]See *The First Annual Report to the President and the Congress of the Advisory Panel to Assess the Domestic Response Capabilities of the Government for Terrorism*

The panel did believe there was a domestic chemical and biological terrorism threat, but it judged possible attacks against U.S. agriculture, small-scale attacks designed to cause panic, and conventional terrorism to be far more likely than the "lower probability/higher consequence attacks" that are the "focus of current policy and preparedness efforts." In fact, the advisory panel warned that focusing so much on the worst-case scenarios was a mistake.

> The guiding assumption has been that smaller-scale, non-mass-casualty events are a lesser-included contingency that can be addressed adequately by preparations for the higher-end mass casualty attacks. This is by no means axiomatic. . . . By continuing a policy that emphasizes high-end threats, there is a very real danger of failing to optimize state and local response capabilities to deal with the more probable terrorist threats confronting the United States today.[25]

The advisory panel, of course, was not asked to assess the foreign chemical and biological weapons threat. Yet, if it had, it is likely that it would have found that in overemphasizing the domestic threat, our government runs additional risks. These would include paying insufficient attention to the threats posed by possible chemical and biological attacks against U.S. forces and facilities overseas, by conventional terrorism generally, and by nontraditional agents.

The point here is not to dismiss the possibility of any particular chemical or biological threat, but rather to weigh how much attention each one deserves. Assuming we are not foolish enough to demand 100 percent protection against all attacks, our medical system, federal and local governments, and military should be able to ensure against a lasting strategic calamity. The key to success, however, will be the same as it was a decade ago in Desert Shield, which is to avoid focusing on the most horrific scenarios at the expense of preparing for the most likely ones.

Involving Weapons of Mass Destruction, Dec. 15, 1999, available online from RAND (http://www.rand.org/organization/nsrd/terrpanel).
[25]Ibid.

BAD MEDICINE FOR BIOLOGICAL TERROR

by Andrew J. Bacevich

In an op-ed published in the *Washington Post* on July 26, 1999, Secretary of Defense William S. Cohen offered the most alarming depiction yet of America's vulnerability in what he called the "grave New World" of biological terrorism.[1] In his lurid depiction of a biological Pearl Harbor, a lethal pathogen carried "across hemispheres in hours" infects "unsuspecting thousands," with devastating results. "Hospitals would become warehouses for the dead and dying. A plague more monstrous than anything we have experienced could spread with all the irrevocability of ink on tissue paper. Ancient scourges would quickly become modern nightmares." The question confronting the United States, Cohen insisted, is not *if* such an incident will occur, but *when*.[2]

Nor is the belief that Americans face the near-certain prospect of a surprise biological attack unique to Cohen. President Clinton himself confessed that worrying about a biological assault against the United States "keeps me awake at night."[3] And over the last two years—ever since *The Cobra Event*, a thriller about terrorists unleashing a deadly toxin in New York City, made it to the top of the presidential reading list—such fears have prompted the Clinton administration as a whole to make biological defense a top priority.[4]

In spite or because of its priority, however, the administration's crash program to prepare for biological war is riddled with contradictions. Growing controversy surrounding one specific aspect of that program—the vaccination of American soldiers against anthrax—is exposing the program's larger flaws. Paradoxically, that controversy also offers a ready-made opportunity to shift to a more sensible alternative course.

[1]This essay originally appeared in *Orbis*, Spring 2000.
[2]William S. Cohen, "Preparing for a Grave New World," *Washington Post*, July 26, 1999.
[3]Judith Miller and William J. Broad, "Clinton Describes Terrorism Threat for 21st Century," *New York Times*, Jan. 22, 1999.
[4]William J. Broad and Judith Miller, "Germ Defense Plan in Peril as Its Flaws Are Revealed," *New York Times*, Aug. 7, 1998.

Soldiers Just Saying No to Anthrax Vaccine

For the most part, U.S. preparations for biological war are proceeding behind the scenes, with federal agencies currently spending several hundred million dollars to stockpile antibiotics and train emergency response teams in major cities. There is one important exception to that rule: the mandatory vaccination against anthrax of more than two million U.S. military personnel, announced with much ballyhoo by Secretary Cohen in December 1997. Apart from shielding American soldiers from the effects of one particular pathogen, this component of the administration's biological warfare program serves a second, larger purpose, which is to publicize this new threat to national security and convey the impression that the Clinton administration is already responding aggressively to it. In short, the anthrax vaccination program is as much about public relations as about military prophylaxis.

This most publicized element of the administration's biological warfare initiative is also the one that has triggered active opposition. Yet those opposing the anthrax vaccination policy are not antiwar activists, crusaders for disarmament, environmental extremists, or crackpots given to paranoid fantasies about government conspiracies. Rather, the opponents, much to the Pentagon's consternation and chagrin, are themselves members of the armed forces.

Citing anecdotal evidence from the field about adverse side effects, these protesters in uniform contend that the vaccine is unsafe and that its potential impact on long-term health is unknown. As a result, since the vaccination program began, a steadily increasing number of service personnel—now totaling more than 300—have refused to be inoculated or have simply left the military to avoid taking the shots.[5] Documented instances of *collective* resistance include the following:

- Seven of thirty pilots assigned to the 115th Fighter Wing of the Wisconsin Air National Guard, along with thirteen other members of that unit.[6]
- Eight pilots, representing 20 percent of the assigned strength of the Connecticut Air National Guard's 103d Fighter Wing.[7]
- Seventeen pilots flying KC-10 tankers with the 79th Air Refueling Squadron at Travis Air Force Base in California and

[5]Thomas D. Williams, "Failed Inspection Slows Military's Anthrax Vaccine Program," *Hartford Courant*, Dec. 15, 1999.

[6]Associated Press State and Local Wire, July 28, 1999 (http://wire.ap.org).

[7]Deborah Funk, "Anthrax Critics Continue to Stand Ground," *Air Force Times*, Feb. 8, 1999.

thirty-two pilots flying C5s with the 301st Airlift Squadron.[8]
- Thirty of fifty-eight pilots assigned to the 97th Airlift Squadron at McChord Air Force Base in Washington State.[9]
- Twenty pilots assigned to the 514th Air Mobility Wing or 108th Air Refueling Wing at McGuire Air Force Base in New Jersey.[10]
- Sixty members of the Tennessee Air National Guard in Memphis, including twenty-two of fifty pilots assigned to the 164th Airlift Wing.[11]
- Two dozen enlisted marines on Okinawa, thirty more at Camp Pendleton, and ten at Twenty-nine Palms, California, with several having been court-martialed and issued bad conduct discharges.[12]
- Twenty-nine sailors on the aircraft carrier *Theodore Roosevelt*, seven on the carrier *John C. Stennis*, and seven more on the carrier *Independence*.[13]

With nearly 400,000 service members having at least begun the vaccination protocol (six injections administered over eighteen months, followed by an annual booster), the Department of Defense characterizes any resistance to the policy as incidental. As to the minor discontent they are willing to acknowledge, Pentagon officials blame the Internet and a malicious campaign of disinformation for misleading "our youngsters."[14]

Yet the most vocal and impassioned critics of the vaccination policy are anything but kids. Indeed, a disproportionate percentage of the refuseniks are pilots, combat veterans, and/or field-grade officers in their thirties and forties. From the Pentagon's perspective, the specific character of opposition complicates matters considerably. To the extent that those questioning the vaccination regime are mature, well-educated professionals who, in the case of the reservists and guardsmen, are also engaged in respon-

---

[8]Tom Bowman, "Military Rebels at Anthrax Vaccine," *Baltimore Sun*, Feb. 27, 1999; David Castellon, "Anthrax Vaccine Draws More Resistance," *Air Force Times*, Mar. 1, 1999.

[9]Tom Bowman, "Anthrax Vaccine Divides Military," *Baltimore Sun*, July 12, 1999.

[10]"More Reservists Refuse Anthrax Vaccine," *Air Force Times*, Aug. 16, 1999.

[11]Lela Garlington, "Nearly Half of the Pilots in Memphis Air Guard Refuse Anthrax Vaccinations," *Memphis Commercial Appeal*, Oct. 5, 1999.

[12]Dwight Daniels, "Anthrax Shots Bad Medicine?" *San Diego Union-Tribune*, June 29, 1999.

[13]Steven Lee Myers, "Armed Services Opt to Discharge Those Who Refuse Vaccine," *New York Times*, Mar. 11, 1999; Steve Vogel, "Sailors Refuse Anthrax Shots," *Washington Post*, Mar. 12, 1999; "16 Gulf Troops Refuse to Take Anthrax Shots," CNN, Apr. 8, 1998 (http://www.cnn.com).

[14]Pentagon background briefing, Aug. 5, 1999 (http://www.defenselink.mil/Aug1999/x08051999_x0805ant.html). Presenters at this briefing were identified only as "senior defense and Army officials."

sible civilian careers, it becomes difficult to dismiss them as naive, misinformed, or easily manipulated.

Furthermore, to the extent that the anthrax inoculation is causing experienced pilots to terminate their military careers, the program may actually be undermining rather than enhancing overall combat readiness. The services are already critically short of trained aviators, and the problem is projected to worsen over the next several years, even as the United States relies increasingly on air power as its preferred military instrument abroad.

Finally, with the Pentagon looking to the National Guard and reserves—in Secretary Cohen's formulation, "forward-deployed forces here at home"—to shoulder the recently revived mission of "homeland defense," an unexpected show of recalcitrance emanating from the ranks of the citizen-soldiers is hardly reassuring. A central element of that mission, as envisioned by defense planners, is specifically to protect the continental United States against biological threats. The unwillingness of reservists to comply with the vaccination policy does not bode well for this initiative.[15]

Yet suspending the vaccinations in the face of protests from the ranks could also prove difficult and costly. For their part, the generals and admirals understandably worry that such a retreat may undermine the integrity of the chain of command, setting a precedent that other service personnel could cite in order to challenge onerous or unpopular orders. More broadly, abandoning the vaccination program could unravel the administration's entire response to biological threats, discrediting a major element of Clinton's self-described legacy.[16]

But there is still another factor. Defense Department officials have draped anthrax immunization in the gauzy rhetoric of "force protection," portraying it as part of the nation's obligation to protect troops sent in harm's way. Cohen himself has made force protection the distinguishing feature of his tenure as secretary of defense. His first major decision, and in some respects his defining act, was to terminate the career of the air force brigadier general in command at the time of the Khobar Towers terrorist bombing in 1996. Although investigators cleared that officer of willful irresponsibility, gross negligence, and dereliction of duty, Cohen concluded that "not enough was done" to anticipate and prepare for an attack, and therefore held the commander on the ground accountable.[17] In doing

[15]Cohen, "Preparing for a Grave New World"; Paul Stone, "Reserve Forces Forge Ahead into New Millennium," Armed Forces Press Service, Aug. 10, 1999 (http://www.defenselink.mil/new/Aug1999/n08101999-9908103.html).

[16]Miller and Broad, "Clinton Describes Terrorism Threat."

[17]Department of Defense news briefing, Subject: Khobar Towers, July 31, 1997 (http://www.defenselink.mil/news/Jul1997/t07311997-t0731coh.html).

so, the secretary made it clear that any oversight with regard to force protection would henceforth be considered a hanging offense. With the lesson of Khobar Towers now etched in the Pentagon's post–Cold War canon of professional standards, Cohen cannot easily exempt himself from its provisions.

Not surprisingly, therefore, the Department of Defense has tenaciously defended its anthrax policy and rejects criticism of the vaccine, licensed by the Food and Drug Administration (FDA) since 1970, as just wrong. "It's safe and reliable," Pentagon spokesman Kenneth Bacon flatly states. "It works and has no side effects."[18] And it is essential, Pentagon officials assert, because at least ten nations possess or are developing biological weapons, with Iraq and North Korea typically cited as the leading culprits for whom anthrax is "the weapon of choice for germ warfare."[19] In the words of one ranking U.S. officer, "It's the poor man's atomic bomb. It's ubiquitous, it's everywhere, it's easy to get a hold of, it's easy to grow."[20] It is also lethal: the projected mortality rate for unprotected human beings who inhale anthrax spores approaches 100 percent.

Senior defense officials, both civilian and military, counter reports of debilitating side effects to anthrax vaccine by insisting that adverse reactions are occurring at a lower rate than with vaccines used to prevent mumps or measles. According to the Pentagon's own statistics, problems are rare.[21] When reactions do occur, they are usually minor, the sort of "[take] two aspirins and see me in the morning kind of things."[22] Emphasizing that they would not subject the troops to undue hazards, civilian and military leaders alike, beginning with Secretary Cohen and each of the joint chiefs, have rolled up their sleeves and been vaccinated themselves. (The commander in chief has declined to indicate whether or not he has himself been immunized.)[23]

As proof of the Pentagon's willingness to go the extra mile, defense officials cite four additional preconditions that Cohen

---

[18]Department of Defense news release, Jan. 22, 1999 (http://www.defenselink.mil/news/Jan1999/n01221999_9901222.html).

[19]William S. Cohen and General Henry S. Shelton, "Anthrax Editorial Did A 'Disservice' To Troops," *Army Times*, July 19, 1999.

[20]Rear Adm. Michael L. Cowan, "DoD News Briefing," Aug. 14, 1998 (http://www.defenselink.mil/news/Aug1998/t08171998_t814ntrx.html).

[21]Through Dec. 13, 1999, the Defense Department acknowledged a total of 559 "adverse events" resulting from the vaccine, most of them categorized as minor. "DoD News Briefing," Dec. 13, 1999 (http://www.defenselink.mil/cgi-bin/dlprint).

[22]Pentagon background briefing, Aug. 5, 1999 (http://www.defenselink.mil/Aug1999/x08051999_x0805ant.html).

[23]Miller and Broad, "Clinton Describes Terrorism Threat."

insisted be satisfied before beginning actual vaccinations: supplemental testing of existing vaccine stocks, a system of tracking all recipients of vaccinations, a comprehensive communications plan to inform soldiers of the program, and a "review of health and medical issues of the program by an independent expert."[24]

Finally, if reassurance and persuasion do not suffice, there is always ridicule. A Defense Department anthrax newsletter mocks soldiers who remain wary of the program as "people who think the 'field' is where a farmer works." According to the army officer who edits the newsletter, "Most of these people have never spent a single moment in harm's way and have no appreciation of what that sacrifice means."[25] Similarly, General Charles Krulak, until his recent retirement as commandant of the Marine Corps, belittled opponents of the vaccine program as people who "are petrified that their penis is going to fall off."[26]

Beyond Safety

In one sense, the anthrax vaccine controversy recalls the standoff that occurred earlier in this decade over the so-called Gulf War Syndrome.[27] First, personnel report the onset of unexplained and

[24]Department of Defense news release, Dec. 15, 1997 (http://www.defenselink.mil/news/Dec1997/b12151997_bt79-97.html).

[25]Maj. Guy Strawder, "Straight Shot," Anthrax Vaccine Immunization Program website, June 9, 1999 (http://www.anthrax.osd.mil).

[26]Darlene Himmelspach, "A Born Leader to the Corps," *San Diego Union-Tribune*, Feb. 23, 1999.

[27]Some of the same Pentagon officials who today insist upon the safety of the anthrax vaccine have themselves suggested a link between the vaccine and Gulf War illness. Lt. Gen. Ronald Blanck, currently the surgeon general of the U.S. Army and an enthusiastic defender of the vaccine, told staff representatives of the Senate Veterans Affairs Committee in 1994 that the "safety [of the anthrax vaccine], particularly when given to thousands of soldiers in conjunction with other vaccines, is not well established. Anthrax vaccine should continue to be considered as a potential cause for undiagnosed illnesses in Persian Gulf military personnel. . . ." Senate Committee on Veterans Affairs, *Is Military Research Hazardous to Veterans' Health?* 103rd Cong., 2nd sess., Dec. 8, 1994, Senate doc. 103-97, p. 35. Investigators with the General Accounting Office (GAO) have likewise linked the two directly. According to a GAO report published in March 1999, researchers have found in the blood of sick Gulf War–era veterans antibodies for squalene, an adjuvant used in some experimental vaccines. (An adjuvant is a substance incorporated into a vaccine to accelerate or enhance a desired immune response.) In testing the effectiveness of various experimental vaccines, the Defense Department has used squalene, which has not been approved by the FDA. The GAO report suggests that government-controlled facilities producing anthrax vaccine on an emergency basis for the Gulf War may have substituted squalene for the approved adjuvant and that it may be "a contributing factor to Gulf War illnesses." Opponents of the current vaccination policy suggest that this same, unlicensed vaccine is part of the stockpile being used at present, accounting for some of the adverse reactions. The Defense Department denies ever using squalene in the production of any vaccine. See GAO, "Gulf War Illnesses: Questions About the Presence of Squalene Antibodies in Veterans Can Be Resolved," GAO/NSIAD Report 99-5 (Washington, D.C.: GAO, Mar. 29, 1999). For a detailed examination of squalene-

incapacitating illnesses shortly after getting vaccinated and present their case to sympathetic congressmen.[28] The media quickly chime in, casting the story in David and Goliath terms. Next, Defense Department officials armed with reams of data respond that whatever the source of complaint, there is no scientifically verifiable link between the reported symptoms and the vaccine. As with the illnesses reported by Gulf War veterans, it seems unlikely that this exchange will yield a definitive conclusion.

Yet, in their dogged search for information relating to the vaccine's safety, skeptics of the program have turned over many rocks and revealed a plethora of concerns that range far beyond safety as such. Those revelations suggest that the program is riddled with mismanagement, reeking with impropriety, and based on a strategy that is manifestly defective. Above all, the concerns call into question the larger policy of preparing for biological war, of which the vaccination program forms an integral part. In short, even if the Pentagon were to sustain its claims that the vaccine has no malign effects, more than sufficient cause exists on other grounds to indict the administration's biological warfare policy. Indeed, a failure to do so might truly jeopardize U.S. national security, because persisting in a foolhardy vaccination program might undermine the trust that soldiers must have in their leaders and deplete actual military capabilities, while misleading the American people as to the true nature of the challenges that they face in the aftermath of the Cold War.

The broader critique of the administration's biological warfare program consists of four major points, listed here in ascending order of importance. First, the Defense Department has entrusted the manufacture of anthrax vaccine to a single firm of dubious reputation. Serious doubts exist regarding the ability of this firm to produce a vaccine that meets established standards of purity and potency, and efforts by the Defense Department to ease those doubts have been less than persuasive.

Secondly, contrary to the public posture maintained by the Pentagon, responsible officials, including qualified medical professionals in government employ, acknowledge that the efficacy of this specific vaccine is subject to question. The Pentagon's prom-

related allegations, see Gary Matsumoto, "The Pentagon's Toxic Secret," *Vanity Fair*, May 1999, pp. 82–98.

[28]See, for example, House Committee on Government Reform, Subcommittee on National Security, Veterans Affairs, and International Affairs, testimony of Capt. Michelle L. Piel, Capt. Jonathan E. Richter, and Staff Sgt. Robert H. Soska Jr., 106th Cong., 1st sess., July 21, 1999 (http://www.house.gov/reform/ns/hearings/testimony/july_21.htm).

ised consultation with an "independent expert" about the vaccination program has not occurred.

Thirdly, immunizing U.S. forces in the field against the putative threat posed by one single strain of anthrax is woefully inadequate, and the "security" ostensibly achieved is illusory. According to the administration's own forecast about the dangers of biological terrorism, many toxins other than anthrax pose at least as great a threat. Furthermore, the likely target of any biological attack, whatever the toxin, is American civilians, not soldiers. By erecting a defensive barrier that relies on yesterday's means and leaving its flanks exposed, the Defense Department is creating a biological Maginot Line.

Fourthly, and most important, the administration's biological defense policy perpetuates the peculiarly American delusion that for every security problem there exists a technological fix. In this instance, the term "fix" becomes especially apt: taking a shot will presumably purge the bad dreams that deprive the president and his secretary of defense of a good night's sleep. Yet the expectation that immunization will nullify the bioterrorist threat conflates strategy with problem-solving. Focused on the imperative of action—inoculating soldiers, training response teams, and stockpiling supplies—this technocratic approach to security is innocent of important broader considerations.

Tainted Source

The sole source of FDA-licensed anthrax vaccine is the BioPort Corporation of Lansing, Michigan. This small start-up firm came into existence in 1998 when it purchased the assets of Michigan Biologic Products Institute (MBPI), a state-owned company with a decidedly mixed record of performance. FDA inspectors had repeatedly evaluated MBPI's procedures for manufacturing and maintaining vaccines and always found them wanting.[29] In March 1997, the FDA issued a "Notice of Intent to Revoke" MBPI's license, but even that did not get MBPI's attention.[30] A follow-up in February 1998 showed continuing deficiencies. During the course of that inspection, the FDA found fault with, *inter alia*,

---

[29]For a detailed accounting of MBPI's dismal performance during inspections, see House Committee on Government Reform, Subcommittee on National Security, Veterans Affairs, and International Affairs, statement by Dr. Robert C. Myers, Chief Operating Officer, BioPort Corporation, Apr. 29, 1999.

[30]House Subcommittee on National Security, Veterans Affairs, and International Affairs, statement by Dr. Kathryn C. Zoon, Center for Biologics and Research, FDA, Apr. 29, 1999.

the effectiveness of the firm's sporicide, the integrity of its filters, and the adequacy of its product testing, labeling, storage, and sanitation. Several lots of vaccine already on hand also failed the inspectors' potency tests. The FDA accordingly found that "the manufacturing process for Anthrax Vaccine is not validated."[31]

Rather than invest the considerable sum required to fix MBPI's problems, the state of Michigan chose to sell it. In September 1998, BioPort bought the troubled company for $25 million. This new company was the creation of three principals: Dr. Robert C. Myers, who had been MBPI's chief operating officer and who continues in that capacity with BioPort;[32] Mr. Fuad El-Hibri, a foreign national who had previously directed Porton Products, Inc., a manufacturer of biological defense vaccines in the United Kingdom; and Admiral William Crowe, former chairman of the Joint Chiefs of Staff. Mr. El-Hibri describes Admiral Crowe as a long-time family friend, but in 1992, Crowe was also a prominent supporter of presidential candidate Bill Clinton and was subsequently appointed ambassador to Great Britain. According to ABC News, Crowe acquired his stake in BioPort without having "invested a penny" of his own money.[33]

Within a month of its creation, BioPort landed a government contract to "manufacture, test, bottle, and store" anthrax vaccine for the Department of Defense. The agreement called for BioPort to produce vaccine exclusively for the government at a price of $4.36 per dose. The nominal value of the contract was $29 million. However, with the total cost of the vaccination program estimated at $130 million over six years, the potential payoff is much greater.[34]

In January 1998, MBPI shut down its plant for renovations that were funded by the Department of Defense, projecting that pro-

---

[31]FDA inspection report on MBPI, Feb. 20, 1998 (http://www.dallasnw.quik.com/cyberella/Anthrax/anthrax1.html). Lots that failed inspection were subsequently quarantined.

[32]In 1996, as MBPI's problems mounted and the sale of the troubled operation was being discussed, Dr. Myers denied any interest in purchasing the company. "I am a state employee and this would be a conflict of interest," he told the *Lansing State Journal* on Nov. 30, 1996. Cited in a memorandum to Democratic members of the House Oversight and Ethics Committee, Michigan State Legislature, from David Oppliger, House Majority Counsel, Re: Sept. 24, 1998, hearing on the sale of MBPI (Sept. 23, 1998).

[33]Howard Rosenberg, "Anthrax Cloud's Silver Lining," ABC News, Mar. 12, 1999 (http://more.abcnews.go.com/onair/2020/2020_990312_anthrax_feature.html).

[34]Assistant Secretary of Defense Sue Bailey, Department of Defense (DoD) news briefing, Aug. 14, 1998.

duction would recommence in January 2000.[35] In early 1999, El-Hibri began petitioning the government to renegotiate BioPort's contract, arguing that if the company were to remain in business it would need to increase the price charged per dose and market anthrax vaccine to outside customers.[36] Citing the lack of alternative suppliers, the Pentagon granted both requests, permitting BioPort to sell 70,000 doses elsewhere *before* meeting its government obligations and to boost the price to $10.64 per dose. The effect was to double the value of BioPort's contract. The Pentagon also agreed to provide the company (which had not yet made delivery on any vaccine) with a cash advance of $18.7 million.[37] In December 1999, the Pentagon announced that BioPort had failed the FDA inspection required to certify its production of anthrax vaccine. FDA inspectors had found some thirty deficiencies in the renovated production facility. Defense officials projected that BioPort would require an additional six to twelve months in order to meet FDA standards. They also announced plans to provide an additional $7–10 million of interim funding to keep BioPort afloat.[38]

In effect, the Pentagon locked itself in a dependent relationship with a company of questionable capabilities, which offered what appeared to be a sweetheart deal to a retired senior officer who happens to be a close supporter of the president. Relying on the same work force and the same plant management as did MBPI, the company inspires little confidence and has already demonstrated its inability to fulfill the terms of a contract it signed just one year ago. Under such circumstances, the skepticism with which some soldiers treat Defense Department assurances that all anthrax vaccine in use meets FDA standards is easily understandable.

[35]Vaccinations administered thus far all use stocks manufactured by MBPI.

[36]House Subcommittee on National Security, Veterans Affairs, and International Affairs, statement by Mr. Fuad El-Hibri, president and chief executive officer, BioPort Corporation, June 30, 1999.

[37]Pentagon background briefing, Aug. 5, 1999 (http://www.defenselink.mil/Aug1999/x08051999_x0805ant.html). On-hand stocks of vaccine, to include four lots "not part of the original DoD stockpile," are sufficient to supply the ongoing vaccination program through Dec. 1999. See House Subcommittee on National Security, Veterans Affairs, and International Affairs, statement by Brig. Gen. Eddie Cain, Joint Program Office for Biological Defense, Apr. 29, 1999. The origin of this vaccine is not clear. However, Pentagon officials acknowledge that in May 1991 the Defense Department contracted with the National Cancer Institute for the bulk production of anthrax vaccine in a quantity amounting to 6.3 million doses. See House Subcommittee, testimony of David Oliver, Principal Deputy Under Secretary of Defense for Acquisition Technology, June 30, 1999 (http://www.house.gov/reform/ns/hearings/testimony/introduction_630.htm).

[38]DoD news briefing, Dec. 13, 1999.

Questions of Efficacy

Even if the vaccine does meet FDA standards, will it actually work? In public, Defense Department officials state categorically that the vaccine is effective. Behind closed doors, the military's own experts are not so sure.

Although the military touts its biological defense initiative as innovative and forward looking, the anthrax vaccine itself is anything but that. Its formula represents old technology dating from the 1950s and was developed not with an eye toward its potential military utility, but for civilian purposes. Specifically, the vaccine was developed to protect tannery workers at risk from handling the hides of anthrax-infected animals. The chief hazard that those workers faced was not the inhalation of anthrax spores, but infection by penetration through the skin, or cutaneously.

In the 1950s, tests involving the work force in four mills in the northeastern United States demonstrated the vaccine's effectiveness against cutaneous anthrax.[39] Although five participants in the test population did develop inhalational anthrax, none of the five had received the vaccine.[40] As Colonel Arthur Friedlander, chief of the Bacteriology Division at U.S. Army Medical Research Institute, noted in 1995, these studies of "humans working in tanneries show protection against cutaneous disease." However, there exists "insufficient data to demonstrate protection against inhalational disease."[41]

Reflecting such concerns, Secretary of the Army Louis Caldera, on the eve of BioPort's purchase of MBPI in September 1998, took the unusual step of indemnifying the manufacturer against any lawsuits arising out of the use of the vaccine.[42] In justifying this action, Caldera explained that producing anthrax vaccine involves "unusually hazardous risks associated with the potential for adverse reactions in some recipients and the possibility that the desired immunological effect will not be obtained by

[39]The test population was quite limited. During the trial, twenty-six workers developed anthrax. Of those twenty-six, twenty-three had not received the vaccine, having been given a placebo or being part of an observational group. Of the remaining three, two individuals were partially immunized and one fully immunized. House Subcommittee on National Security, Veterans Affairs, and International Affairs, statement by Dr. Kathryn C. Zoon, Apr. 29, 1999.

[40]Each of the five had either received a placebo or was in an "observational" group that received neither the vaccine nor a placebo.

[41]Department of the Army, Joint Program Office for Biological Defense, Memorandum, Subject: Minutes of the Meeting on Changing the Food and Drug Administration License for Michigan Department of Public Health (MDPH) Anthrax Vaccine to Meet Military Requirements, Nov. 13, 1995.

[42]With regard to the management of the anthrax vaccination program, the army serves as executive agent for the entire Department of Defense.

all recipients." Caldera's memorandum continued: "There is no way to be certain that the pathogen used in tests measuring vaccine efficacy will be sufficiently similar to the pathogen that U.S. forces might encounter to confer immunity."[43] Stripped of "bureaucratese," the language employed by Caldera is unambiguous: depending on the circumstances, the vaccine might work or might not.

"Nonsense," Defense Department spokesmen reply: the secretary's memorandum is routine, boilerplate meant to satisfy the concerns of Pentagon lawyers and not reflective of Caldera's actual assessment of the vaccine's efficacy.[44] They remind critics that Secretary Cohen had ordered a comprehensive external review of the vaccine before implementing the vaccination program. Indeed, according to Rudy De Leon, under secretary of defense for personnel and readiness, "We asked an outside expert panel, led by the dean of the medical school at Yale University, to take a fresh look at the vaccine."[45]

Upon examination, that external review turns out to be much less than advertised. The "expert panel" was in fact a single individual, Dr. Gerard N. Burrow, and he is not the dean of Yale's medical school, but a member of the faculty with an area of specialization remote from biological warfare. He is a professor of obstetrics and gynecology. Although Burrow did give the proposed vaccination program a clean bill of health, when asked to testify before a congressional subcommittee regarding that evaluation, he begged off, claiming that his schedule would not permit him to appear in Washington. Instead, he sent a letter explaining that he had accepted Cohen's invitation to evaluate the program simply "out of patriotism." He added that he had made it clear "that I had no expertise in Anthrax."[46]

A New Maginot Line

Even if the vaccine works, does the anthrax vaccination program constitute an effective defense against the threat most likely to face the United States?

---

[43] Secretary of the Army Louis Caldera, Memorandum of Decision, Subject: Authority under Public Law 85-804 to Include an Indemnification Clause in Contract DAMD 17-91-C-1139 with Michigan Biologic Products Institute, Sept. 3, 1998.

[44] Apart from anthrax, the most recent government indemnification of a vaccine manufacturer occurred in 1976 and involved the notorious swine-flu vaccine. Daniels, "Anthrax Shots Bad Medicine?"

[45] Staff Sgt. George Hayward, "DOD Officials Say Anthrax Vaccine Safe, Effective," Apr. 16, 1998 (http://www.af.mil/news/Apr.1998/n19980416_980507.html).

[46] Letter, Gerard N. Burrow to Congressman Christopher Shays, Apr. 26, 1999.

Notwithstanding the Pentagon's designation of anthrax as the "poor man's atomic bomb," the Clinton administration acknowledges that adversaries bent on using biological agents as terror weapons can choose from a veritable smorgasbord.[47] For several of these alternatives, the mortality rate approaches that of anthrax, and for some there exists no known cure. Among the candidates are smallpox, botulism, bubonic plague, and the ebola virus.[48] In the widely quoted assessment by Kathleen Bailey, a former official with the U.S. Arms Control and Disarmament Agency, all it would take to produce a potent biological arsenal using one of these pathogens would be 225 square feet of laboratory and $10,000 worth of equipment.[49] Indeed, U.S. intelligence agencies believe that Iraq and North Korea are already developing the capability to weaponize smallpox.[50]

For true believers in biological terror, the challenges of employing such an arsenal, although not trivial, are by no means insurmountable. Jessica Stern, formerly with the Clinton administration's National Security Council, recounts tests conducted by the U.S. Army in the 1950s and 1960s to demonstrate the feasibility of releasing biological weapons offshore or in subways or of employing crop dusters to spread toxins. She speculates about terrorists employing chemical or biological agents to contaminate the nation's water supply or its stocks of "cola, milk, and baby food."[51] Although Stern does not minimize the practical difficulties inherent in such operations, she leaves the clear impression that a resourceful terrorist would find ways to overcome them.

Given such a hydra-headed threat, what benefit derives from protecting less than 1 percent of the population against a single pathogen? According to Rear Admiral Michael L. Cowan of the Joint Staff, "Having the vaccine sort of takes the atomic bomb away. There's no point in dropping it if it's not going to harm any-

[47]Bradley Graham, "Clinton Calls for Germ War Antidotes," *Washington Post*, May 21, 1998. The training of reservists who form Rapid Assessment and Initial Detection teams (the quick-response component of "home defense") features several non-anthrax scenarios. They include botulism delivered by balloon and a nerve agent in an exploding trash can. Bradley Graham, "Sneak Attack Detectives Prepare to Prowl," *Washington Post*, Aug. 28, 1999.

[48]Jessica Stern, *The Ultimate Terrorists* (Cambridge, Mass.: Harvard University Press, 1999), pp. 164–65.

[49]Cited in Leonard A. Cole, "The Specter of Biological Weapons," *Scientific American*, Dec. 1996 (http://www.sciam.com/1296issue/1296cole.html).

[50]William J. Broad and Judith Miller, "Government Report Says 3 Nations Hide Stocks of Smallpox," *New York Times*, June 13, 1999. See also D. A. Henderson, "Bioterrorism as a Public Health Threat," *Emerging Infectious Diseases*, July–Sept. 1998 (http://www.cdc.gov/ncidod/EID/vol4no3/hendrsn.htm).

[51]Stern, *The Ultimate Terrorists*, pp. 52–53.

body." But the implication that inoculating troops at Fort Hood or Camp Lejeune will frustrate an anthrax-equipped terrorist is absurd. Terrorists bent on mayhem are unlikely to target military installations in the first place. Far "softer" and more lucrative targets are readily available, ranging from the New York subway to the ventilation system of a high-rise building in any American city. As an antiterrorist measure, a program of selected inoculation will at best provide a reaction force that is protected against anthrax and can therefore respond to the disaster. But if that is the requirement, then the priority of vaccinations should go not to soldiers, but to police, fire fighters, and medical personnel—none of whom are protected under the administration's biological defense policy.

Furthermore, even assuming that anthrax is the terrorist's "weapon of choice," the strain actually employed may well differ genetically from anthrax found in nature. In other words, it may differ from the strain against which the existing vaccine was tested in the 1950s. As Caldera's precisely worded memorandum acknowledged, "There is no way to be certain that the pathogen used in tests measuring vaccine efficacy will be sufficiently similar to the pathogen that U.S. forces might encounter to confer immunity." Indeed, potential adversaries have been hard at work developing ways to modify anthrax, and according to Ken Alibek, a former deputy director of the Soviet Union's biological weapons research program, Soviet researchers succeeded in developing a genetically altered strain of anthrax by the 1980s.[52]

If the threat of bioterrorism depicted by Cohen and others in the administration really exists, then terrorists calculating when, where, and how to strike can choose from a wide range of options. The vaccination program currently in place will have its promised effect only if adversaries confine themselves to the particular biological weapon of *our* choosing (anthrax as found in nature) employed according to *our* preferred scenario (against U.S. troops). That assumes a willingness to accommodate American desires hardly to be expected even from a Saddam Hussein.

Defending the anthrax vaccination program, Secretary Cohen, the arch-proponent of force protection, has told his troops, "I would be derelict in my duties sending you out in an environment in which you weren't properly protected."[53] But if Cohen has assessed the bioterrorism threat accurately and if prophylactic

---

[52]William J. Broad and Judith Miller, "Defector Tells of Soviet and Chinese Germ Weapons," *New York Times*, Apr. 5, 1999.
[53]Linda D. Kozaryn, "Duty-Bound to Order Anthrax Shots, Cohen Says," Mar. 9, 1999 (http://www.defenselink.mil/news/Mar1999/n03121999_9903103.html).

vaccination is essential to deflect that threat—two very large and dubious assumptions—it is not soldiers who are principally at risk, but civilians.[54] Only if the United States implemented a *nationwide* program of vaccination against *all* likely pathogens might terrorists armed with the "poor man's atomic bomb" calculate that there is no point in using it.

Strategies of Illusion

In fact, barring the profoundly improbable discovery of some universal vaccine, it is not at all clear that an emphasis on vaccination makes sense, no matter how broad the population selected for immunization. The search for quick-fix solutions leads only to a dead-end, as previous American experience with weapons of mass destruction suggests.

With its discovery of an imminent biological threat, the Clinton administration would have Americans believe that they are confronted with something altogether new. Yet that is not the case. As the General Accounting Office, the investigative arm of Congress, reports, "The nature and magnitude of the military threat of biological warfare has [sic] not changed since 1990."[55] What is new at this time when the United States reigns supreme in the realm of *conventional* warfare is the Pentagon's heightened awareness of this *unconventional* threat. That threat has long existed, but in the old days went largely ignored.

Taking at face value the rhetoric employed by administration officials to describe that threat, the United States finds itself today in a position of naked vulnerability. This was precisely the perception in 1949 when the Soviet Union detonated its first atomic device. The government's response to that vulnerability (which we now know to have been exaggerated, at least into the 1960s) was civil defense. Building enough shelters and stockpiling enough water, rations, and medical supplies would enable people to survive a nuclear attack, or so the optimistic propaganda of the day led Americans to believe.

[54]Interestingly, while the vaccination of all U.S. forces is mandatory, it remains optional for Defense Department civilians actually assigned to duties where the risk of exposure to anthrax exists. A directive issued by the Defense Threat Reduction Agency, which conducts inspections worldwide related to weapons of mass destruction, permits "Emergency Essential" civilian staff to deploy on missions abroad without immunization. The only requirement is that the individual must "execute a 'Statement of Informed Declination' attesting to the Agency's offer of anthrax immunization and the employee's decision to decline." Defense Threat Reduction Agency, "Policy Memorandum 99-22, DTRA Anthrax Immunization Program," July 23, 1999.

[55]House Subcommittee on National Security, Veterans Affairs, and International Affairs, testimony of Mr. Kwai Chan, director of special studies and evaluations, National Security and International Affairs Division, GAO, Apr. 29, 1999 (http://www.house.gov/reform/ns/hearings/testimony/mrchan4-30.htm).

But civil defense was an exercise in self-delusion. The notion that the federal government, its vast resources notwithstanding, could engineer a defense against nuclear war was preposterous. To the extent it diverted resources from more relevant measures that *did* avert a nuclear exchange (such as early warning, a robust and credible deterrent, flexible and responsive conventional capabilities, arms control, and confidence-building measures), the misplaced emphasis on civil defense may actually have been dangerous. It only fed the public fear of Armageddon, fueling political hysteria that complicated the efforts of Presidents Truman and Eisenhower to formulate a reasoned, coherent Cold War strategy.

The Clinton administration's impassioned call to erect a barrier against biological terror recalls that earlier infatuation with civil defense. This time, instead of protection for the masses, the government is offering inoculation only for a select few. But as with civil defense, this search for absolute protection is illusory, serves to block consideration of sounder alternatives, and—as in the early Cold War—may inadvertently encourage panic. The requirement is not for more impassioned rhetoric, but for a different approach.

A Way Out

In Congress, skepticism about the anthrax vaccination policy is growing. Congressman Christopher Shays (R-Conn.) has held hearings that are highly critical of the program, and two bills are currently pending that would take the matter out of the Pentagon's hands altogether. HR 2548, "The Department of Defense Anthrax Vaccination Moratorium Act," introduced by Congressman Benjamin A. Gilman (R-N.Y.) in July 1999, would halt anthrax immunizations until independent studies have verified the safety of the vaccine. HR 2543, "The American Military Health Protection Act," introduced that same month by Congressman Walter Jones Jr. (R-N.C.), would make anthrax immunization voluntary until an improved vaccine becomes available. But the Pentagon should act first, defusing the impending readiness crisis caused by concerns about vaccine safety and thereby creating an opportunity to reevaluate its entire biological warfare strategy. Thanks to the misadventures of BioPort, defense policymakers can reverse course without having to admit openly that their strategy was flawed. BioPort's failure to meet its obligations provides sufficient basis for the Defense Department to cancel its contract with the struggling manufacturer. That action would provide the necessary pretext to suspend the anthrax vaccination program pending the identification of a reliable supplier of high-quality vaccine. Admittedly, that will likely take a considerable period of time.

That action would, of course, leave the United States without a ready source of anthrax vaccine, apart from the remnants of the MBPI stocks. As an interim defense against anthrax, the Defense Department should shift its emphasis from prophylaxis to treatment, administering antibiotics and vaccine to any soldiers exposed to the disease. This, in fact, is how the Pentagon had intended to treat unvaccinated soldiers had Saddam Hussein employed anthrax against U.S. forces during the Persian Gulf War. One particularly promising antibiotic is ciprofloxacin. Indeed, on the eve of Operation Desert Storm, Defense Department medical experts were touting ciprofloxacin as "an effective treatment against anthrax provided that it is taken immediately after exposure and the SM [servicemember] also completes the anthrax vaccination series as soon as possible."[56] Relying on antibiotics reinforced with vaccine offers real advantages over vaccine alone. Unlike the vaccine, antibiotics are effective against multiple strains of anthrax, complicating efforts by adversaries to design a variant that cannot be treated.[57]

Of greater importance, both the president and the secretary of defense should restate unambiguously the intention of the United States to *retaliate massively* in response to any attack with biological weapons against Americans. That threat should encompass any state involved directly or indirectly in supporting terrorists who employ biological (or, for that matter, nuclear or chemical) weapons, thereby depriving would-be perpetrators of sanctuary and bases from which to mount such an attack. As was the case with the nuclear threat during the Cold War, there is no substitute for a credible promise of punishment: swift, potent, and unerring.

Yet all of that is, in a sense, the easier part of the problem. The larger challenge is to restore to U.S. national security policy the sense of proportion it currently lacks, as exemplified by the Clinton administration's preoccupation with a possible biological Pearl Harbor. Indeed, such preoccupations have become a signature of U.S. policymakers in the post–Cold War era: tending obsessively to operational and tactical details as a pretext for dodging fundamental strategic issues.

The issue taking precedence over all others derives from one

[56]DoD information paper, Subject: Anthrax Inoculation Message from USCINCCENT, Dec. 10, 1990.
[57]Office of the Surgeon General, U.S. Army, "Rationale for Antibiotics in Prophylaxis Against Inhalation Anthrax," n.d. (Sept. 1991), declassified Oct. 31, 1996.

singular fact: the dominance of the international order by a highly ideological nation that is dedicated not simply to its own defense, but to the universal adoption of the values that it espouses. As the United States embarks upon a new century, the success of that project—which policymakers since Woodrow Wilson have characterized as providentially mandated—has become a predicate of genuine national security.

Throughout the last decade, however, progress made toward fulfilling the aims of that project—a world that is peaceful, democratic, and respectful of human rights and free enterprise, with the United States presiding as ultimate arbitrator—has been at best uneven. The frequency with which the Clinton administration has found itself obliged to employ U.S. military forces to warn, coerce, punish, and occupy offers the best measure of how limited this progress has been.

Certain of their own good will and of the universality of American values, policymakers have a hard time knowing what to make of those who take exception to the further spread of American power, ideals, culture, and lifestyle. Given the benign intentions of the United States, opposition can only be explained as perverse or irrational. Thus, the looming fears of terrorists who kill mindlessly, of paranoid dictators lobbing nuclear-tipped missiles at American cities, and hackers who for a lark might shut down the nation's electronic infrastructure. Thus, as well, the paradox of a growing sense of U.S. insecurity at a time when actual threats are, by any objective measure, lower than at any point since the 1930s.

In short, defining the "threat" as bioterrorism—much less rogue states, cyber-anarchists, or religious extremists—is to gloss over the larger point: even with the chief ideological alternatives off the board, the project of global transformation to which the United States has committed itself is not inspiring spontaneous compliance. Fixating on the problem of fending off a biological calamity—a danger that has existed virtually unnoticed for decades—enables policymakers to avert their eyes from the larger, disconcerting truth that there is no end in sight to the exertions that Americans will be obliged to make in pursuit of President Clinton's interpretation of the Wilsonian vision.

Are the aspirations implied by that vision feasible? What will it cost to fulfill them? How much are Americans, citizens as well as soldiers, willing to pay? However commendable their concern for protecting U.S. forces, the duty that American policymakers are called upon to fulfill, and dare not neglect, is to address precisely those larger questions.

Asymmetrical Adversaries

by Winn Schwartau

Attrition is generally considered to be "the American way of war," inasmuch as the United States has been able to bring to bear overwhelming firepower thanks to its industrial and technological superiority.[1] But what American-style warfare generates more than anything is *paper*. The conventional wisdom in the halls of the Pentagon is that developing the average American weapon system generates between five and ten million pieces of paper, while "big ticket" items such as the M1 tank, B-2 bomber, or the Advanced Tactical Fighter may take twenty years to get from concept to battlefield and generate over 200 million pieces of paper. All that paper means that a large number of paper-pushers are needed to fight the war. To support the paper-pushers, other people have to buy the paper, pens, and computers, and still others (the bean counters) have to count how much paper the paper-pushers are pushing, and still others (the filing clerks) must sort it all out and make it accessible.

The new breed of potential adversaries that challenge U.S. military power in the post–Cold War era, however, do not need to generate a single shred of paper in order to vex an American-style bureaucratic war machine. They need only strap together some discarded military hardware and make of it the terrorist's equivalent of a "Saturday night special." Better yet, they may simply download a file of aggressive source code from the Internet or even buy the (readily available) *Anarchist's Cookbook* in order to learn how to manufacture explosives on the scale of the bomb in Oklahoma City. What do they have to fear? That their superpower adversary will threaten to escalate its paperwork? In truth, the fewer Western-style cost/benefit analyses involved in their calculations and the simpler their chains of command, the greater their efficiency. As David Shukman has summed it up, "While Western militaries struggle for a decade on average to acquire new weapons, a country with commercially available computer equipment and *less rig-*

[1]This essay originally appeared in *Orbis*, Spring 2000, and arose from the Foreign Policy Research Institute conference "America the Vulnerable: Three Threats and What to Do about Them," Philadelphia, Pa., Oct. 7–8, 1999.

orous democratic and accounting processes could field new systems within a few years. It is the stuff of military nightmares."[2]

The End of Symmetry

The best way to appreciate perfect symmetry in a conflict situation is to contrast the typical board game with real-world warfare. In games such as chess, checkers, Chinese checkers, Stratego, or the Japanese pebble game *go*, two opposing forces with identical resources begin in mirror-image positions, and the outcome of the game is determined by the players' skills alone. In backgammon, by contrast, the rolling of dice introduces the element of luck to an otherwise symmetrical conflict, just as in real war many extraneous factors such as weather, topography, and morale can render an otherwise "fair fight" unequal. But both sides possess roughly the same equipment and play by the same rules.

Such was the fundamental nature of war throughout early modern and modern history. To be sure, in World War I the Germans broke (or rewrote) the rules when they employed mustard gas, and weaker opponents in imperial conflicts such as the Boer War, Cuban insurrection, and Filipino war against the United States resorted to guerrilla tactics. But the weapons and "game pieces"—cannon, rifles, and soldiers—remained largely symmetrical. In the same fashion, while the Germans invented a new style of war in World War II, the Blitzkrieg, that conflict continued the pattern of industrial, symmetrical war in which millions of men fought for territory, matching tank against tank, bomber against bomber. Once again, new weapons were invented that appeared to revolutionize war, such as the German V-2 rockets and especially the atomic bomb. But after the onset of the Cold War, the Soviets soon developed their own nuclear weapons, both sides raced for the intercontinental ballistic missile, and symmetry was reestablished. By the 1960s, Secretary of Defense Robert S. McNamara heralded this symmetry in his doctrine of Mutual Assured Destruction and extended deterrence.

Now, it seems, the mathematical and moral certainties of symmetrical war-gaming are giving way to a "postmodern era" in international conflict. U.S. warplanes bury the Iraqi Republican Guard under a million tons of sand and deliver destruction on Serbia with hardly a casualty. What is more, no current adversary can even aspire to meeting NATO forces on a "level" playing field.

[2]David Shukman, *Tomorrow's Wars* (New York: Harcourt Brace, 1996), emphasis in original.

It is in response to such asymmetry that those who are resistant to U.S. hegemony have pursued asymmetries of their own. In a recent book called *Unrestricted War*, the Beijing regime declared that since it cannot possibly win a conventional conflict with the United States, it intends in case of a conflict to target U.S. civilian infrastructures that control critical financial systems and transportation, communications, and power grids.[3] One of the authors, Colonel Wang Xiangsui of the Chinese air force, amplified those sentiments in August 1999. "War has rules, but those rules are set by the West. . . . If you use those rules, then weak countries have no chance. . . . We are a weak country, so do we need to fight according to your rules? No."[4] Future adversaries can be expected to seek asymmetries allowing them to confront superior opponents such as the United States by embracing an "indirect approach." The Chinese colonels who wrote *Unrestricted War* also suggested that Serbian president Milosevic would have strengthened his cause by launching terrorist attacks against NATO and U.S. interests in Italy.

Asymmetry gives terrorists their strength. They operate outside of accepted international behavior and according to value systems radically different from those of the United States, Europe, or even Russia. For instance, some of today's non-state combatants operate according to a "warrior clan" ethos reminiscent of Japanese samurai or medieval crusaders, a philosophy at odds with the ethic of modern, professional armed services. Culturally, the modern West has difficulty comprehending a value-based approach that legitimates atrocity as a weapon of war, such as when Serbian soldiers employ rape as a way to undermine the will of their opponents. Indeed, Colonel Charles Dunlap, a lawyer with the U.S. Air Force, was a master of understatement when he said, "Our likely future opponents will be unlike ourselves."[5]

How Western nations have handled such asymmetries up until now illustrates the legal and cultural constraints that they place on themselves. A trial of the terrorists accused of complicity in the Lockerbie tragedy finally began in late 1999—ten years after the event—a perfect example of a civil, symmetrical response to an asymmetrical attack. How many terrorist acts will it take to alter such behavior and provoke an asymmetrical response from a Western nation?

[3]Col. Wang Xiangsui and Oiao Liang, *Unrestricted War* (Beijing: PLA Literature Arts Publishing House, Feb. 1999), trans. Foreign Broadcast Information Service.
[4]John Pomfret, "China Ponders New Rules of 'Unrestricted War,'" *Washington Post*, Aug. 8, 1999.
[5]Private conversations with Col. Dunlap.

The Fish Tank

The Santa Fe Institute, a prominent think tank fostering inter-disciplinary analyses, recently staged a revealing asymmetrical game. First, it designed an artificial, digital "fish tank" bounded only by the quantum uncertainties of silicon storage inside memory chips. Next, it invited players to introduce artificial life forms into the fish tank to observe how they coexisted, and which life forms lived the longest and healthiest lives. "A-lifers" (the self-designation of students of artificial life) from around the world participated by contributing their favorite digital life forms while the experimenters watched to see which thrived, multiplied, or died out either from their own programmed failings or from inter-action with other life forms. Over a prolonged period, one life form consistently dominated: the one with the simplest set of encoded rules. Its first instruction read, "My species will always play nice with you. I will never be aggressive toward you. I will make every attempt to cooperate and work with you and everyone in our (global) fish tank." The second and last read, "If you mess with me, I will annihilate you without any warning." The rules that govern foreign and defense policy in Western nations do not allow them to function that way today. Western nations cannot tolerate televised bloodbaths, nor in any case do they have an adequate definition of what "mess with me" really means. Terrorism is considered a crime, not an act of war, and the legal system gives elaborate rights and privileges to "criminals" not accorded enemies at war. The fish tank experiment, however, should provide insight into foreign policy, no matter how jingoistic it may at first appear.

Fundamentals of Information Warfare

Information warfare (IW) is a prominent type of asymmetrical strategy that is likely to emerge in the near future, and it can be waged at three different levels of intensity.

Class I information warfare is aimed at the individual. In cyberspace all are guilty until proven innocent, personal privacy is not legislated, and even names and buying habits are bartered and sold by commercial concerns for profit. Each year some 20,000 Americans are victims of identity theft. Thus, in time of conflict, nothing prevents a military adversary from researching senior NATO leaders (or soldiers in the field) and threatening their families back home, turning users' very trust in the contents of computers and the algorithms running them into a tool that can be used by miscreant marketers, common criminals, or foreign enemies to "get at" them.

Class II information warfare comprises industrial and economic espionage by states or non-state organizations. Thus, British Airways can steal (and has stolen) customers from Virgin Atlantic through simple theft of its data base. But the techniques can include eavesdropping on telephone or cellular calls, Internet sniffing, password cracking, and electronic breaking and entering. According to the FBI, 122 countries conduct online industrial and economic espionage against the United States, with the resulting losses to Americans of approximately $300 billion per year.

Class III information warfare is conducted by one nation against another and can include cyberterrorism by organized groups, organized militia-like groups, or narco-terrorists possessing the same high-end snooping devices as governments. China's declaration of "Unrestricted War" certainly fits this category, as does Russia's announcement that IW is second in seriousness only to nuclear war.

Under predominant military thought, hacking one's way to victory is asymmetrical, and it has taken many years for the U.S. military to be willing to play in this new, virtual arena. But not everyone agrees that the threat is sufficient to abandon the old, symmetrical rules. Colonel Dunlap, for one, has "never been an advocate of the position that there is the very great threat of computer network attack," because in reality "it is much more difficult to do." Perhaps the threat is not "nearly as great as some of the zealots would say," but the asymmetry of IW nevertheless makes it potentially appealing.[6]

Asymmetrical adversaries thrive on simplicity, not complexity. They shun the hierarchical, three-dimensional structure of the industrial age in favor of the far more efficient, two-dimensional leadership models adopted by many terrorist groups. Asymmetrical adversaries do not fill reams of paper with justifications. They do not attempt to build a paper trail to justify their acts at some later date to historians, judges, pundits, or armchair experts. They just do it. According to Dunlap, "Many low-tech opponents are often unfazed by orthodox calculations of what is militarily doable." If, in the commercial sector, breaking the mold or accomplishing the undoable is what breeds success and huge financial reward, why should we expect anything less on the battlefield?

We tend to miscalculate the real ability of opponents to devise low-cost, low-tech methods to offset capabilities of technologically superior adversaries. Effective psychological operations, media manipulation, atrocities, genocide, and unrestricted assaults against civilians are familiar methods used by groups that employ

[6]Transcript of the Foreign Policy Research Institute conference, "America the Vulnerable: Three Threats and What to Do about Them."

widely available technology, but apply to its use a different set of values than those prevailing in the West. Yet the West has developed neither the military imagination to streamline its conventional (hierarchical, paper-intensive) way of war nor the political will to deter or defend against asymmetrical threats.

Another skeptic is Martin Libicki, a senior RAND analyst. "If this threat is so dire," he asks, "why haven't we seen anything really, really large take place?"[7] But according to that reasoning, we should only worry about disasters after they occur. Such a complacent approach scarcely prevailed during the Cold War, when the dangers of nuclear war were keenly anticipated in advance of some "really, really large" event.

At the criminal level, we are aware of a certain amount of computer hacking and can only speculate about how much goes undetected. True, an electronic Pearl Harbor has thankfully not occurred yet. But tests such as Eligible Receiver, run by the National Security Administration, suggest that widespread damage can occur from an asymmetrical adversary as isolated as North Korea. What is more, asymmetrical commercial adversaries do all sorts of things Americans only wish they could do. Private foreign companies are often backed by government subsidies to increase global competitiveness. Product dumping is not illegal in many countries. Banking and disclosure laws tend to be more stringent in the United States than overseas. Spying and espionage are more a matter of the nature of business, although Americans still recite, "Gentlemen don't read other gentlemen's mail." But the world is not populated by gentlemen, and the U.S. government's Economic Espionage Act of 1996 does nothing more than threaten commercial spies with a $10 million fine. Such a deterrent is a trifling amount in industries measured in the tens of billions of dollars. When the national economic hemorrhage from Class II IW is estimated at $100–300 billion and the rest of the world asks why the rules of global capitalism are set by the United States, whose population constitutes a mere 4 percent of the population of the earth, asymmetrical attack is bound to be the norm, not the exception.

Yet Washington is, if anything, an accessory to such crime. As a result of certain environmental laws, mandatory disclosures of U.S. companies' trade secrets subsequently become part of the public domain, because trade secrets and proprietary information are not considered worth protecting in the manner of military intelligence. The U.S. Patent and Trademark Office veritably trumpets the latest innovations in American technology before the rest of the world.

[7]Conference transcript.

Above all, when an American company comes under assault (cybernetic or otherwise) by an adversary (domestic or international), it finds itself virtually handcuffed to a legal system unequipped to deal with Internet crime and high-tech espionage, and offering no reasonable chance of recovery or restitution. So what is the victim company to do when law enforcement is either unable or unwilling to help? Many companies are saying that the only way to balance the asymmetry of the threat against the inadequate legal response is to engage in self-help and "fight fire with fire." American law enforcement agencies, however, say that if they catch an American firm aggressively defending itself, they will prosecute it.

Vigilantism is perhaps not the most desirable means of self-protection, but the alternative is victimization. That is why other countries are actively building vigilante-like response mechanisms to both physical and virtual assaults. Israel tolerates nothing, and France is notorious for its one-upmanship in commercial warfare. Other European countries are taking similar stands and wondering why the United States refrains from active defense of its intellectual and physical wealth. Some in the Congress say, "We have to set an example. We're not going to stoop to their level." But if the Pentagon deploys the SEALs, Special Forces, and Delta Forces to deter or respond to asymmetrical threats, why does Washington shrink from treating IW in the same fashion? One way or another, the United States needs to balance the odds, or it will lose by forfeit.

Ten Questions about Cyber-War

There are no easy answers to the challenges of asymmetrical conflict, but neither are those challenges new. When I myself briefed a disbelieving Congress, Pentagon, and White House in 1991 about the specter of cyberterrorism and danger of an "electronic Pearl Harbor" I was labeled a "Chicken Little." Nearly a decade later, there is no more margin for inactivity. To continue to ignore the realities of asymmetrical personal digital assaults, global economic espionage, and terrorist or nation-state conflict is to repeat the mistakes the U.S. government made in the 1990s when it spent hundreds of millions of dollars on studies and task forces, but, out of arrogance or apathy, accomplished little.

Asymmetrical conflict is now the norm, and just as the maxim "Change is the only constant" holds true, asymmetrical assault is the only strategy that makes sense for erstwhile allies as well as enemies, since they cannot compete under the traditional rules. That is why the so-called revolution in military affairs (RMA) is far *more* profound than even the Pentagon realizes.

What should have been (and now must be) done? To begin with, U.S. authorities need to find answers to at least the following questions, offered here as a springboard for debate, constructive criticism, and inspiration.

1. As a matter of policy, should proportional response remain the moral principle defining U.S. proactive defense, inasmuch as it gives the asymmetrical adversary the advantage of knowing the contents of the U.S. "policy box" and our sociopolitical limitations? Or should America once again threaten nonproportional response (including massive retaliation) as the only way to keep adversaries at bay? After all, it worked in the fish tank.

2. Should U.S. response to asymmetrical attacks continue to be shaped by the country's sensibilities alone, in secret or open debate, or is it time to play by international "rules" (or lack of them) to create a more even playing field?

3. Many asymmetrical adversaries are nongovernmental organizations (NGOs) hiding behind the industrial era's concepts of physical borders and national sovereignty. The offensive asymmetrical adversary (terrorist) who physically hides inside the border of a nation-state that may or may not be friendly knows that the United States can do little. Thus, whereas in Egypt a murderer encounters a swift and harsh police response, a terrorist on American soil is treated with kid gloves as a conventional criminal. Is it time for Americans, if they really believe in globalization, to protect their interests globally?

4. Does the existing international court system need to be changed to meet the realities of asymmetrical conflicts? Can laws that deal directly with the nature of modern asymmetry evolve to new standards?

5. If a corporation or NGO finds itself under a virtual attack, and law enforcement—for whatever reason—chooses not to involve itself, should that organization be permitted to take the law into its own hands?

6. What sort of dynamic defenses, in contrast to a classic fortress mentality, can be mounted against IW attacks?

7. Today it is illegal for a company to disarm an online assailant, so that the company has no choice but to either absorb the blow and do nothing or else harm its functionality through elaborate layers of enhanced security. How can laws be rewritten to permit the electronic arms of adversaries to be electronically removed?

8. The December 1948 U.N. Declaration of Human Rights

specified privacy as a citizen's guarantee. Can we now agree that passage of the Electronic Bill of Rights, put forth in 1994 and adapted by Vice President Al Gore in 1998, is overdue?[8]

9. The rear-echelon attack as discussed by former general John Sheehan is a serious U.S. military weakness. The military uses unclassified civilian infrastructure for many of its operations, yet protection for these systems is out of the control of the military. Is it not high time that the government examine its options, short of nationalization of infrastructure, for defending civilian systems against hostile attacks?

10. Colonel Dunlap thinks that we should continue to treat terrorists as criminals and give them all of the rights of any conventional criminal, unless there is "clear demonstration that the Republic is about to come unravelled."[9] But does not defining information assaults (especially if launched by agents of a foreign power) as mere criminal actions by individuals send a very bad message about our national will to protect ourselves?

Conclusion

Redefining sovereignty, the RMA, and indeed the global culture in order to counter the asymmetrical IW threats that face the American nation, companies, and citizens is a task that can no longer be shirked. We need to ask more of the tough questions above and challenge the nation and international community to search for synergy among the needs of individuals, corporations, and nation-states. Only one person is needed with the broad vision and courage to begin to make the necessary changes. That evangelist, it must be said, will doubtless be vilified for forcing a complacent public and government into a controversial morass and shunning political expedience. But there is no other way to escape the mind-numbing paperwork Americans seem always to force upon themselves before taking the most rudimentary defensive action. Nor can one wait for Congress to act while the world moves into the future at Internet speed and adversaries of the United States adjust much more quickly than Americans themselves. Whether such an evangelist will emerge remains to be seen. But history will judge the years 1995–2005 very harshly if the United States abdicates its responsibility, or looks the other way, or caters to special interest groups. Americans must take to heart the task of defending their right to determine their own nation's fate, or that right will pass into the hands of myriad asymmetrical enemies.

---

[8]Winn Schwartau, *Information Warfare* (New York: Thunder's Mouth Press, 1998).
[9]Conference transcript.

THE RISKS OF A
NETWORKED MILITARY

by Richard J. Harknett and the JCISS Study Group

Lost in the welter of daily crises—Serbian atrocities, Chinese espionage, North Korean nuclear programs, and Iraqi intransigence—is the big story about American defense policy.[1] Away from the headlines, as the United States designs a security policy for the twenty-first century, two basic facts of long-term consequence have emerged. The first is that present and foreseeable defense budgets are simply not large enough simultaneously to support the current tempo of military operations worldwide, the high level of training and readiness that makes American skill at warfare second to none, and the modernization of the current arsenal. The second fact is less widely recognized, but just as certain, and it has important implications for how we deal with the first. Notions of an information technology–driven "revolution in military affairs" (IT-RMA) are now deeply embedded in American defense planning, but despite their intuitive attractiveness, these ideas are dangerously misguided.

American national security planners, informed by an influential group of academics and retired military officers, are pushing a dramatically new vision of conflict in the twenty-first century. These visionaries argue that the combination of advances in computer processing, microelectronics, surveillance, and precision weapons technologies will permit a fundamentally new way of war. After reviewing the challenges for ensuring national security in the next century, the blue-ribbon National Defense Panel, for example, endorsed an aggressive transformation of the American military. The IT-RMA, it concluded, permits and demands a new force structure that "radically alter[s] the way in which we project power," reducing reliance on industrial-age military forces such as heavy ground units and aircraft carrier battle groups.[2] The Clinton

[1]This essay is a multi-authored product of the Joint Center for International and Security Studies. Co-authors include Stephen Biddle, Jan Breemer, Daniel Deudney, Peter Feaver, Benjamin Frankel, Emily O. Goldman, Chaim Kaufmann, William C. Martel, and Edward Rhodes. This essay originally appeared in *Orbis*, Winter 2000.

[2]National Defense Panel Final Report, "Transforming Defense: National Security in the 21st Century" (http://www.dtic.mil/ndp), p. 33.

administration's 1998 *National Security Strategy for a New Century* also calls for such a transformation.[3] IT-RMA proponents argue that the United States cannot act like the early-twentieth-century army that boasted the world's finest horse cavalry while armored tanks rumbled in the distance. The United States now has the world's finest tanks, they argue, but the hum of computers in the background is deafening.

Advocates recognize that such a new force structure will require a very different allocation of service roles and missions among the army, navy, and air force. If it can accomplish this, however, enthusiasts predict that the IT-RMA can rocket the United States into a permanent position of unchallenged leadership in world politics. Moreover, as pressures grow to maximize the utility of every dollar spent on defense, the IT-RMA presents itself as the solution that will preserve U.S. leadership without straining the pocketbook or risking (too many) lives, a radical technological and organizational leap that could solve the defense budget and modernization problems in one fell swoop.

But should the United States, today's leading military power, pursue a revolution that challenges the basis of the very system it currently dominates? The promise of the IT-RMA is offset by significant potential difficulties that do not seem easy to overcome. Before altering U.S. military power to take advantage of what Joseph Nye and William Owens have called "America's information edge," policymakers need to examine the end state carefully.[4]

We conclude that the end state is a major and unnecessary gamble. Given the military preeminence that the United States would be exchanging for an IT-RMA, the burden of proof rests on the advocates of radical change to show that the gamble is worth the risks. Close inspection of the case for IT-RMA reveals a series of ad hoc assumptions about perfect training, perfect coordination, and perfect innovation. Its advocates, furthermore, have yet to address the possibility of unanticipated side effects and new vulnerabilities.

A far more prudent approach than revolution is a "go-slow" approach to defense planning for the twenty-first century that emphasizes the preservation of near-term readiness while exploring the opportunities of an evolutionary transition. Incremental military adaptation has served this country well over the last gen-

[3]*National Security Strategy for a New Century*, Oct. 1998 (http://www.whitehouse.gov/WH/EOP/NSC/html/documents/nssrpref.html).

[4]Joseph Nye and William Owens, "America's Information Edge," *Foreign Affairs*, Mar./Apr. 1996, pp. 20–36.

eration, and before the United States abandons it for a leap into the unknown, policymakers should have a better idea of where they are going to land. Despite budgetary pressures to do otherwise, the United States should not commit itself fully to a drastic shift until the new concepts, weapons, and organizations have demonstrated, through extensive experimentation, that their vaunted effectiveness can meet real security challenges. Absent further evidence, the prudent course is to skip the revolution and stick with evolutionary innovation.

The Revolutionary Argument

Technological advances in the ability to process, organize, and disseminate information are defining America's vision of the approaching millennium. In the most popular view, evolving information capabilities form the basis for fundamental changes in social and economic practices, organizational structures, and military affairs. The digitization of information processing is expected to cause a fundamental shift in the way societies pursue wealth and power, and leaders across the political spectrum have touted their unbounded optimism for the revolution. According to President Clinton,

> the invention of the steam engine two centuries ago and the harnessing of electricity ushered in an industrial revolution. . . . [T]oday, the invention of the integrated circuit and computer and the harnessing of light for communications have made possible the creation of the global Internet and an electronic revolution that will once again transform our lives . . . [as we] enter the new millennium ready to reap the benefits of the emerging electronic age of commerce.[5]

Former Speaker of the House Newt Gingrich talks just as enthusiastically about how the "lessons of the information age" should guide policy decisions.

The U.S. defense community has picked up on these presumed lessons and connected them to centuries-old military maxims about the value of information. The military theorist currently in vogue is the ancient Chinese writer Sun Tzu, whose philosophy of war is captured in the admonition: "Know the enemy and know yourself; in a hundred battles you will never be in peril." In defense circles, information-revolution enthusiasts hold out the possibility of knowing the disposition and movement of both opposing forces and one's own to a degree to which Sun Tzu could

---

[5]Office of the Press Secretary, Text of the President's Message to Internet Users, July 1, 1997 (http://www.pub.whitehouse.gov/uri-res/12r?urn:pdi//oma.eop.gov.us/1997/7/1/4.text.1).

not even have dreamed. The goal is to replace Clausewitz's "fog of war" with total transparency across the battlespace of air, land, sea, and space.[6]

According to these IT-RMA proponents, the integration of information technologies will provide the United States with major military advantages. The combat value of fighting forces will be multiplied through information superiority—the payoff of a "system of systems" that connects remote sensors, soldiers in the field, commanders, and weapon platforms, thereby allowing the military to locate, target, engage, assess, and reengage with speed and efficiency. Total battlespace transparency will allow the United States to close out enemy options and overwhelm an opponent's capacity to take decisive actions in combat. The technologies that will underpin this military power are promised to require fewer weapons and deployed troops, and, very important, to jeopardize the lives of fewer American soldiers.

This image of the future is best captured in the Defense Department's *Joint Vision 2010*, which, according to General John Shalikashvili, then-chairman of the Joint Chiefs of Staff, lays out a blueprint for military doctrine and force structure in the new century. The document's core premise is that emerging technology will grant U.S. forces "information superiority," enabling them to prevail in anything from major war to low-intensity conflict to peacekeeping and humanitarian operations.[7]

Dominance across the spectrum of conflict is precisely what the United States needs, information enthusiasts argue, in part because the end of the Cold War has not ushered in an era of order and stability. On the contrary, regional rogues such as Saddam Hussein threaten vital American interests; international crime syndicates eat away at the internal fabric of American society; terrorists imperil American lives at home and abroad; and civil wars and ethnic conflicts cause mass migrations of refugees, threatening the stability of key allies and trading partners.

According to IT-RMA enthusiasts, new information-based methods and organizations will produce a flexible military able to adapt to any contingency in an uncertain world. This is not the military of the Persian Gulf War, but a fully networked, omniscient fighting force with global reach and a full spectrum of responses.

---

[6]Sun Tzu, *The Art of War*, ed. James Clavell (New York: Delta, 1988); Carl von Clausewitz, *On War*, ed. Michael Howard and Peter Paret (Princeton, N.J.: Princeton University Press, 1984).

[7]Joint Chiefs of Staff, *Joint Vision 2010* (1996) (http://www.dtic.mil/doctrine/jv2010/jvpub.htm).

Drawn from lessons of corporate restructuring around information technology, a networked military will function by way of organizational and command structures radically different from those that typify the traditional, hierarchical armed forces. According to IT-RMA proponents, since information content and connectivity have the potential to shape economic, political, and military realities in the next century, the United States should exploit the comparative technological advantage that it now enjoys and further develop the processes, norms, and organizations to maintain its predominance. However, three broad objections to this perspective must be raised. First, efforts to promote an IT-RMA will create significant vulnerabilities that do not currently exist. Secondly, an IT-RMA is unlikely to provide useful responses to the threats that will probably pose the greatest challenges to the United States. Finally, it risks triggering a backlash against U.S. foreign policy, even among allies.

The Revolution Creates New Weaknesses

Enthusiastic supporters of an IT-RMA argue that restructuring forces to take advantage of information technology can significantly reduce the uncertainty inherent in military operations and the inefficiencies common to large organizational action. Networked information systems will provide, according to this view, a shared sense of fluid military situations among all levels of command. Troops will know clearly where they are in relation to friendly and enemy soldiers and will have detailed information concerning the behavior and dispositions of enemy forces. Armed with such data, troops and commanders should be able to discern the probability that enemy soldiers can achieve their objectives or prevent the U.S. forces from achieving their own. Information superiority is expected to leave the enemy paralyzed and easy prey for coordinated, low-cost surgical strikes. Shared battlespace awareness will purportedly enhance efficiency by giving every actor access to all the best information the U.S. side possesses. If an entire military force, from the most junior foot soldier to the commander in chief, shares a common understanding of the whereabouts of enemy and friendly forces, mistakes such as "friendly fire" casualties or unintended collateral damage can be averted and military power brought to bear with precision.

For this shared sense of battlespace to be maintained during combat, of course, access to information will have to be relatively easy and comprehensive. Individuals must be able to connect to the information network in a variety of ways, and redundant access points must be available. What many of its advocates fail to acknowledge is that the changes the IT-RMA requires create the risks of a loss of information security, a reduction in force resilience, and significant management and organizational problems.

The Access/Security Tradeoff. If shared battlespace awareness can provide a critical, perhaps even decisive advantage, opponents will find that the data infrastructure and the data themselves make exceedingly valuable targets. The incentive to "eavesdrop" on, contaminate, or disrupt the information flow of the American military will be enormous. In the Persian Gulf conflict, Iraqi leaders did not fully appreciate the significance of highly advanced surveillance planes or networked computer communications, but it would be imprudent to expect that the next opponent will make the same mistake. Each access point into the system of systems will be a potential Achilles' heel in need of protection.

It is here that the tension between easy access and robust security creates a dilemma. Because networks are supposed to have a seamless quality—once in the network, one can see almost everything—an adversary who has gained access will be able to steal, change, or destroy critical information freely and swiftly. By contrast, within a traditional hierarchical organization, an opponent that impersonates an infantry soldier would have great difficulty discovering essential information simply because his rank would restrict access. The very nature of non-hierarchical information systems means that penetration of one point of defense could provide access to enormous amounts of information or even unleash havoc throughout the information system. The opportunity to exploit the seamless quality of networked communication is amplified by the requirement that direct access be relatively easy. The problem is straightforward: it is easier to protect access to the filing cabinet if ten people have one key each than if a thousand people have five keys each.

One solution to this access/security problem is to recompartmentalize information so that the access of the private differs from that of the general. But this reintroduces hierarchy into information processing, essentially un-networking the network and forgoing the benefits of seamless sharing of information. Another solution might be to keep a seamless network, but with fewer access points and restrictions for certain individuals or ranks, but again this would undermine shared awareness. A third response would be to maintain comprehensive access and seamless networking, but erect a very active and robust defense. IT-RMA proponents assume that reliable defense against enemy exploitation of information system vulnerabilities is possible. They may be correct, given the potential for encryption, passwords, and layers of firewalls to foil an opponent's attacks on an information system. The problem, however, lies not in developing effective countermeasures, but in the seamless incorporation of those countermeasures during combat. Can we expect that, in response to an assumed enemy penetration, an effective defensive software patch can be introduced in such a way that all friendly forces are able to update their access procedures quickly and maintain connections while the intruder is forced out of the system? For comparison, just consider the compatibility problems created when a new version of a word-processing program is introduced into a small office group.

The issue is not whether it is possible to defend information operations, but whether it can be done without undermining the whole point of the network. Opponents need not gain ascendancy over the information system in order to frustrate the system's owner. All they have to do is persist long enough and force the creation of so many firewalls that the system no longer functions as designed. Recent navy wargames produced this result. In its efforts to protect the network, the American side effectively unnetworked the network by recompartmentalizing access—that is, it did the enemy's job! Every step toward protecting information is a step away from shared awareness. Finding the correct mix of security and access will be a daunting task.

Individual empowerment and the leveling of hierarchy also raise the possibility of conscious misuse. The access/security dilemma involves keeping unauthorized persons out of the network, but a more serious problem occurs when someone who is authorized to be in the system "goes south." Since it is much easier to move through an information system in a networked organization than it is in a hierarchical one, the potential for individuals to cause harm increases markedly. Ideological dissenters or simply disgruntled employees may seek to crash the system, leave time bombs that can be activated in the future, corrupt information, or engage in internal conspiracy, theft, or espionage.

Traitors and malcontents have always existed in militaries, but until now the problem has been manageable because, with few exceptions, the amount of damage an individual could inflict without great effort was marginal. Enemies within may have been able to pass along some narrow intelligence, scuttle a few weapons, or persuade a few others not to carry out their duty. Moreover, the greater the effort to do harm, the more likely a traitor would be caught by authorities. The empowerment associated with network organization dynamics changes this balance. Actions of individuals can have a ripple effect throughout the organization and occur at much greater speed. Consider what the likes of the Oklahoma City bombing perpetrators or the white supremacist group at Fort Bragg could do in the future with easy access to comrades in a million-person military. The number of malcontents and misfits is likely to remain small, but a single individual with access to critical nodes might be able to bring an entire system down. Individual empowerment means that lone rogues in the armed forces would not even need to recruit collaborators, dramatically reducing their risk of getting caught. Deterring such action becomes difficult, if not impossible. As the former director of the National Security Agency, Lieutenant General Kenneth Minihan, has noted, "Unstructured attacks are occurring against our networks every day, but unfortunately, most are not even detected." When they are, he said, "we rarely know who the attacker was."[8] Imagine what the few spies that have inflicted serious damage, such as Jonathan Pollard, John Walker, Aldrich Ames, and Ronald Pelton, might have accomplished with wider and easier access.

Future opponents are unlikely to miss this opportunity. The National Defense Panel notes that adversaries will try asymmetric strategies to exploit American vulnerabilities and we must assume that all weaknesses cannot be completely eliminated. A recent report by the Center for Strategic and International Studies cites Pentagon experts who conclude that "well-coordinated attacks by fewer than 30 computer virtuosos . . . with a budget of less than $10 million, could bring the United States to its knees."[9] If even relatively small efforts can have such sweeping effects, then increasing the Pentagon's dependence on the very systems such strategies target could be a dangerous gamble.

The Loss of Resilience. IT-RMA is often touted as a force multiplier. In fact, it will have to be, considering the reductions in force structure that will be needed to pay for the new technology.

---

[8]Quoted in Anthony Kimery, "When the Night Comes Crashing," *Military Information Technology*, vol. 3, issue 1 (1999), p. 12.

[9]*Cybercrime . . . Cyberterrorism . . . Cyberwarfare . . . : Averting an Electronic Waterloo*, Report of the CSIS Global Organized Crime Project (Washington, D.C.: Center for Strategic and International Studies, 1999), p. xiii.

The result will be a smaller military that depends on high volumes of quality information merely to survive, much less succeed. If the information turns out to be unavailable, corrupted, insufficient, or misinterpreted, then the much smaller IT-RMA force structure could be in big trouble. Today's massive forces provide an insurance policy against unforeseen setbacks. If the breaks go against American forces, they currently are large and diverse enough to recover. Thus, if an opponent checks the U.S. deep-strike air force with unexpected electronic countermeasures, he can still be defeated in close combat; if the enemy stops the marines with mines and obstacles on the beaches, he can still be pummeled from the air; if the enemy resorts to guerrilla tactics, U.S. infantry can pursue him. On the other hand, a force radically restructured to exploit new information technology by definition puts more of its eggs in the deep-strike basket. If the enemy's tactics outflank technology, an IT-RMA military may lack the size and diversity to compensate. To take a single example, the initial plan for intervention in Kosovo, for political reasons, involved air operations only. Force restructuring could mean that in the future other options may be unavailable or prohibitively costly. Today's forces are resilient. A radically restructured IT-RMA force would be much less so.

A less risky alternative could allow the United States to incorporate RMA information assets within the current force structure, which may well make the force more robust. However, maintaining two distinct organizational forms, one hierarchical and one networked, might prove problematic. In addition, this could not be done without major budget increases. Much of the IT-RMA's political appeal rests on its claim to square the circle of growing commitments and shrinking budgets by letting the United States do more with less. If all it offers is to do more with more, there may be few takers on Capitol Hill.

Organizational Problems. The problems of access/security and resilience are tied to a third problem that goes to the heart of the change being planned. The true revolution in military affairs is not only about weapons and doctrine, but about radical organizational change. Of all modern social institutions, the military has come closest to the ideal form of a bureaucratic hierarchy, in which information is tied to function, and function to rank. The responsibilities of a general require a different amount and type of information than do the duties of a private. Each possesses the information needed to perform his or her job and not much more.

The transformation of the military into a networked organization fundamentally alters the relationship between information and function. *Joint Vision 2010* states that "new technologies will allow increased capability at lower echelons to control more lethal forces . . . thus leveraging the skills and initiative of individuals."[10] The document envisions empowered individuals exercising "maneuver, planning, and coordination . . . which were normally exercised by more senior commanders in the past." In the Persian Gulf War, for example, majors in Riyadh with secure fax machines and friends on Washington staffs could get information to which only generals had access in past wars. The scrambler phone shifted control of the flow of information to lower echelons of command than ever before, and this trend is likely to accelerate.

There are, however, troubling costs associated with extending this empowerment fully. In a non-hierarchical structure based on equal access to information, the notion of "higher" authority becomes problematic. This creates two mirror-image concerns. The first is intense micromanagement, that is, the potential for central authorities—civilian as well as military—to make every decision. If an American president, who is ultimately accountable, after all, has complete awareness of a military situation, it may be difficult to pass up the chance to take control himself. The network might thus function as a "hyper-hierarchy," wherein top leaders reach down to orchestrate action at the lowest levels. Perhaps, given full knowledge of the battlespace, such intervention by the centralized command might not have the deleterious effects that have been associated with past examples of micromanagement, such as Lyndon Johnson's selecting bombing targets in Vietnam or Jimmy Carter's intervention in Desert One. Yet even with more information, the prospect of a president's making tactical decisions between Rose Garden ceremonies is not necessarily desirable. Among other consequences, such a ratcheting up of control would deny junior officers meaningful authority and responsibility and be certain to lead to morale problems. In the long run, it may give way to a mindset that is not conducive to effective leadership. In the U.S. Navy, for example, where there are currently only 1.6 ships for every admiral, the potential for hyper-hierarchy may create a serious challenge for command structures and rules.

The leveling of traditional hierarchical structure also creates the converse danger of macromanagement: the temptation of

---

[10]*Joint Vision 2010*, p. 15.

actors in the field to make decisions that should be made by higher authorities. Giving the troops a "god's-eye view" through direct access to satellites and other remote sensors may encourage them to act independently. Instead of more information leading to greater coordination, a breakdown of discipline could result. Will soldiers who are fully informed that they are outnumbered, surrounded, and without hope of timely support hold their positions? Even for courageous and well-trained troops, there is a difference between being ordered to hold a position when the risk is great but ambiguous, and doing so in the full knowledge that it is suicide. Complete knowledge may demoralize rather than embolden the troops. To be sure, the dire truth might be withheld, but then troops might interpret an information blackout as proof of their impending doom. In sum, empowering troops with better information could produce enormous, perhaps insurmountable, challenges to discipline.

Pressures for micro- and macromanagement grow out of the different interests of actors within the network. The problem, simply stated, is that having the same information does not necessarily lead actors to reach the same conclusion about how to respond. A president will view information through political-strategic lenses; the field commander, through operational lenses; and soldiers, through tactical and personal lenses. Flattened, highly networked command structures, however, do not in and of themselves privilege particular lenses or viewpoints. Without a perfect integration of political-military goals throughout the network, without a fusion of perspectives and views, and without the development of new command rule sets that clearly determine who makes decisions, the potential for different actors with the same information to make conflicting choices will surely exist. Advocates of full battlespace awareness assume that shared information will translate into (indeed, will equate with) a convergence of interests and perspectives, but common sense and experience suggest that this is not so.

The redesigning of military institutions to take advantage of the information revolution will also create sweeping cultural and practical problems for the military services, problems that need to be addressed carefully. One of the objectives of military training is to create a military ethos, a particular view of the world. The creation of this unique social institution has been possible, among other reasons, because of its members' physical isolation on military bases, although students of civil-military relations differ on the optimal degree of separation during peacetime. A networked military that allows greater individual initiative will have to contend with closer connections between the military and civilian worlds even as the gap in understanding between these worlds widens.

This interconnection may boost morale, but could also erode it, particularly during combat. Once deployment is made and hostilities are in progress, a barrage of e-mail from concerned friends and relatives who are getting critical reports on an operation from local news broadcasters (who have their own satellite feed from the operation) can, at the very least, distract soldiers in the field. Add to that the home front's arsenal of fax machines, cell phones (a problem with which the Israeli military has had to contend), and e-mail pagers, and the traditional divide between the military and home front—a divide upon which a system of discipline rests—becomes blurred. The professional military will begin to take on the feel of a virtual militia, for which the conduct of military operations competes with concerns and responsibilities at home and on the job: when the crops are ready, the pitchfork replaces the gun. The main advantage of a professional structure is dependability, but a professional military electronically connected to home may behave quite "unprofessionally" in combat.

Of course, total isolation during combat is not necessary. During the Second World War, mail call and movies were important, controlled distractions. The problem with networked integration is that commanders will have a hard time controlling the flow between the home front and the battlefront. The problem will intensify if the gap between civilian society and military institutions, as measured in values, attitudes, and life experiences, continues to grow. Civilians and the military may simultaneously have tighter communication links and increasingly disparate worldviews. Civilians, who increasingly know nothing about combat, will have the ability to tag along and chat with the troops, hardly a beneficial situation when American forces face prolonged combat conditions.

The military must also be concerned about the flow of information back to the home front. Stateside family and friends can cause problems, even unintentionally, by the way they use information gleaned from the deployed troops. An example of this concerns the rescue of air force captain Scott F. O'Grady, who was shot down in Bosnia in 1995. The rescue pilot e-mailed his pilot buddies describing the rescue in vivid detail, including sensitive information on American operational methods. Someone forwarded the message to another friend, who forwarded it again, and within hours a conversation that would have been a harmless diversion at the officers' club bar twenty years ago became a globe-circling security violation.

The negative aspects of individual empowerment can be eliminated by increasing the level of professionalism of the individual soldier, but this too is problematical. Even if we grant that 99.9 percent of military personnel are above distraction, that leaves a thousand weak links in a million-member organization. To this must be added the further complications created as the Defense Department increasingly contracts with civilian technicians to install, maintain, update, and repair complex technical systems. Civilian electronic engineers and software developers cannot be expected to have the same discipline demanded of the fighting forces, and the integration of people who may not carry what Eliot Cohen calls the "warrior's ethos" could increase the risk of internal conspiracy, theft, and espionage.[11] The flow of e-mail traffic out of national weapons laboratories, which was highlighted in the recent charges of Chinese espionage at Los Alamos, indicates a different cultural perspective on information between the scientific community and the military, even among that portion of the scientific community that is dealing with critical national security data.

All the offsetting costs listed so far will be exacerbated by the deployment of American forces as part of a coalition effort. An alliance-wide information network will have even more potential access points in need of defense and a membership that by definition involves different cultural values and national interests. Different levels of training and equipment are also likely to impair access and hinder the development of a shared awareness. Already, one of the greatest concerns among NATO allies is common interface standards and interoperability with U.S. military technology. The United States' NATO allies simply cannot afford to keep up. If allies' access is limited for security reasons, it will reduce the ability to work together effectively. Burden-sharing resentments may also emerge if in future joint actions the United States contributes the advanced technology while its allies, with their more traditional and relatively larger fighting forces, are left to provide the troops whose lives are at risk.

[11]Eliot Cohen, "A Revolution in Warfare," *Foreign Affairs*, Mar./Apr. 1996, pp. 37–54.

The Wrong Response to Security Threats

Given the potential for so many new vulnerabilities, the transformation of the military is clearly fraught with risks. Perhaps, if the security challenges of the future required radically new responses, these risks would be acceptable. However, in light of the current U.S. position as unchallenged superpower, caution and restraint seem far more prudent. A revolutionary transformation in the security infrastructure cannot be justified until it is demonstrated that information superiority solves real problems and permits U.S. armed forces to accomplish real-world missions better. Upon closer examination, however, it appears that the IT-RMA would leave the military ill equipped to counteract the dangers most likely to threaten U.S. security.

Information technology may contribute the most added value in the case of major theater wars, but those are precisely the threats that today's U.S. forces are most clearly able to handle. Current U.S. military superiority is overwhelming and is unlikely to be challenged soon, and American defense spending is roughly equal to that of the next ten top defense-spending countries combined (most of which are U.S. allies), plus such rogue states as North Korea, Libya, and Cuba. Success in the Persian Gulf War reveals that the United States can integrate information technologies and exploit them to great effect without the radical organizational and operational changes called for in the IT-RMA vision. Enthusiasts warn that because the IT-RMA is embedded in, indeed led by, the communications revolution in the commercial world, peer competitors can emerge quickly. But it is rather improbable that another state could rise as a threat more quickly than the United States could adapt to face it. This is not a call for standing still, but for slower, value-added defense planning. If the most important national security threat can already be handled with the means at hand, why revolutionize, particularly when the change might come at the cost of declining preparedness for that threat?

Some argue that an information-enabled military would deal more effectively with low-intensity conflicts. If correct, this would truly be important, since the most likely threats facing the U.S. military will involve instability among or the collapse of weak states. A critical problem, however, is that these scenarios will likely involve urban settings and opponents who are indistinguishable from the civilian population. As in Kosovo, the proximity between military targets and civilians may prevent planes from dropping their bombs or lead to the accidental killing of civilians.

Opposing forces could rely on widely available low-tech means to communicate, defend themselves, and inflict damage, or they could adopt the Serbian tactic of hiding forces in churches and schools. Organizational structure may be so simple or horizontal that isolation of leaders could be irrelevant. Alternatively, the adversary may have the sophistication to understand and exploit American technological and political vulnerabilities.

In any of these scenarios, there is no technological panacea. The fact that the United States could easily monitor the movement of Serbian forces in and out of Kosovo was only marginally helpful in dealing with the root causes of the crisis. Dominant battlespace awareness will do little to alter the centuries-old animosities and political struggles that give rise to such ethnic conflicts. In these cases, it is "boots on the ground" or the gunboat conspicuously offshore, and not information superiority, that restores short-term order and negates the military capacity of adversaries. NATO keeps the peace in Bosnia by means of soldiers on street corners backed by tanks and aircraft, not by radically transformed organizational structures and concepts. Indeed, if an embrace of the IT-RMA results in reductions in force levels, it may have the unintended consequence of reducing America's ability to deal with the low-intensity conflicts that seem likely to dominate in the foreseeable future.

In addition to improving U.S. capabilities to undertake major theater wars and low-intensity conflicts, enthusiasts argue that American sensors and communication systems can enhance such monitoring operations as arms control verification, scientific and environmental studies, refugee tracking, and everything collectively known as "military operations other than war." It is true that peace operations can be aided by more effective information collection, analysis, and dissemination. Additionally, intelligence-gathering capabilities for combatting terrorism and international crime will surely benefit from the greater use of information technologies. But none of that requires a radical restructuring of military forces. Indeed, doing so along the lines suggested by IT-RMA proponents may prove counterproductive because of the aforementioned vulnerabilities such an organization creates. It is hard to imagine a terrorist group taking on a combat brigade, but easy to imagine it taking down a computer network.

A final argument offered in support of the IT-RMA is that thinking of war and peace in traditional military terms simply misses the point about an information edge. Alvin and Heidi

Toffler, William Owens, and Joseph Nye have contended that command of the information environment may be used to prevent genocide and ethnic clashes before they start, thus obviating the need to send troops to intervene. The United States, for example, could suppress inflammatory radio messages, denying nationalist leaders the ability to incite their populations. In the case of Rwanda, Nye and Owens wrote in *Foreign Affairs*, the United States could have "exposed the true actions and goals of those who sought to hijack the government and incite genocide, which might have contained or averted the killing."[12]

While propaganda can be effective, advocating the IT-RMA as an antidote to global instability mistakes content for context. The mindset necessary to grab a machete and hack another human being to death does not emerge overnight in response to a voice on the radio, but from much deeper fears and calculations. Indeed, information that contradicts an individual's preexisting conceptual mindset is itself likely to be rejected as propaganda rather than accepted as truth. American computers, satellites, and info-warriors will not stop Christian southern Sudanese and Arab Muslim northern Sudanese from hating and killing each other. An information-driven U.S. military will be no more effective in dealing with these problems than traditional militaries—but it will be smaller, more expensive, and more thinly stretched.

The Balance of Power Still Matters

A final reason for caution in approaching the IT-RMA is the international reaction it is likely to generate. In the late 1980s it was popular to observe that American power was in decline. One of the stronger objections to this school of thought was offered by Nye, who argued that the unique appeal of American democracy and free-market economics could translate into "soft power," that is, the ability to achieve foreign policy goals through attraction rather than coercion.[13] He concluded that the growth in American soft power could offset declines in military and economic predominance. In their 1996 *Foreign Affairs* article, Nye and Owens moved one step further, arguing that with an intelligent strategy America could actually increase its overall power relative to the rest of the world. They called on the United States to "adjust its defense and foreign policy strategy to reflect its growing compar-

[12]Nye and Owens, "America's Information Edge," p. 33.
[13]Joseph Nye, *Bound to Lead: The Changing Nature of American Power* (New York: Basic Books, 1990).

ative advantage in information resources."[14] Implicit in this strategy is their notion that other nations will view American power as benign or, failing that, as incontestable. According to Nye and Owens, the "United States can use its information resources to engage China, Russia, and other powerful states in security dialogues to prevent them from becoming hostile. At the same time, its information edge can help prevent states like Iran and Iraq, already hostile, from becoming powerful."[15]

But as suggested earlier, clarity of information does not guarantee a convergence of interests. Information advantages may enhance the U.S. ability to shape relationships, but they do not alter basic interests. Recent protests in response to the American-led NATO strikes against Serbia suggest that people disagree even about the need to resist so repugnant a policy as ethnic cleansing. Some countries may ultimately trust the United States to wield its strength benignly, but the history of international politics suggests that few states will be willing to accept uncritically and passively such preponderance of power. Some states, including friends and allies, may coalesce to try to offset an American hegemon.

Enthusiasts of the information revolution claim that, in a break with past patterns of international politics, American hegemony will not prompt a countervailing balance of power. The Tofflers talk about "the end of equilibrium (not history)." As they argue in the book *War and Anti-War*, numerous "theories about the global system tended to assume that it is equilibrial, that it has self-correcting elements in it. . . . The entire theory of balance of power presupposed . . . restoring equilibrium. . . . Yet none of these assumptions apply today." They warn that "the promise of the twenty-first century will swiftly evaporate if we continue using intellectual weapons of yesterday."[16] Yet, just as information does not equate to shared goals within a single organization, there is little evidence that information suspends or transforms the interests of states. Even when certain goals can be agreed upon, reasonable state leaders may disagree on how to achieve them. France and the United States agreed that international law against war crimes should be upheld, and they shared information as to the whereabouts of war criminals in Bosnia. This did not lead, however, to agreement on how to proceed, and better information would not have transcended their disagreements. Nye and Owens write that

---

[14]Nye and Owens, "America's Information Edge," p. 23.
[15]Ibid., p. 22.
[16]Alvin and Heidi Toffler, *War and Anti-War: Survival at the Dawn of the 21st Century* (Boston: Little, Brown and Co., 1993), pp. 249–50.

"the information advantage can strengthen the intellectual link between U.S. foreign policy and military power."[17] However, given other nations' fears of U.S. domination, a revolutionary technological leap could easily be viewed in, say, China or Russia as evidence of open-ended U.S. ambitions and clearly at odds with a political grand strategy of benign engagement. Allies' acquiescence in an American hegemony will last only as long as the United States can reassure them of the complementarity of American interests and their own.

A Revolution Today Is Premature

Although the benefit of a restructured American military is marginal for many missions, carries significant off-setting costs, and might encourage balancing by adversaries and unease among friends, defense planners are moving forward with the IT-RMA. The Joint Chiefs of Staff has produced a *Concept for Future Joint Operations* that requires fundamental organizational and operational change.[18] Political leaders in both parties accept the argument that incrementalism is "dangerous thinking," and the National Defense Panel calls for "aggressive transformation." Why does the revolutionary consensus continue to grow? The obvious (and cynical) reasons are threat inflation throughout the defense and policymaking communities, traditional service rivalries, and the attendant bureaucratic politics. But one could just as well expect that those quarters would favor existing institutional arrangements and practices rather than the shifting of resources—and power—to new programs and services. Nor does the attraction of technological revolution derive from the short-term perspective from which American politics tends to suffer. On the contrary, the current push for a radical change in military planning and force structure is remarkable because it is coming at the *expense* of parochial service interests and *despite* the short-term preoccupations of most leaders.

There are in fact five reasons why defense planners want a revolution. The first is that analysts have tended to misinterpret the Gulf War as a victory of technology. Although U.S. technology was unquestionably impressive in that conflict, the victory was the result of a fortuitous mix of superior American might and generalship with a good dose of Iraqi incompetence. The readiness level of American troops, created through rigorous and superior training,

[17]Nye and Owens, "America's Information Edge," p. 20.
[18]Joint Staff, *Concept for Future Joint Operations* (http://www.dtic.mil/doctrine/jv2010/concept.htm).

was especially critical. The second and third reasons for support of an IT-RMA are that the pursuit of innovation has become institutionalized, combined with a generally positive societal view of technological progress. These two factors reinforce each other. The Defense Advanced Research Projects Agency alone has a budget that exceeds the individual defense spending of all but the top twenty-two countries in the world, and its sole purpose is to innovate. Such bureaucratic players' vision of the future resonates in a larger political environment and culture that accepts all "progress" as good. Consider the difference between industrial America's emphasis on cars of the latest model-year and the current information-age cycle in which hardware and software are declared obsolete within months of hitting the stores. In the defense community as in America at large, to move slowly is not to move at all. The fourth reason is that information technology has become the most common means by which to gauge both competence and success. Here, too, the IT-RMA argument parallels social norms. In the 1950s Americans measured themselves in terms of their automobiles' horsepower; now the standards are gigabytes and RAM. Finally, and perhaps most significantly, support for revolutionary change in the military has unmistakable political appeal. If leaders worry about remaining engaged in world affairs but do not have sufficient domestic political support to cover the financial and human costs of such a commitment, they are likely to be open to a solution that promises them engagement with less sacrifice.

None of these appeals, however, address the costs and concerns detailed here. The information-age enthusiasts insist that the United States should overturn a system it already dominates and push to radically expand America's advantage. This is both unnecessary and dangerous. The United States has reached a pinnacle of world power without exhausting itself, and dire predictions of decline have proven groundless. Relative to most developed countries, the U.S. economy continues to show resilience and its military remains without peer. The United States is not only ahead, but it is well positioned, provided that readiness is maintained, to respond quickly to any threat that might arise.

The normal process of evolutionary adaptation is perfectly adequate to the times and is a safer and wiser response to new technology. The kind of incremental change that has characterized U.S. defense planning for more than a generation is a better—if less exciting—bet than radical transformation. The revolution can wait.

THE DEFENSE TASK FORCE

Co-Chairmen
Hon. John F. Lehman, J.F. Lehman & Company
Harvey Sicherman, Foreign Policy Research Institute

Project Coordinator
Michael P. Noonan, Foreign Policy Research Institute

Rapporteurs
Eliot A. Cohen, School of Advanced International Studies, Johns
    Hopkins University
John Hillen, Island ECN, Inc./Foreign Policy Research Institute
Donald Kagan, Yale University
Williamson Murray, Institute of Defense Analysis
Keith B. Payne, National Institute for Public Policy
Winn Schwartau, Interpact, Inc.
Don M. Snider, U.S. Military Academy
Henry Sokolski, Nonproliferation Policy Education Center
Col. Harry G. Summers Jr., U.S. Army (ret.), deceased

Conference Participants
Deborah Avant, George Washington University
Andrew J. Bacevich, Boston University
Richard K. Betts, Columbia University
James Burk, Texas A&M University
Elaine Donnelly, Center for Military Readiness
Col. Charles Dunlap, U.S. Air Force
Maj. Christopher Gibson, U.S. Army
Daniel Gouré, Center for Strategic and International Studies
Eugenia Kiesling, U.S. Military Academy
Michael Krepon, Stimson Center
Joshua Lederberg, Rockefeller University
Martin Libicki, RAND Corporation
Walter A. McDougall, University of Pennsylvania/Foreign Policy
    Research Institute
Mackubin Thomas Owens, U.S. Naval War College
Hon. Everett Pyatt, consultant
David Rapoport, University of California at Los Angeles
Thomas E. Ricks, *Washington Post*
William Rosenau, SAIC
David Alan Rosenberg, National Defense University
David R. Segal, University of Maryland at College Park
Lt. Gen. Bernard E. Trainor, U.S. Marine Corps (ret.), formerly of
    the Kennedy School of Government, Harvard University
Hon. Dov S. Zakheim, SPC International

Biographical Notes on the Editors and Authors

John F. Lehman is chairman of J.F. Lehman & Company, a private equity investment firm, and was formerly an investment banker with PaineWebber Inc. Prior to joining PaineWebber, he served for six years as secretary of the navy. He served twenty-five years in the naval reserves. Dr. Lehman's books include *Command of the Seas* and *Making War*.

Harvey Sicherman is president of the Foreign Policy Research Institute. He worked as special assistant to Secretary of State Alexander M. Haig Jr. (1981–82), consultant to Secretary of the Navy John F. Lehman (1982–87), consultant to Secretary of State George P. Shultz (1988), and served on Secretary of State James A. Baker's Policy Planning Staff (1990–91). Dr. Sicherman has written numerous books and articles on U.S. foreign policy.

Andrew J. Bacevich is professor of international relations at Boston University, where he also serves as director of the university's Center for International Relations. He is a graduate of the U.S. Military Academy and received his Ph.D. in American diplomatic history from Princeton. He has been an International Affairs Fellow with the Council on Foreign Relations, a National Security Fellow at the Kennedy School of Government, and a Visiting Fellow of Strategic Studies at Johns Hopkins University. Prior to beginning his academic career, Dr. Bacevich served for twenty-three years as an officer in the U.S. Army.

Eliot A. Cohen is professor of strategic studies at the Paul H. Nitze School of Advanced International Studies, Johns Hopkins University. After receiving his doctorate in political science from Harvard he taught there and at the Naval War College before coming to SAIS in 1990. The author of numerous books and articles, he directed the U.S. government's official study of air power in the 1991 war with Iraq, the Gulf War Air Power Survey. In addition to serving on various editorial and advisory boards, he is the founding director of the Center for Strategic Education at SAIS.

Andrew P. N. Erdmann, an affiliate of the John M. Olin Institute for Strategic Studies, recently completed his Ph.D. in history at Harvard University. He is revising for publication his dissertation, a study of how Americans' understanding of "victory" changed during the twentieth century. He is also editing a volume of recently released recordings from before, during, and after the presidency of Dwight D. Eisenhower for the Presidential Recordings Project of the Miller Center of Public Affairs, University of Virginia.

Richard J. Harknett is associate professor of political science at the University of Cincinnati and directed the efforts of the Joint Center for International and Security Studies (JCISS) Study Group on Information Warfare. The **JCISS Study Group** co-authors are: Stephen Biddle, University of North Carolina, Chapel Hill; Jan Breemer, Naval Post-Graduate School; Daniel Deudney, Johns Hopkins University; Peter Feaver, Duke University; Benjamin Frankel, editor of *Security Studies*; Emily O. Goldman, University of California, Davis; Chaim Kaufmann, Lehigh University; William Martel, Naval War College; and Edward Rhodes, Rutgers University.

John Hillen is vice president at Island ECN, Inc., an alternative trading system on Wall Street. A former U.S. Army officer and public policy scholar, he is a decorated combat veteran of the Persian Gulf War with a doctorate from Oxford. He has held fellowships at several think tanks in Washington, D.C., and is a contributing editor at *National Review*. He is the author of the critically acclaimed book *Blue Helmets: The Strategy of U.N. Military Operations* (Brassey's, 1997) and numerous articles in publications such as *Orbis* and *Foreign Affairs*.

Donald Kagan is Hillhouse Professor of History and Classics at Yale University. He is co-author with Frederick W. Kagan of *While America Sleeps* (St. Martin's Press, 2000). He is also the author of a four-volume history of the Peloponnesian War and of *On the Origins of War and the Preservation of Peace* (Doubleday, 1995).

Williamson Murray is professor emeritus at Ohio State University and is presently serving as senior fellow at the Institute of Defense Analyses.

Keith B. Payne is president and founding research director at the nonprofit National Institute for Public Policy, and also serves as an adjunct professor at Georgetown University and at Southwest Missouri State University. He is the editor-in-chief of

Comparative Strategy: An International Journal and the author or co-author of over seventy published articles and fourteen books. Dr. Payne's most recent book is *Deterrence in the Second Nuclear Age* (University Press of Kentucky, 1996).

Sam C. Sarkesian is professor emeritus, Loyola University Chicago. He has published a number of books and articles on national security, unconventional conflicts, and military professionalism. He served for over twenty years in the U.S. Army with service in Germany, Korea, and Vietnam, including duty with Special Forces, airborne, and infantry units. He taught at the U.S. Military Academy from 1962 to 1966.

Winn Schwartau is president of Interpact, Inc., an international security consulting firm focusing on security awareness programs and cyber-gaming, and founder of www.infowar.com. A prolific writer and speaker, he has over twelve books and a thousand articles to his credit. Most recently, the acclaimed *Cybershock* (Thunder's Mouth Press, 2000) provided a nontechnical examination of hacking and security, and *Time Based Security* (Interpact Press, 1999) created a new paradigm for measuring security in any network.

Don M. Snider is professor of political science at West Point, teaching seminars in military innovation/adaptation and civil-military relations. He has been a member of the civilian faculty of the U.S. Military Academy since 1998, having previously held the Olin Chair in National Security Studies from 1995 to 1998. Earlier, he completed a military career that included three combat tours in the Republic of Vietnam and, much later, service on the staff of the National Security Council. He retired from the Office of the Chairman, Joint Chiefs of Staff, in 1990. Dr. Snider's current research and publications focus on military culture and ethics, the gap between the military and American society, officership, and U.S. security policy towards Europe.

Henry Sokolski is executive director of the Nonproliferation Policy Education Center, a nonprofit educational organization based in Washington, D.C., and teaches graduate school courses on proliferation issues at Boston University's Institute of World Politics. He recently served on the Commission to Assess the Organization of the Federal Government to Combat Proliferation and on the Central Intelligence Agency's Senior Advisory Board. He was Deputy of Nonproliferation Policy at the Pentagon during the George H. W. Bush administration.

Harry G. Summers Jr. was a colonel in the U.S. Army and a veteran of the Korean and Vietnam Wars. Twice decorated for valor and twice wounded in action, he went on to hold fellowships and chairs at the Army War College, Marine Corps University, and the University of California at Berkeley. He was also a critically acclaimed columnist and commentator for television and radio. Among his many books are the classic critique of the Vietnam War *On Strategy*; the *Vietnam War Almanac* (1985); and *On Strategy II* (1992), which the *New York Times* called "the best of any gulf war book to date." Col. Summers passed away on November 14, 1999.

About the Foreign Policy Research Institute

Mission

Since 1955, the Foreign Policy Research Institute has used scholarly insight to develop and promote policies that advance U.S. national interests.

Who We Are

The scholars of FPRI include a former aide to three U.S. secretaries of state, a Pulitzer Prize–winning historian, a former president of Swarthmore College (and a Bancroft Prize–winning historian), and two former staff members of the National Security Council. Our distinguished trustees have served at the highest levels in national government and the private sector. Affiliated scholars are active in diverse disciplines including political science, history, economics, law, management, religion, sociology, and psychology.

What We Do

We conduct research on the pressing issues of the day as well as on the oft-overlooked questions and developments that are crucial in the long term. Our publications include the quarterly world-affairs journal *Orbis* and weekly bulletins that reach thousands of people around the globe. A critical component of our programs is education—for the scholar, the general public, and especially the classroom teacher. "Teaching the teachers" and helping them place international politics within larger historical and cultural contexts is one of our most important goals. Through publications, seminars, conferences, and lectures, we serve the community and the nation, the policymaker and the educator, Wall Street and Main Street.

Does It Matter?

It matters to the policymaker, who lacks the time to give serious reflection to long-term trends shaping America's choices abroad; it matters to the media, who rely on outside expertise to make sense of complex developments in foreign lands; it matters to the educator, who needs informed preparation to teach the next generation; it matters to the student, who will soon be a leader; and it matters to the public, whose children may be sent off to war and whose taxes will pay the bills. As FPRI founder Robert Strausz-Hupé once said, "A nation should think before it acts," and that is where FPRI makes its mark.